Angriff
WESTLAND

DILIP SARKAR

Angriff
WESTLAND

DILIP SARKAR

FOREWORD BY

HIS ROYAL HIGHNESS
PRINCE ANDREW, DUKE OF YORK

RAMROD PUBLICATIONS

This book is respectfully dedicated to
Laurence *Peter* Sweet (above) and Maxwell Fitkin,
both killed on October 8th, 1940,
when the shelter at Don Harrison's
corner shop in Preston Grove, Yeovil,
suffered a direct hit.

Contents

DEDICATION _____ 4

FOREWORD _____ 7

INTRODUCTION _____ 9

PROLOGUE _____ 11

THE DEFENDERS _____ 23

THE ATTACKERS _____ 55

TARGET WESTLANDS _____ 79

BLACK MONDAY _____ 89

STÖRFLUG TO WORCESTER _____ 125

ANGRIFF WESTLAND _____ 135

THROUGH THE LOOKING GLASS _____ 155

APPENDIX 1 _____ 167

APPENDIX 2 _____ 173

APPENDIX 3 _____ 175

APPENDIX 4 _____ 179

APPENDIX 5 _____ 181

ACKNOWLEDGEMENTS _____ 183

BIBLIOGRAPHY _____ 187

BUCKINGHAM PALACE

Mr Sarkar has written an excellent book on a facet of the Battle of Britain which for understandable reasons has not always been given the recognition it deserved. His is a well researched account of that part of the Battle which was fought over the West Country. As a naval officer and a practising pilot in the Fleet Air Arm I have both served at Portland and accumulated many flying hours in Westland Helicopters. I have also in the course of my service in the Royal Navy come to know the West Country well and I found Mr Sarkar's account of events in the Autumn of 1940 to be of special interest. For those who wish to be better informed about that part of the Battle of Britain which was fought well away from its central focus over London "Angriff Westland" is required and compelling reading.

Introduction

It has long been an ambition of mine to contribute to existing literature relating to the Battle of Britain as fought over the West Country and by the oft neglected fighter squadrons of Fighter Command's 10 Group. *Angriff Westland* will, I hope, be seen to throw new and accurate light on three particular daylight raids which occurred during the Battle of Britain's fifth phase, also an area much neglected by latter day historians. This has been achieved by using many sources of reference, but in particular I hope that the reader will find most interesting the first-hand accounts by aircrew from both sides of the Channel in addition to those of the ones who either watched the combat from terra firma or had the misfortune to be bombed. For the historian of this period, as time marches relentlessly on, the opportunity to obtain such accounts is becoming increasingly infrequent.

I have also found it essential to include much background information prior to discussing the raids in any detail, to provide the reader with a depth of knowledge necessary to fully appreciate each raid in context, to know what it was like to be a fighter pilot or a groundcrew member in 1940, how both air forces operated and why this air battle was being fought.

Through the Looking Glass describes how my friends and I went about researching this book, which I hope will prove interesting and perhaps be of help to others, as may be the appendices with their statistics.

Whilst researching the MECO raid, retired nursing sister and eye-witness Margaret Hayton sent me the following remarkable poem, apparently written by Thomas Gray some 200 years before the Battle of Britain; as Margaret said, it seemed like a prophecy, and certainly sets the scene for the pages which follow:-

> The time will come when thou shalt lift thine eyes
> To watch a long-drawn battle in the skies;
> While aged peasants, too amazed for words,
> Stare at the flying fleets of wondrous birds.
> England, so long the mistress of the sea,
> Where wind and waves confess her sovereignty;
> Her ancient triumphs yet on high shall bear
> And reign, the sovereign of the conquered air.

Dilip Sarkar, Worcester, March 1994

Prologue

For the first three months of 1940 little happened. The Soviets finally overwhelmed the Finns, and U-Boats continued to attack Britain's North Atlantic shipping, but elsewhere the *Phoney War* persisted. With the exception of the Czechs and the Poles, few people had suffered unduly from the conflict so far. In early April Hitler attacked Denmark and Norway, drawing Anglo-French forces into a hopeless campaign in Norway's inhospitable terrain. A month later came the long-awaited attack on France, but taking the Allies by surprise with classic *Blitzkrieg* tactics. Highly mobile panzer divisions advanced through the *impassable* Ardennes towards the Channel coast, paralysing the Allied command system and cutting off the British Expeditionary Force in a pocket around Dunkirk. While the evacuation of over 330,000 Allied troops may have gone down in history as a *glorious defeat*, the reality was catastrophic. Hitler looked set for a complete victory against all those who opposed him. On June 10th, Mussolini's Italy also declared war on the Allies and thus extended the conflict to Africa and the Mediterranean.

When France asked for an armistice shortly afterwards, Hitler hoped that Britain would follow suit. The British Government had other ideas, however, as the Prime Minister, Winston Churchill, had already proclaimed:-

'Even though large tracts of Europe and many old and famous States have fallen, or may fall into the grip of the Gestapo and all the odious apparatus of Nazi rule, we shall not flag nor fail. We shall go on to the end. We shall fight in France. We shall fight on the seas and oceans, we shall fight with growing confidence and growing strength in the air. We shall fight on the beaches, we shall fight on the landing-grounds, we shall fight in the fields and in the streets, we shall fight in the hills, we shall never surrender.'

Hitler still made vain attempts to persuade the British to ask for terms, but by July, 1940, had decided that preparations must be made for the seaborne invasion of England. Clearly the foundations had been laid for what was to be a fight to the death.

Thirteen divisions of the German Army, each some 19,000 strong, moved to the Channel coast as the vanguard of a landing force of 39 divisions. Plans were made for the disembarkation in Kent and Sussex of 125,000 men during the invasion's first three days. To carry this force across the *Kanal*, the German navy assembled a makeshift invasion fleet comprising some 170 large transport vessels, 1,500 barges, and several hundred tugs, trawlers, motor boats and fishing smacks. As the Kriegsmarine was hopelessly inferior to the Royal Navy in warships of every category, the German service chiefs agreed that *Operation Sea Lion* would only be feasible if the Luftwaffe had defeated the Royal Air Force and gained total air supremacy prior to the fleet setting sail. The Luftwaffe could then dominate the landing-ground's sea approaches and thus repulse the Royal Navy.

Reichsmarschall Hermann Goering, the German Air Minister and Commander-in-Chief of the Luftwaffe, believed that the RAF could be crushed within a month of launching a major aerial assault. He estimated that Britain's air defences, south of a line from London to Gloucester, could be wiped out in just four days, meaning that replacement fighter squadrons would have to be moved down from the north, and these too would be annihilated. With Fighter Command thus defeated, Britain's remaining air and naval bases would be defenceless against aerial bombardment.

The British Government had no knowledge of these plans, but rightly assumed that an invasion would be attempted when Hitler's peace offers were firmly rejected. To meet this threat, two incomplete armoured divisions and the strongest of some 27 infantry divisions took up position south and east of a line from Lyme Bay to the Wash. By mid-summer, thousands of civilians and soldiers alike toiled to construct the stop-lines of anti-tank obstacles guarding London, the Midlands and industrial north. The Royal Navy had assembled a striking force of 36 destroyers, held ready from the Humber to Portsmouth. However, it could not be guaranteed that an invasion fleet would be sighted before it reached the coast, and, even it were, a seaborne striking force might not arrive in time to prevent German troops landing en masse. Therefore the success or failure of Britain's air defences, which alone could prevent the enemy from gaining the air supremacy so essential for invasion, was the decisive factor. As Hitler therefore prepared to undertake the first occupation of the British Isles by a foreign power in 874 years, on June 18th, Winston Churchill stirred the nation:-

'What General Weygand called the Battle of France is over. I expect that the Battle of Britain is about to begin. Upon this battle depends the survival of Christian civilisation......The whole fury and might of the enemy must very soon be turned upon us. Hitler knows that he will have to break us in this island or lose the war. If we can stand up to him, all Europe may be free and the life of the world may move forward into broad, sunlit uplands. But if we fail, then the whole world, including the United States, including all that we have known and cared for, will sink into the abyss of a new Dark Age made more sinister, and perhaps more protracted, by the lights of perverted science. Let us therefore brace ourselves to our duties, and so bear ourselves that if the British Empire and its Commonwealth last for a thousand years, men will still say "This was their finest hour".'

Since the fall of France, Britain, an island fortress under siege, had diverted its all important ocean supply convoys from routes threatened by German air attack. Local convoys, however, still had to travel along the east coast and through the English Channel. Air Chief Marshal Sir Hugh Dowding, the Commander-in-Chief of Fighter Command, was therefore compelled to devote hundreds of sorties a day to protection of this vital merchant shipping, although at the time he wished to conserve his strength for the great air battle ahead. Even so, between July 10th, recognised as the starting date for the 16 week aerial conflict already named by Churchill, and August 12th, 30,000 out of nearly five million tons of such shipping fell victim to air attacks between Land's End and the Nore. During this first phase of the Battle of Britain, the Luftwaffe attacked shipping on a daily basis, and dog-fights were seen, each involving over 100 aircraft. The fighting had in fact, however, commenced before July 10th; on the previous day, the Hurricanes of 151 Squadron were involved in bitter combat some 20 miles north-east of Margate with a formation of enemy aircraft numbering over 100. One of the Hurricane pilots was Pilot Officer Jack Hamar, a successful young veteran of the Battle of France, who later reported the following:-

'At 1540 hrs a large number of enemy aircraft in several waves were sighted flying NW at about 10,000'. It was impossible to attack the first wave, which consisted of He 111 bombers, because of the large number of escorting fighters which were very near us. Red 1 therefore ordered line astern and attacked the nearest formation of fighters which consisted of 12 Me 110s. A No 1 fighter Attack was used, and after Red 1 had broken away after attacking the rear Me 110, I closed to 150 yards and gave it a 5 second burst. I saw my bullets tearing into the fuselage and wings of the enemy aircraft, which staggered badly. I then had to break away quickly as the air seemed full of enemy aircraft. I then saw bombs exploding near the convoy which I approached at full throttle. I chased a section of three enemy aircraft away from the northern end of the convoy but failed to get into a position to open fire. I then continued to patrol the convoy for about fifteen minutes as the air had by this time been cleared of the enemy. No ships in the convoy had been hit, so I returned to base as my fuel was running low.'

Hamar's victim, shared jointly with three other pilots, was an Me 110 of III/ZG26; the two crew members remain *vermisst* (missing).

The world's press already eagerly monitored the aerial skirmishes over the Channel. On Sunday, 14th July, Charles Gardner, a BBC reporter, made broadcasting history when he gave an exhilarating eye-witness account of an air battle over a convoy observed from the cliffs of Dover. His remarkable report thrilled many, but angered others who felt that the subject of mens' lives was not a topic to be aired on the level of a cup final:-

The spider's web of condensation trails which often represented the Battle of Britain to those on the ground.

'There are three Spitfires chasing three Messerschmitts now. Oh, boy! Look at them going! Oh, look how the Messerschmitts! - Oh, boy! That was really grand! There's a Spitfire behind the first two. He will get them. Oh, yes. Oh, boy! I've never seen anything so good as this!'

On August 12th, Reichsmarschall Goering finally decided that the air assault on Great Britain itself should commence in earnest the following day, August 13th, dubbed *Adlertag*, or Eagle Day. In his proposed *Adlerangriff*, or Eagle Attack, he planned that as of Adlertag, when the Battle of Britain moved into its second phase, formations of 50 bombers, heavily escorted by fighters, should attack by day airfields, radar stations, ports and aircraft factories in the south of England. Single-seat Me 109 fighters were to assist by clearing a path for the bombers, but were not rigidly tied to an escort role. Due to an overcast sky on the morning of Adlertag, Adlerangriff was postponed, but the orders were given too late to prevent several units from taking off. Although operations after midday were better co-ordinated, they were no more successful as not one objective of any importance was destroyed. The Luftwaffe lost 45 aircraft against 13 by Fighter Command.

On August 15th, all three *Luftflotten* (Air fleets) on the Western Front made concerted attacks on targets from Northumberland to Dorset. The Luftwaffe planners wrongly believed that their attack in the north would meet with little opposition due to the British having been forced to make good losses suffered in the south by reinforcing with those squadrons from northern England. The more northerly raiding force, consisting of 63 He 111s of I and III Gruppen KG26, escorted by 21 Me 110s of I/ZG76, was actually intercepted east of the Farne Islands by Flight Lieutenant Ted Graham and 11 other Spitfires of Acklington's 72 Squadron, the first of five Spitfire and Hurricane squadrons to attack the raiders from bases between Catterick in Yorkshire and Drem on the Firth of Forth. The more southerly raid, directed against the airfield at Driffield, and comprising 50 Ju 88s of KG30, was engaged by 616 Squadron's Spitfires and the Hurricanes of 73 Squadron's 'B' flight. The defenders claimed eight enemy aircraft destroyed in what became known as the *Junkers Party*. However, the enemy managed to destroy 10 RAF bombers on the ground. Meanwhile, attacks in southern England caused some damage to fighter stations and two aircraft factories, but suffered similarly heavy losses in the process. To the Luftwaffe, August 15th, 1940, became known as *Black Thursday*.

Particularly following *Adlertag*, Goering concluded that his single-seat fighters must be used primarily to give close cover to his bombers. Quite rightly, he also realised that he could not hope to win the battle unless Fighter Command was drawn into the air and destroyed piecemeal. Therefore it was decided that Fighter Command's airfields would be heavily attacked. During the next fortnight, Goering gave Generalfeldmarschall Albert Kesselring, commander of Luftflotte 2 in northern France, with airfields closest to England, the majority of his single-engined fighters and all of Luftflotte 5's bombers from Scandinavia. Luftflotte 5's heavy fighters then went to Luftflotte 3, commanded by Generalfeldmarschall Hugo Sperrle, which was to make harrassing attacks by day and prepare for the nocturnal destruction of Liverpool. The previously much vaunted Ju 87 *Stuka*, which although had created a legend when used as flying artillery against ground forces, had proved no match for the fast Spitfires and Hurricanes, and so was from hereon held in reserve to support the actual invasion. On Adler Tag, 609 Squadron's Spitfires had so decimated a formation of Stukas over Lyme Bay that Flying Officer John Dundas, a pre-war journalist, was moved to record in the squadron diary that August 13th was *'a particularly bad day for the species Ju 87.'*

From there on the Battle of Britain became largely a duel between Generalfeldmarschall Kesselring, and Air Vice-Marshal Keith Park, commanding Fighter Command's No 11 Group covering London and south-east England. In Park's seven sectors ranging from Suffolk to West Sussex, he had 21 Spitfire and Hurricane squadrons, and could count upon being reinforced by a further five from Leigh-Mallory's 12 Group and two or more from Brand's 10 Group. This gave Park a total of some 300 fighters against the 600 under Kesselring's command.

Further heavy attacks were made against airfields, radar stations and other objectives in southern England on August 16th and 18th. Many caused heavy casualties and serious administrative inconvenience, but overall Britain's capacity to continue the fight was unimpaired. After a five-day lull from August 19th-23rd, on August 24th, the third, and most crucial phase of the battle commenced, and Park faced concentrated attacks by powerfully escorted bomber forces on airfields which he could not afford to leave unprotected. Attempts to defend these valuable objectives, however, continually drew his precious fighters into clashes with Kesselring's *jagdfliegern* (fighter pilots), and for a time the Germans appeared to be gaining the advantage. Between August 24th and nightfall on September 6th, Fighter Command lost 286 aircraft. Five forward airfields and six sector stations in 11 Group were so seriously damaged that Park feared another week of such sustained attacks might have jeopardized the defence of London yet to come. One of the important fighter stations hit during that time was Hornchurch, to the north-east of London, home of 54, 222 and 603 (Spitfire) Squadrons. On August 31st, the station diary recorded:-

'Mass raids continued to be made against our aerodromes, again starting early in the morning. The first two attacks were delivered at 0830 and 1030 hrs respectively and were directed at Biggin Hill, Eastchurch and Debden. The third attack was delivered at Hornchurch, and although our squadrons engaged, they were unable to break the enemy bomber formation, and about thirty Dorniers dropped some one hundred bombs across the airfield. Damage, however, was slight, although a bomb fell on the new Airmens' Mess which was almost completed. The only vital damage, however, was to a power cable, which was cut. The emergency power equipment was brought into operation until repair was effected. Three men were killed and eleven wounded. 54 Squadron attempted to take off during the attack and ran through the bombs. Three aircraft were destroyed, one being blown from the middle of the landing field to outside the boundary, but all three pilots miraculously escaped with only minor injuries.

'The fourth attack of the day was also directed at Hornchurch, and once again, despite strong fighter opposition and anti-aircraft fire, the bombers penetrated our defences. This time, however, their aim was most inaccurate, and the line of bombs fell towards the edge of the aerodrome. Two Spitfires parked near the edge of the aerodrome were written off, and one airman killed. Otherwise, apart from the damage to dispersal pens, the perimeter track and the aerodrome surface, the raid was abortive, and the aerodrome remained serviceable. Our squadrons, which had a very heavy day, accounted for no less than nineteen of the enemy and a further seven probably destroyed. 603 Squadron alone were responsible for the destruction of fourteen enemy aircraft. Although we lost a total of nine aircraft, either in combat or on the ground, only one pilot was lost.'

Although the German *jagdverbande*, or fighter formations, fought hard, the Me 109 was not designed as an escort fighter. With precious little fuel available for combat over England as it was, with the fighters now tied so inflexibly to escorting the slower bombers, and the jagdfliegern therefore constantly jiggling their throttle levers to keep pace with their slower charges, thus burning more fuel in the process, the situation became exacerbated. On their return flights across the Channel to their bases in France, the Me 109 pilots must have almost constantly monitored their fuel gauges. Oberleutnant von Hahn of I/JG3 reported, *'There are only a few of us who have not yet had to ditch in the Channel with a shot up aircraft or stationary airscrew.'* Leutnant Hellmuth Ostermann of III/JG54 wrote: *'Utter exhaustion from the English operations had set in. For the first time one heard pilots talk of the prospect of a posting to a quieter sector.'* A survivor, Oberleutnant Ulrich Steinhilper of JG52, has more recently written of *Kanalkrankheit* (channel sickness), the symptoms of which were the feigning of mechanical failure so as not to risk combat over England. It should be remembered that while Fighter Command was hard pressed to defend its nation alone, the German aircrews in the west had been under virtually constant pressure since the blitzkrieg

An Me 109 which only just made the French Coast

had begun several months earlier.

Although Fighter Command had lost 286 aircraft during this hard-fought phase, the Luftwaffe lost 380. For the Germans, replacement aircraft were not so quickly forthcoming, so by early September Luftflotten 2 and 3, weakened by combat losses and extended by the round-the-clock offensive, were in danger of losing the capability to make repeated daylight strikes against well defended targets. For the RAF, casualties had also produced a shortage of trained and experienced pilots. Training units dramatically cut courses so as to provide replacements rapidly, but many of these young pilots, most with just 10 hours experience on Spitfires or Hurricanes, and probably none in air-to-air firing, were flung into the crucible of battle that Indian summer to die at the hands of battle-hardened *experten*. Leutnant Ostermann was just one young jagdflieger who had learned some hard lessons in combat with British fighters since

the Battle for France. At the end of August, 1940, his unit, JG54 *Grunherz*, was constantly flying escort sorties to bombers, or flying *Freie Jagd* (fighter sweeps) across the Channel as far as London. During a huge dogfight between the Me 109s of his Gruppe and Spitfires, Ostermann saw a comrade being pursued by a British fighter: *'At once I flung my machine around and went down after them. Now I was about 200 yards behind the Tommy. Steady does it - wait. The range was much too far. I crept slowly nearer till I was only a hundred yards away, and the Spit's wings filled my reflector gunsight. Suddenly the Tommy opened fire and the Me in front of him went into a dive. I too had pressed the firing button after having taken careful aim. I was only in a gentle turn as I did so. The Spit caught fire at once and with a long grey plume of smoke dived down vertically into the sea.'* 22-year-old Ostermann went on to score 102 victories, the majority in the east, before being killed in action over Russia in 1942.

Max-Hellmuth Ostermann pictured wearing the Knights Cross with Oak Leaves and Swords shortly before his death in action when 24 years old.

On the night of August 24th, German bombers bound for the aircraft factory at Rochester and oil tanks at Thameshaven made a navigational error and dropped their bombs on Central London. This action, despite Hitler's orders that his bombers were not to attack the British capital, heralded a new phase in the fighting. Churchill immediately ordered Bomber Command to attack Berlin, and four such raids were made during the next 10 days. Hitler was furious, and responded to the Reichstag: *'Since they attack our cities, we shall wipe theirs out.'*

The fourth phase in the Battle of Britain, which represented a turning point for the defenders, commenced on Saturday, 7th September. On the afternoon of that day, Goering stood on the cliffs at Cap Blanc Nez with Kesselring and Bruno Loerzer, the

General Officer Commanding II Air Corps, and watched a massive formation of his fighters and bombers droning overhead towards England. As Fighter Command's controllers anxiously monitored the progress of the approaching enemy formation, understandably they assumed that the Sector airfields were again the target. Such a huge attack could well have delivered the telling blow. At 4.17 pm 11 RAF squadrons scrambled, and by 4.30 pm every squadron in the London area was airborne, 21 in total. East of Sheppey the defenders intercepted the enemy, almost a thousand aircraft flying in a formation stepped up one and a half miles high and occupying 800 square miles of sky. As the formation forged its way up the Thames Estuary, without the usual separation into smaller groups, each to attack a different target, it became obvious to Fighter Command that the airfields were to be spared; the target was London. Hundreds of bombs crashed down on docklands east of Tower Bridge. As the fire of London later illuminated the night sky, the raiders returned in a constant stream from 8.10 pm until 4.30 am. By the raid's end, some 1,800 Londoners were dead. The capital's defiant inhabitants proclaimed *'London can take it'*, and in so doing won the admiration of the free world. In failing to direct such a concentrated attack against Park's airfields, Goering had made a major tactical blunder. The price Goering paid was defeat in the Battle of Britain. Keith Park later wrote:-

'It was burning all down the river. It was a horrid sight. But I looked down and said: "Thank God for that", because I knew that the Nazis had switched their attack from our fighter stations thinking that they were knocked out. They weren't, but they were pretty groggy.'

The bombers returned to London on September 9th, 11th and 14th. On the last date Hitler, having been warned by his Naval Staff that air superiority had yet to be won, postponed the invasion until September 17th, hoping that a few extra days would tip the scales decisively in Goering's favour.

On Sunday, September 15th, Kesselring launched what proved to be his last attempt to gain a decision in daylight over London. Dawn on the great day found most of southern England shrouded in grey mist, but as the sun climbed higher the fog rapidly evaporated. By 8 am visibility was excellent. The fine weather heralded the onslaught which Fighter Command wisely anticipated. Before 11 am, German reconnaissance aircraft had probed the Straits of Dover and the east coast of Kent. From first light onwards standing patrols of Spitfires and Hurricanes had been up over the coast from Harwich to Land's End. Each sector station kept one squadron at readiness to take off at a moment's notice. At 10.50 am the British radar stations reported an enemy formation massing south-east of Boulogne, and five minutes later all of 11 Group's squadrons were at readiness. At 11.33 am an enemy formation crossed the coast between Dover and Folkestone, being followed three minutes later by two further hostile plots between Dover and South Foreland. The raiders' targets were London's gasworks and other industrial objectives. To parry this thrust, 20 of Park's squadrons were airborne, reinforced at Big Ben's midday stroke by the five squadrons of the Duxford

Wing. Such was the ferocity of Fighter Command's attack on the one hundred Dornier 17s of KG76 that the main formation was broken up before the target was reached. Consequently the enemy bombed at random across southern England. Two bombs fell on Buckingham Palace; the already popular King and Queen were undoubtedly now in the front line alongside the commoners of the East End. Hardly had this first mass attack been dispersed, however, than the radar stations discovered further enemy formations assembling in the Pas de Calais. Between 2.10 and 2.34 pm, eight or more German formations crossed the English coast bound for London. Visiting the 11 Group Operations Room at Uxbridge, the Prime Minister enquired of Air Vice-Marshal Park the number of reserves available; *'None, Sir'*, came the reply. If the number of British fighters defending London that morning had caused the Luftwaffe consternation, then the afternoon's 31 squadrons would doubtless do even more so. Fighting amongst the mêleé of cutting, thrusting aircraft, was Squadron Leader Brian Lane DFC, the 23-year-old Commanding Officer of 19 Squadron; he later described the number of enemy aircraft encountered over the capital as *'infinite.'* Having lit fires in Woolwich, Barking, Stepney, Stratford Gasworks, West Ham, Penge, and at a petrol depot in West Ham Park, the Luftwaffe withdrew, constantly harried by the defending fighters. With the threat to London now over, 27 He 111s attacking Portland were dealt with by just six Spitfires, and six squadrons and accurate anti-aircraft fire frustrated an intended raid on the Supermarine factory at Woolston by the low-level bombing unit, Erprobungsgruppe 210. The thwarted attack marked an end to the day fighting on what is now annually celebrated as *Battle of Britain Day*. Fighter Command claimed

Squadron Leader Brian Lane DFC, the 23-year-old Commanding Officer of 19 Squadron (centre) clearly shows the strain of battle having recently landed from a combat during September 1940. He is wearing the Mae West lifejacket and a silk neckscarf, the latter now synonymous with wartime fighter pilots. At left is Flt Lt 'Farmer' Lawson DFC, and at right Flt Sgt George Unwin DFM.

Author's Collection

the destruction of 185 enemy aircraft, although postwar research indicates the figure to be nearer 58. Nevertheless, against this amount Fighter Command lost just 28 aircraft destroyed. The day's events showed conclusively that the Luftwaffe was still not within measurable distance of gaining the air supremacy required for Operation Sea Lion.

On Tuesday, 17th September, 1940, British Intelligence intercepted a German High Command signal ordering dispersal of invasion facilities; Hitler had postponed the proposed invasion of Great Britain indefinitely.

As the German bomber offensive failed further, the jagdfliegern, frustrated by their inflexible close escort role, hoped that as a consequence they would once again be able to hunt down the RAF on fighter sweeps over southern England. Goering had other ideas, however, and issued orders that the aircraft of one Staffel in each Gruppe of every Jagdgeschwader should be converted to carry a single SC250 bomb, and thus become *Jabos*, or fighter-bombers. The operational value of fighter-bombers could not be denied, but only presupposing a surplus of aircraft. Adolf Galland, Kommodore of JG26 *Schlageter*, felt strongly that to use a fighter for such a role when the fighter arm was already inadequate to achieve air superiority, was *'putting the cart before the horse.'* The damage that such a small force of single-bomb carrying aircraft could achieve was negligible, but the RAF were unable to ignore such raids. Their value, therefore, was more of a nuisance nature, the jabos acting as *bait* to lure the RAF to intercept and clash with the unfettered fighter escort. The first of these raids was directed against London on September 20th, and the Controllers were not surprisingly caught out, having ignored the incursion as a fighter sweep until bombs crashed down on the City of London. Many RAF squadrons were scrambled too late, and as they desperately clawed for height over the Thames Estuary, the Me 109s fell on them. In the ensuing mêleé, II/JG2 bounced the Spitfires of 222 Squadron, flying in their neat vics of three. Oberleutnant Hans *Assi* Hahn took careful aim and fired. Seconds later Pilot Officer Laurie Whitbread was hurtling earthwards to his death. Altogether Fighter Command lost four pilots killed that day in addition to several others wounded. The Luftwaffe lost just one Me 109, and had given the RAF a salutary reminder of how dangerous the *Emil* could be when playing the hunter.

It can be appreciated from the foregoing that essentially the Battle of Britain was, on the British part, fought to deny Germany the air superiority essential to a seaborne invasion. However, the conflict did not suddenly end when the embers of fires lit in London on September 15th had smouldered to ash, or even when Hitler indefinitely postponed his conquest and turned his territorial ambitions eastward. Instead, on October 1st, the battle moved into a fifth and final phase which, so far as British history is concerned, lasted until Thursday, 31st October, 1940. Students of this stirring period of our modern history will be aware that despite this, many accounts of the Battle of Britain peter out after the September 15th climax over London, virtually dismissing the often bitter fighting that took place until the summer of 1940 finally

Flt Lt 'Tommy' Smart of 65 Squadron climbing aboard his Spitfire Mk IIA in late 1940. Note the pilot's canvas oxygen mask and parachute harness detail, and the aircraft's 'weathered' wing leading edge, 'fishtail' exhausts, and doped patch protecting each machine gun port.

Author's Collection

ended, and indeed generally pass over the importance and historical significance regarding much of the fighting over the West Country. As the capital city, London was clearly a target of paramount importance to the Luftwaffe, as were the airfields in south-eastern England. It cannot be doubted, therefore, that Air Vice-Marshal Park's 11Group, covering that very area, bore the brunt of the battle. However, in addition to the contribution made by the famous, but controversial, 12 Group Duxford Wing, it should be remembered that 10 Group's squadrons, covering the West Country, not only reinforced 11 Group during the London battles on many occasions, but also fought their own independent battle over Wessex. On September 25th, German bombers attacked and caused considerable damage to the Bristol Aeroplane Company works at Filton; two days later the raiders returned and attacked the Parnall Aircraft Company at Yate, on which occasion the enemy came off second best. These two attacks are excellently documented by my friend Kenneth Wakefield in his *Luftwaffe Encore* (see bibliography). *Angriff Westland* deals with two further significant occasions when West Country air raid sirens wailed during the Battle of Britain, on September 30th, and October 7th, when elements of Luftflotte 3 were briefed to attack the Westland aircraft factory at Yeovil in Somerset. So as to fully illustrate the tactics of the fifth phase, the one and only air attack against the Midland city of Worcester is also examined in detail for the first time. The many adventures, and tragedies, that subsequently befell no less a number of people on these three occasions, follow in the pages hereafter. *Angriff Westland* will, I hope, provide a lasting reference to these events that might otherwise have gone unrecorded in their entirety.

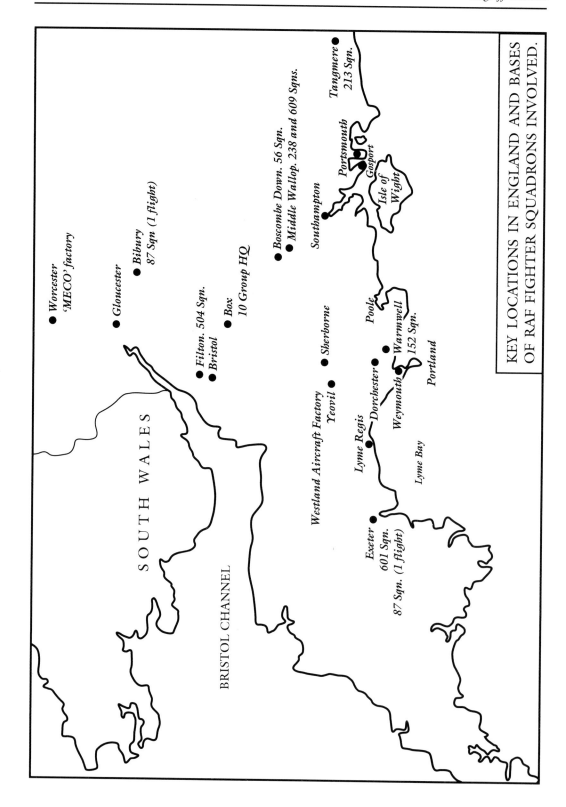

Tangmere
213 Sqn.

Boscombe Down. 56 Sqn.
Middle Wallop. 238 and 609 Sqns.
Southampton

Portsmouth
Gosport
Isle of
Wight

Worcester
'MECO' factory

Gloucester

Bibury
87 Sqn. (1 flight)

Filton. 504 Sqn.
Bristol

Box
10 Group HQ

Sherborne

Poole

Warmwell
152 Sqn.

Westland Aircraft Factory

Yeovil

Dorchester

Weymouth

Portland

Lyme Regis

Lyme Bay

SOUTH WALES

BRISTOL CHANNEL

Exeter
601 Sqn.
87 Sqn. (1 flight)

KEY LOCATIONS IN ENGLAND AND BASES
OF RAF FIGHTER SQUADRONS INVOLVED.

The Defenders

In 1936, the Air Ministry decided to divorce control of the home-based fighter force from that of the bomber force by setting up Fighter Command with headquarters at Bentley Priory, a large rambling house on the outskirts of London. This reform had important consequences.

Air Chief Marshal Sir Hugh Dowding, the first commander of the air defences in their new form, was a veteran fighter pilot himself, having commanded the British fighter wing at the Battle of the Somme in 1916. Between 1930 and 1936 he had played an important part in the decision to adopt Mr R.A. Watson Watt's scientific proposals. In January 1935, Watson Watt of the National Physical Laboratory gave air defence a new dimension by proposing that electromagnetic radiation should be used to detect and locate approaching aircraft. A month later he used the British Broadcasting Corporation's short-wave transmitter at Daventry for a practical demonstration of the device which became known as Radio Direction Finding (R.D.F., later called radar). By the summer of 1940 the United Kingdom's approaches were guarded by a chain of R.D.F. stations extending from Sumburgh in the Shetland Islands, down the east coast, along the south coast, and up the west coast to Strumble Head in Pembrokeshire. Dowding integrated radar into a new system of defence, which, it is fair to say despite certain limitations, was the best in the world.

Fighter Command's Commander-in-Chief had also helped bring the air defences up to date by insisting that the experience gained by designers and aircraft manufacturers with racing aircraft during the Schneider Trophy contests should be applied to the design of high performance fighters. This Reginald Joseph Mitchell and Sydney Camm did to great effect, the results being the Spitfire and Hurricane. In 1935, Squadron Leader R.S. Sorley of the Air Ministry, after inspecting mock-ups of the new aircraft, proposed that the Government should underwrite the cost of tools so that the manufacturers could prepare for mass production whilst the prototypes were being completed and tested. This far-sighted proposal was declined, but the Air Ministry did modify their specifications to give the designers maximum scope. Eventually, for example, both fighters were armed with eight .303 Browning machine-guns, as opposed to the four or six originally requested. By August 1940 about four-fifths of the fighter force was equipped with the two new aircraft in the proportion, as is perhaps still not widely appreciated, of three Hurricanes to two Spitfires.

The strategic thinking of the time was not of defence but of offence, i.e. *the bomber will always get through*. Dowding, in his new position, however, argued that although the fighter force should not expand at the bomber's expense, a powerful bomber force would be useless unless the fighter force were strong enough to ensure that its commander did not lose a decisive battle before the bomber force commander had time to fight one. In 1938 the Government agreed to give priority to the production of fighter aircraft. As late as 1940, Lord Beaverbrook, the Minister of Aircraft Production, was criticized for delaying the expansion of the bomber force by insisting on the highest possible output of Hurricanes and Spitfires.

In 1939, the authorities calculated that Dowding would need 53 fighter squadrons to defend the British mainland, the fleet at Scapa Flow, and coastal merchant shipping. When war broke out he had 39 squadrons, including four Hurricane squadrons which went to France with the B.E.F. 18 new squadrons were formed soon afterwards, and others later, but further moves to France reduced the home strength to 36 squadrons. On May 16th, 1940, Dowding wrote a letter to the Government making it clear that if his strength was reduced any further, the air defence of Britain could not be guaranteed. Churchill respected these views, and no more squadrons were sent across the Channel. Especially important was that not one single Spitfire had left England for French bases, and so Dowding's Spitfire squadrons, which were blooded over Dunkirk, remained comparatively intact for the coming decisive aerial conflict. By July, Fighter Command's strength had risen to 54 squadrons, increasing to 60 by September at the height of battle.

For the air defence of Great Britain, Fighter Command divided the British Isles into four Group areas, each with its own commander and headquarters but answerable directly to Dowding at Bentley Priory. London and the south-east of England became No 11 Group, commanded by Air Vice-Marshal Keith Park. Air Vice-Marshal Trafford Leigh-Mallory's 12 Group protected the Midlands and the north of England, and Northern Ireland was the responsibility of Air Vice-Marshal Richard Saul's 13 Group. No 10 Group, covering the West Country and South Wales, commanded by Air Vice-Marshal Sir Quintin Brand, became operational on July 8th, 1940, and its headquarters were at Rudloe Manor, Box, in Wiltshire. It is with 10 Group that this book is principally concerned.

Brand was also a Great War fighter pilot and had won the DSO, MC and DFC. He actually shot down a German Gotha on one of the war's last raids. With General Sir Pierre van Ryneveld he made the first flight from England to the Cape in 1920. The flying time was some 109 hours and as a result of this adventure Brand was knighted. From 1932-1936 Sir Quintin was Director General of Aviation, Egypt, from 1937-39 Director of Repair and Maintenance, and from 1940-41 Commander of No 10 Group (he retired from the service in 1943 and died in 1968).

The keystone of defence, however, was undoubtedly the network of Watson Watt's R.D.F. stations, Observer Corps posts and centres, operations rooms, radio-telephony transmitters, landlines and ancillary devices which made up the system of early warning and control. By the summer of 1940, the radar chain around the United Kingdom consisted of 22 *Chain Home* stations, supplemented by 30 *Chain Home Low* stations. These stations were positioned to ensure, at least in theory, that every aircraft approaching Britain from the east, south, or south-west would be detected by at least two stations. The existence of these stations with their 350' lattice masts became known to the Germans before the war, but Goering's advisors believed that those who worked the equipment would be unable, at times of stress, to distinguish between large and small formations, and that the system would break down if large numbers of aircraft approached the country simultaneously. Thus the actual effectiveness of the early-warning system remained a well-kept secret. The great strength of the system was its ability to direct fighter squadrons against specific attacks as they developed, rather than dissipate effort in flying constant standing patrols awaiting the enemy.

All of the radar stations, except those in 10 Group which reported to the Western Filter Room at Group Headquarters, passed their information by direct landline to the underground Filter Room at Bentley Priory. There the information was sifted by filterers and filter officers, displayed on a gridded map and passed by tellers through closed speech circuits both to the adjacent Command Operations Room and to those of appropriate Groups and Sectors. It took just four minutes between a radar operator observing a plot to its appearance in the operations rooms.

The 'Beauty Chorus' at the 10 Group Operations Room

After incoming aircraft had crossed the coast, the Observer Corps was responsible for tracking their progress. Observer Posts reported to Observer Centres connected by landline with the Command Operations Room. It was from the latter that instructions were issued to local authorities when to sound sirens warning the populace of approaching hostile aircraft. Tactical control, however, was delegated to the Groups and Sectors who issued orders directly to stations and squadrons, in addition to the Gun Operations Rooms which tied anti-aircraft guns to the system.

In each Group Operations Room, at least one Controller was always on duty. He looked down on the huge gridded map of the Group area and its surroundings. Aircraft approaching or crossing the area were represented by coloured plaques manipulated by WAAFs, the famed *Beauty Chorus*, armed with magnetized wands and through headphones linked to a teller at an Observer Centre or Filter Room. Facing the Controller across the table was a *totalisator* which showed at a glance the location and readiness state of the squadrons at the various Sector Stations and other Group airfields.

The Group Controller's job was to decide what course of action to adopt in respect of each raid that threatened his area. Subsequently he would give appropriate orders to Sector Headquarters and Gun Operations Rooms. His responsibilities were clearly heavy.

A Sector Operations Room was generally situated within the perimeter of the corresponding sector station. For example, 10 Group's Sector Station at Middle Wallop, inland of Southampton, was also home to the Sector 'Y' Operations Room. Each Sector Operations Room was linked by landlines and loudspeaker systems to the aircraft dispersal points where pilots on duty waited to fly. It was also linked with one or more radio-telephony transmitters, placed far enough away to ensure that intercepted transmissions did not reveal its whereabouts. The Sector Commander, or Controller, brought his squadrons to readiness, or sent them into the air, in accordance with the orders received from Group. Once the squadrons were airborne, he was responsible for giving them orders and information with the express intention of placing them in a favourable position from which to attack the enemy. Controllers and formation leaders used a special R/T code: *Scramble* meant take off urgently, *Pancake* meant land, *Angels* corresponded to height measured in thousands of feet, and *Bandits* were aircraft identified as hostile. A *Bogey* was an as yet unidentified plot. Pilots were directed by the provision of a compass heading, or *Vector*, expressed in degrees, or by reference to landmarks given codenames. *Buster* was for the fighters to travel at top speed, and *Liner* was cruising pace. When the formation leader cried *'Tally Ho!'*, the controller knew the enemy had been sighted and that battle was about to be joined.

'Scramble!' *Pilots of 601 Squadron sprint to their Hurricanes in a scene repeated many times during the war years on both sides of the channel.*

Chris Goss Collection

Regarding tactics, during the Battle for France, including the air operation covering the Dunkirk evacuation, Fighter Command had tried to put into practice the months of training in textbook attacks comprising smart, tight formations. These actually proved disastrously unsuitable for fast modern air combat. Due to the tight formations, of either vics of three aircraft or sections in line astern, with each aircraft therefore in close proximity to its neighbour as specified by the Fighter Command Area Attacks, the RAF pilots were unable to search the sky for the enemy without fear of risking collision. Thus in the early days many RAF pilots went to their deaths not knowing what had hit them. These traditional sections of three aircraft, in both the vic and line astern attitude, were also highly vulnerable to attack from both above and behind. The First World War rules of attacking from above and out of the sun were as valid in 1940 as during 1918. When a *tail-end Charlie* was added to the formation, criss-crossing the sky and protecting the rear, he proved most vulnerable of all. Peter Fox, a 19-year-old Hurricane pilot with 56 Squadron during the Battle of Britain remembers that '*on October 10th, 1940, a Czech, Sergeant Hlavac, and myself were both weaving as Tail-end Charlies; he was somehow shot down but I did not even see him attacked.*' The Fighter Command *book*, which foresaw orderly queues of fighters in line astern peeling off one by one to attack lone enemy bombers which were flying straight and level, had to be re-written. Owing to Britain and Germany being beyond the range of their respective single-engined types, fighter versus fighter combat had just not been anticipated. What could not be predicted were Hitler's modern ground tactics that took his armies to the Channel ports in an unprecedented period of time, thus providing bases for his fighters in France which placed England, and even London itself, within their range. The Luftwaffe, however, had fought in the Spanish Civil War during the mid-1930s and there developed its fighter tactics to deadly and flexible effect. The basic German tactical formation was the *Schwarm* of four aircraft, flying loosely in line abreast, stepped up and giving mutual cover (and also more difficult to spot than tight clusters of aircraft). In such a loose formation the sky could easily be scrutinized for the enemy without fear of collision. When combat commenced the Schwarm broke into pairs, leader and wingman, known as the *Rotte*. Eventually these tactics would be adopted by the RAF and in fact remain the basis of fighter combat today. Understandably it took time for Fighter Command to adapt, but slowly RAF fighter formations developed marked similarities to those of the *jagdwaffe*, 152 Squadron being credited as being the first squadron to adopt the pairs and fours system. Other squadron commanders pioneered their own techniques, such as Squadron Leader Gerald Edge, a veteran of the French campaign and commander of 253 Squadron during September 1940, who became an enthusiastic exponent of the head-on attack against German bombers. But whilst squadrons gained such experience the hard way, there was surprisingly little exchange of information between them.

When 10 Group became operational, Air Vice-Marshal Brand had a number of day squadrons at his disposal, namely the Spitfires of 92 Squadron at Pembrey in South Wales, and 234 at St Eval in Cornwall, in addition to the Hurricanes of 87 and 213 Squadrons at Exeter. Also, one flight of 247 Squadron's Gladiator biplanes were stationed at Roborough, near Plymouth. In August, the Sector Station at Middle Wallop and its satellite at Warmwell, just inland of Weymouth, were transferred from

11 to 10 Group which gained four more squadrons: the Hurricanes of 238, the Blenheims of 604, and the Spitfires of 152 and 609 Squadrons. There was, however, an almost constant rotation of squadrons for various reasons. On August 14th, 234 Squadron's Spitfires also arrived at Middle Wallop and were involved in heavy fighting until withdrawn to St Eval, in Cornwall, on September 8th. During the same week, two squadrons were sent to reinforce 11 Group on a permanent basis, 92 at Biggin Hill, and 213 at Tangmere. 249 Squadron had spent two weeks at Boscombe Down, also in 10 Group, between August 14th and September 1st, during which time, on August 16th, its Flight Lieutenant James Brindley Nicholson won the only Victoria Cross ever awarded to a fighter pilot. On September 1st, however, 249 was replaced by another Hurricane unit, 56 Squadron. 601 Squadron's Hurricanes arrived at Exeter on September 7th. Following the successful German attack on Filton of September 25th, the next day 504 Squadron's pilots flew their Hurricanes from Hendon to reinforce 10 Group at Filton. 87 Squadron was ostensibly based at Exeter, but in fact had one flight of Hurricanes detached to Bibury, in Gloucestershire, to afford some protection to the aircraft industry at Gloucester and Oxford.

During the German attack on the West Country made on the afternoon of Monday, 30th September 1940, 56, 238, 504, 609, 152 and 87 Squadrons of 10 Group intercepted the enemy with 213 Squadron from Tangmere. On Monday, 7th October, when the Germans returned to the area, 56, 238, 152 and 609 Squadrons were again in action, in addition to 601. It is with those units, therefore, that this book is concerned.

A fighter squadron consisted of 12 aircraft and pilots, excluding reserves, divided into two flights, 'A' and 'B', each normally led by a Flight Lieutenant. The flights were then further divided into two sections of three aircraft, each trio of fighters having its own leader and being identified by a colour. 'A' flight consisted of Red and Yellow Sections, and 'B' flight of Blue and Green. Each section was numbered from 1-3, 1 indicating the leader. *Blue 1* would therefore identify the leader of 'B' flight's Blue Section. Each squadron was identified by its own two code letters, which were applied to the fuselage of every aircraft, and individual aircraft within the squadron by a single letter, A to K for 'A' flight and L to Z for 'B'. *UM-M* would therefore have been a Spitfire of 152 Squadron's 'B' flight. Each squadron also had its own radio call sign which the controller would use - *Maida Blue 1* would therefore be the leader of Blue Section in 152 Squadron's 'B' flight. A squadron was commanded by a Squadron Leader, who, in addition to flying duties, was responsible for administration, through his adjutant, and general smooth operation of the unit as a whole. During the Battle of Britain it was not uncommon for the Commanding Officer to be under 25 years old (and known as the *old man*), whilst his youngest pilot may have been no more than 18. Pilots were of both commissioned and NCO rank. In the air it was experience that counted, so frequently sergeants would be Section Leaders whilst their numbers 2 and 3 were officers. On the ground, however, commissioned and NCO ranks were segregated, officers living in the Officers' Mess, and NCO pilots in the Sergeants' Mess. Also a part of the overall squadron would be the Intelligence Officer, or *spy*, and the essential groundcrews who maintained, armed and repaired the aircraft.

Fighter pilots during the summer of 1940 faced a very uncertain future. They never knew when the order to *Scramble* would come. The tempo and atmosphere of a front line fighter station were those of suspense. If the weather was clear then chances were that action would come sometime and suddenly, in the middle of a game of chess, whilst drinking a cup of tea, or when lighting a cigarette - perhaps the last. The telephone became the pilots' master and its ring would often herald action. The operational centre of the squadron was the *dispersal*, usually a wooden hut in which was situated an orderly and the all-important telephone. There were also 12 beds on which the pilots rested when on readiness. Outside, the aircraft were dispersed as a precaution against bombing. The machines were always left facing the centre of the airfield so that the pilots could take off with a minimum of delay. During the daytime the pilots usually left their parachutes on top of the port wing, with the straps hanging down under the leading edge. This meant that they could dash under the wing, seize the two shoulder straps, pull the pack of the parachute off the wing and then move towards the cockpit. Leather flying helmets, ear-phones plugged into their sockets, were left in the *office* on either the reflector gunsight or control column top. The pilot

19 Squadron's Pilot Officer Richard Jones personifies an entire generation of fighter pilots - youthful and optimistic. Note the Spitfire's reflector gunsight and rearview mirror, and the pilot's leather flying helmet, goggles, canvas oxygen mask, and yellow lifejacket.

Author's Collection

would probably be wearing leather flying boots and thick socks to insulate against the cold in his unheated cockpit at high altitude (although some preferred to fly in shoes to achieve a greater *feel* over the controls), and his yellow *Mae West* life jacket. When in action a pilot's head and face would be protected by his flying helmet, canvas oxygen mask which covered the nose, mouth and cheeks, and goggles which covered the eyes. His hands would also be protected by leather gauntlets. Looking like some knight in a medieval tournament, the pilot was thus afforded some protection against fire. Some also preferred to fly with the sliding cockpit canopy open, so as to facilitate a quick escape from the confines of a blazing aircraft. The customary, and now legendary, brightly coloured silk scarf was actually not a pose but another safety precaution. Buttoned-up, stiff uniform shirt collars caused the fighter pilot considerable discomfort as he constantly turned his head from side to side, and up and down, searching for the enemy. The open neck and silk scarf, however, proved much more practical, not least because neck-ties had been found to shrink in seawater. On the ground the fighter pilots' sign was the classic undone top tunic button.

238 Squadron's pilots worked a four day cycle. On the first day, the pilot would be on *Stand By* and therefore ready to fly within 1 hour. On the second he would be *Available* and ready to fly in just 15 minutes. On day three, he would be at *Readiness*, which meant immediately available for take off. The fourth day was the *Stand Down* when each pilot could leave the aerodrome with the flight commander's permission. However, a flight of operational pilots still had to be retained on that day which was also used for training.

56 Squadron's Pilot Officer 'Taffy' Higginson at 'Readiness', 1940.

Author's Collection via Wg Cdr FW Higginson

The British fighters' standard armament was eight .303 Browning machine-guns, each carrying a supply of 300 rounds and with a rate of fire of 1,200 rounds per minute. Ammunition belts were made up with a mix of bullets: ball, armour piercing and incendiary. The Browning was generally true up to 300 yards range, after which gravity imposed *bullet drop*. Many pilots had their guns harmonised to converge at 250 yards, thus producing a lethal cone of fire. Directly in front of the pilot's line of vision was the reflector of his gunsight, on which projected illuminated *cross-hairs*. These lines could be adjusted manually according to which type of enemy aircraft was involved. If the bars simultaneously touched both wingtips then the true range could calculated automatically. However, in a twisting, turning dogfight such methodical operations were impractical. The gunsight was usually therefore pre-set to the wingspan of a particular enemy aircraft type and thereafter used as a guide only. Wing Commander Bob Doe DSO DFC RAF Retd recalls that *'It is incredibly difficult to judge range in the air and I found experience to be the only real help.'*

Connected to each fighter was a mobile starter battery, astride which sat in readiness the *erks* - RAF slang for mechanics. The groundcrews, the chief of whom was invariably a senior NCO known as *Chiefy*, were accommodated nearby in tents along with all those personnel associated with squadron maintenance, such as petrol bowser crews, armourers, wireless servicing crews and aircraft fitters. Together these men constituted Britain's front line.

A snapshot of 56 Squadron's Hurricanes taken at North Weald around May 1940. Note the parachute slung onto the nearest aircraft's wing leading edge and trolley 'acc' plugged in.

Author's Collection via Wg Cdr FW Higginson

152 *Hyderabad* Squadron had seen action during the Great War but was disbanded in 1919. The Squadron re-formed at Acklington on October 2nd, 1939, and was initially equipped with obsolete Gladiator biplanes which were exchanged for Spitfires in December. To defend the Portland Naval base, on July 12th, 1940 the Squadron flew south to Warmwell, were it remained throughout the Battle of Britain. Warmwell had opened in May 1937 and was first known as RAF Woodsford, situated south of the Wareham to Dorchester railway and stretching nearly a mile westwards from Woodsford Crossing. The watch office lay halfway along the northern boundary and later looked out across the grass airfield at a row of dispersal pads on the western half of the field. Two Bellman hangars were built in the south-east corner, adjacent to the camp site, and seven blister hangars were added later.

Ray Johnson, an armourer with 152 Squadron during the Battle of Britain

Author's Collection via Ray Johnson.

A member of 152 Squadron's groundcrew was 19-year-old Ray Johnson, an armourer who had joined the Squadron at Acklington. He moved south with the squadron to Warmwell, and vividly recalls those days:-

'And then it happened. What is now known as the Battle of Britain started. 152 Squadron moved south from Acklington to Warmwell in Dorset. An advance party, including myself, was flown down in a Handley Page Harrow, which was a high-wing monoplane, to Warmwell which was a grass airfield inland of Weymouth and not far from the army camp at Bovington. It was actually adjacent to the spot where Lawrence of Arabia was killed on his motorcycle. Warmwell was in fact a pre-war practice camp, using the nearby Lulworth Cove bombing and gunnery ranges. The station master, a Group Captain, had the whole station on parade a week or so after our arrival. We had up until then operated from the concrete apron in front of the hangars, but his speech altered all that; it went something like this: "One of these days in the not too distant future, the Hun is going to appear over those Purbeck hills and knock three kinds of shit out of us. Therefore 152 Squadron is going to disperse to the far side of the airfield and thus try to ensure that as little damage as possible is occasioned. The hangar will only be used for major inspections and repairs". He was right about being hit. We were, several times, but luckily nowhere near as badly as some airfields in the London area.

'The Squadron's duties were in defence of the Portland Naval base, Southampton docks, Yeovil aircraft factory, and throughout 152 Squadron managed to give a good account of itself. 152 Squadron must have accounted for fifty or sixty confirmed victories. They were certainly hectic days, from dawn to dusk we were at dispersal. It seemed as though we were always at "readiness", but obviously this was not so. Re-arming, re-fuelling, daily inspections (of aircraft) all seemed to follow each other without pause. It was certainly thrilling to see your aircraft return with its gun ports in the wing leading edges open and black streaks down the undersides of the wings indicating that it had been in action. Very often there was a victory roll before the undercarriage was lowered and the pilot brought it in to land. Sometimes, though, your aircraft did nor return, and you were left wondering what had happened to it. Sometimes a Spitfire would land badly shot up. One such incident occurred when Flight Lieutenant Boitel-Gill crashed his Spitfire right into the corner of the airfield. The aircraft was absolutely riddled, we counted more than seventy holes, that is points of entry, and lost count. His undercarriage could not be lowered and neither could his flaps. Boitel-Gill, known as "Bottle", was one of those unflappable types, he never rushed, always appeared casual. He was a veteran cigarette smoker, using a long cigarette holder that he always carried. This time, after alighting from the wreck, he calmly placed a cigarette in the holder and said "I thought that I'd better put it in the corner out of the way", as I have said, he was a really cool customer.

'Another incident, Flying Officer Graham "Cocky" Cox landed with his head and shoulders protruding above the cockpit, his seat supports having collapsed either due to enemy action or violent evasive manoeuvres. The seat was resting on the elevator and rudder controls. Flying Officer Christopher "Jumbo" Deansley was another who had a

lucky escape, two in fact, twice crashing into the sea and being rescued each time. He later became a night fighter pilot and survived the war.

'One day Jerry started to concentrate his attacks on the airfields, and Warmwell did not escape. We saw a formation of about a dozen twin-engined aircraft approaching at 8-10,000' and drop their loads. It was all over in a matter of minutes. They were pretty accurate; the hangar and a number of aircraft were either destroyed or damaged, and then delayed action bombs kept exploding over the next few days. There was also a number of casualties amongst the ground personnel. As practically all our waking hours were spent at the dispersal point at the wooded end of the airfield, for years after in any panic the standard call was "Away to the woods".

'On another occasion towards the end of that long, hot, summer, half a dozen of us were having a snack in the canteen run by the WRVS, which had better food than the NAAFI, but a lone enemy aircraft bombed and strafed the camp at zero feet. It was a day of particularly poor visibility and I remember diving under one of the heavy hardwood tables, which were standard equipment in those days. A radiator from the heating system landed on top of it, again, some were more lucky than others.

'A sad loss during the Battle of Britain was that of 21-year-old Pilot Officer Douglas Shepley, who had only been married for six weeks. His elder brother, a Flight Lieutenant, had already been lost over Dunkirk. His sister, a nurse, had been lost at sea when the SS Lancastrian was bombed and sunk. His family lived at Woodthorpe Hall, near Sheffield. His wife, "Biddy", and his parents raised a fund to buy a Spitfire, and a pub near the hall is, to this day, still called the "Shepley Spitfire".

'From the beginning the Squadron's mascot was a white bull terrier known as "Pooch". Now, "Pooch" was not an easy animal to get on with and if he only suspected that you were afraid of him that was sufficient to make your life a misery and a continual hazard. A very good mate of mine, the squadron parachute packer, was one of these, and amongst his duties was a daily visit to the pilots' dispersal tent to carry out his inspection. I am sure that "Pooch" heard or sensed this coming from afar, and it was the duty of whoever was there to grab "Pooch" and picket him down. To do so was indeed difficult, for he had been known to move a NAAFI wagon given a strong rope and enough encouragement! "Pooch" even until then had had a somewhat colourful career having previously belonged to a Canadian officer pilot stationed at Digby. The pilot was with the RAF on some kind of scheme. When he returned to Canada "Pooch" was given to Tommy Thomas who gave the dog to his wife as a present. For some time, understandably, she was scared stiff of the dog but eventually they became very attached. When 152 re-formed in 1939, Tommy became commander of 'B' flight and remained so until he was promoted to Squadron Leader and posted as a controller to Middle Wallop, Warmwell's sector station. His good lady had by this time relinquished ownership of "Pooch" who was taken over by 152 and Flying Officer Graham "Cocky" Cox in particular. Now "Cocky" was equivalent in weight and strength to "Pooch", but luckily his disposition was more docile! He and the dog became great friends. Wherever the Squadron went until sometime in 1942, "Pooch" was there and in *every place the pilots sought out female companionship for him, so much so that I am sure he had more than all of the rest of the squadron put together! I recently saw a photograph of "Pooch", taken somewhere in SE England in 1944 and by which time he was looking a little the worse for wear.*

'*During the late summer and early autumn of 1940, the invasion of this country was more than a distinct possibility. The pros and cons and whys and wherefores have been voiced and written about many times elsewhere, so I will not go into that here, but suffice to say that the possibility eventually receded, and as the days shortened so did daylight air activity and we were given a little time off. Bus trips into neighbouring Bournemouth and Weymouth were arranged, and in the evenings we would visit hostelries in the more immediate vicinity, such as at Woodsford, Puddletown, Broadmaine and Dorchester. Pilots had their own haunts, although occasionally our paths would cross, such as at the Gloucester Hotel in Weymouth which was popular for all ranks. I managed a week's leave for the New Year of '41. When I returned I discovered my promotion to the exalted rank of LAC. The corresponding increase in pay was again greatly appreciated. In February 1941 the pilots very kindly threw a party for the ground crews, and of course included themselves, at the Gloucester Hotel. It was a very heavy night indeed and a number of us had to have a whiff of oxygen for breakfast the following morning! Squadron Leader Boitel-Gill, on such occasions, would take up a Spitfire and treat us all to a session of aerobatics. One such "air test", as these flights were officially called, included another Spitfire flown by Flight Lieutenant Dennis David, who finished the war with a score of 20. After a mock dogfight the aircraft disappeared, then reappeared flying very low towards dispersal at just 300', wing-tip to wing-tip, apparently trying to get lower than the other. When they landed Dennis David immediately made for the pilots' hut. It is said that he went to his quarters for a change of underclothing, and this could be true, for I believe the last bodily function before a violent death is the evacuation of the bowels. In this instance his propeller blade had been damaged which did not do the engine any good.*

'*As frequently happened, there were unfortunate occurrences. On April 1st, 1941, of all days, we had a visitation by a nuisance raider. One of our pilots, Sergeant Fawcett, was killed by a single bullet whilst seated in the Sergeants' Mess. During the previous November a young pilot joined us, Pilot Officer Allen, he made a good job of a crashed landing but not so lucky a second time when he went into some forest at Durweston near Dorchester after having been with us just a fortnight. The cynics on occasions such as this, and there were many at this time, said that it all went to prove that if your name was on it it would find you wherever you were.*'

152 Squadron was commanded by Squadron Leader Peter Devitt, formerly a member of No 600 Squadron of the Royal Auxiliary Air Force based at Hendon. Called up to full-time service in August 1939, Devitt first served in Tangmere's Operations Room before being given command of 152 in February, 1940, by which time he was 27 years old and married with two children. Devitt had made his money before the war with Lloyd's. Pilot Officer Roger Hall described him as '*a debonair sort of person, an excellent pilot and very capable leader.*'

Formal 152 Squadron line up taken early in the Battle of Britain. Those in the rear row are senior ground staff NCOs.

Middle Row: left to right -

Sgt (later Plt Off) HJ Ackroyd, Sgt EE Shepperd, Plt Off RM Hogg, Plt Off Brian (IO), Plt Off IN Bayles, Plt Off AR Watson, Plt Off W Beaumont, Plt Off C Warren, Plt Off ES Marrs, Plt Off FH Holmes, Sgt JK Barker & Sgt LA Reddington.

Seated:

Sgt AW Kearsey, Plt Off TS Wildblood, Flg Off Laverick (Adj), Flg Off PG St G O'Brian, Flt Lt DPA Boitel-Gill, Sqn Ldr PK Devitt (CO), Flt Lt FM Thomas, Flg Off ES Hogg, W/O Deverill (Eng Off), Plt Off GJ Cox, Sgt KC Holland.

Author's Collection via Ray Johnson

Amongst the squadron's other pilots was 20-year-old Pilot Officer Eric *Boy* Marrs, a regular officer and product of Cranwell. *Boy* was to become an *ace*, having destroyed more than five enemy aircraft, and received the Distinguished Flying Cross in January 1941. Seven months later, however, he was dead, shot down by anti-aircraft fire over Brest. One of his Battle of Britain victories was a Ju 88A-1, *L1 + XC*, of Stab II/LG1, which was engaged on a sortie to bomb Speke airfield on September 17th, 1940. The Ju 88 was attacked by 152 Squadron's Blue Section, led by Marrs and comprising Flying Officer P.G. St. G. O'Brian, and Sergeant K.C. Holland. The raider crashed whilst attempting a forced landing at Ladywell Barn, near Warminster, at 2 pm. Leutnant O. Heinrich was killed, but the remainder of the crew, including the pilot, Major Heinz Cramer, the Gruppenkommandeur and holder of the Knights Cross, were captured. After the war, Marrs's diary was published in *The Aeroplane*, and he wrote the following of Cramer's demise:-

'On Tuesday I was leading a section of three and we were ordered on to a Ju 88 bomber near Bath. I attacked first and hit the radiator of his starboard engine with my first burst. Glycol poured out in white streams and his starboard motor finally packed up. The other

two Spitfires then attacked in order and then we each nibbled around attacking when we could.

'*He then managed to reach the clouds, which were thick, puffy cumulus. I followed into one but lost him. The other two went around and found him again. When I lost him I circled round but noticed a strange smell. I looked down and saw slight fumes arising from under the dashboard. During the scrap I had noticed an aerodrome with big runways standing out and showing up well. I made for it, and as I was still at about 12,000' I was able to make it easily. My engine began shuddering violently, making the whole aeroplane shake. It then seized up solid. I then noticed that my aerodrome was covered with small, square concrete blocks to prevent German transport aeroplanes landing. I had to come down and was able to pick a spot more or less free from blocks, where I landed without damage to the aeroplane. The aerodrome (Colerne) was just being built, hence the concrete blocks. I inspected my aeroplane and found one bullet through my oil cooler. I had lost my oil and the engine had seized up.*

'*When I got back to Warmwell I found that the 88 had come down at Imber. The next day we three who had shot it down motored up to inspect it. We arrived at 5 pm. It was in very good condition and we were extremely interested. There were four bullet marks on the back of an armour-plated seat. We arrived to find quite a crowd all round the machine, though kept at distance by a rope. We were able to climb all over it and see where our bullets had gone and where I had hit his radiator. We stayed two hours then pushed off to Salisbury.*'

Pilot Officer ES 'Boy' Marrs DFC of
152 Squadron.
Author's Collection via Allan White

Major Heinz Cramer,
Gruppenkommandeur of II/LG 1
Author's Collection via Allan White

The Sector Station of Middle Wallop boasted both a Hurricane and a Spitfire squadron, 238 and 609 Squadrons respectively. Like 152, 238 had also fought during the First World War, disbanding in 1922. Re-formed at Tangmere on May 16th, 1940, the Squadron was first equipped with Spitfires but changed to Hurricanes in June. As was the practice with Wallop based squadrons, 238 often operated daily out of Warmwell, nearer the coast. On September 30th, however, the Squadron moved to the new airfield at Chilbolton, a satellite to the east of the Sector Station. The squadron diary recorded on that date:-

'In this way, the 238th Squadron of the line entered the depths of Hampshire countryside to a common, where, in the bright, early autumn weather, they renewed their guard and saw the thorns and trees changing colour, so as to bring to mind the lines:-

Royal the Pageant Closes,
Lit by the last of the sun,
Opal and ash of roses,
Cinnamon, amber and dun.'

Sergeant LG Batt of 238 Squadron.
Author's Collection via Flt Lt LG Batt

238 Squadron's identification letters were *VK*, and during the Battle of Britain the unit lost 17 pilots. From June 1940 the squadron was commanded by Squadron Leader Harold Fenton who had initially received a short service commission in 1928. Between

1933 and the outbreak of war, Fenton was a flying instructor on the Reserve List. Like many other squadron commanders at this time, Fenton had no combat experience. Nevertheless he led from the front, sharing in the destruction of a Do 17 on July 21st, and ditching in the Channel a few days later after attacking an He 59 floatplane during a search for a missing member of his squadron. Wounded, Fenton re-joined the squadron on September 13th. On the 26th, he forced landed at Lee-on-Solent following combat with Me 110s during the attack on Southampton's Spitfire factory. Towards the end of September, Fenton had several experienced fighter pilots under his command, including his flight commanders, Flight Lieutenant Michael Lister Robinson, who had joined 238 from 601 on September 28th, having already destroyed several enemy aircraft, and Flying Officer Bob Doe, formerly a Spitfire pilot with 234 Squadron until joining 238 on September 27th. 20-year-old Doe had already destroyed 12 enemy aircraft by that time. His efforts during the Battle of Britain were to place him high on the list of *aces* during 1940 and earn him both a DFC and Bar.

238 Squadron informal line up at Chilbolton, 1941. The known Battle of Britain pilots are,
from left to right:
2nd, Sgt P Pearson; 7, Plt Off PJ Morgan; 8, Plt Off JR Urwin-Mann; 16, Plt Off VC Simmonds.
Author's Collection via Air Cdre HA Fenton

609 *West Riding* Squadron of the Auxiliary Air Force had been formed at Yeadon in February 1936. The Auxiliaries were largely men of wealth who flew for pleasure at weekends. In time of war, however, the Auxiliary units supplemented the strength of the regular air force, their personnel distinguishable by the gold *A* on their collars, and, so legend has it, slightly longer hair than the norm and a disregard for red tape! 609 Squadron received the Spitfire in August 1939, when based at Catterick, and first engaged the enemy en masse over Dunkirk, during *Operation Dynamo*, whilst flying from Northolt. On July 6th, the squadron moved south to Middle Wallop to provide

further protection to the Royal Navy at Portland. Over Dunkirk 609 had suffered its first losses. It must be understood that these Auxiliary squadrons, whose pilots all hailed from the same local areas and in some cases had known each other since childhood, perhaps felt these early losses even more keenly than the regular squadrons. This was certainly the case with 609, and on June 22nd, 27-year-old Squadron Leader HS *George* Darley, a regular officer who had held a commission since 1932, took command of the Squadron with the express intention of ensuring that it overcame this depression. Darley immediately embarked upon a harsh training programme at Middle Wallop, although the Squadron was also in the front line. In the opening shots of the Battle of Britain, during which 609 fought in numerous skirmishes over the Weymouth and Portland areas, the Squadron fared little better. During the preceding nine weeks, which included Dunkirk, the squadron had lost nine pilots, including seven of the 12 Auxiliary officers called up in August 1939. However, on Adlertag the squadron's fortunes changed dramatically during their annihilation of the Stukas over Lyme Bay. From that point on the squadron's combat claims exceeded their losses. Replacements had actually meant, however, that this, with many other Auxiliary units, became somewhat more cosmopolitan, by August boasting amongst its pilots three American volunteers (all sadly killed later), and two Poles who had escaped the defeat of their homeland to continue the fight.

Pilots of 609 Squadron snapped shortly after landing at Warmwell following combat during the Battle of Britain. At extreme left is possibly Sgt AN Feary, centre is Plt Off David Crook. Note the motorcycle, Spitfire with trolley 'acc' plugged in and ready to go again, and other Spitfires dispersed around the airfield.

Chris Goss Collection

A long-standing member of 609 Squadron was Pilot Officer David Crook. Born at Huddersfield in 1914, and educated at Leys School, Cambridge, young David was being groomed to join the family business of manufacturing leather and wooden sports goods. During the summer holiday of 1933 he took flying lessons at Ganton, near Scarborough, going solo after eight hours dual experience. In October 1937 he joined the Auxiliary Air Force and was commissioned into 609 Squadron. After completing his service flying training, Crook re-joined the squadron at Northolt in time for the Dunkirk air battles. A married man, Crook was also a talented writer. In 1942 *Spitfire Pilot* was published, being his first hand experiences as a fighter pilot during 1940 and written from the diary he recorded at the time. Whilst that title is well known to those familiar with the literature of the period, perhaps less so is Crook's second book, a wartime thriller entitled *In Pursuit of Passey.*

609 Squadron's David Crook, author of 'Spitfire Pilot', pictured later in the war whilst a flying instructor and shortly before his death in a flying accident.

Author's Collection via Hessling.

During the defence of the Parnall aircraft factory at Yate on September 27th, 1940, 609 Squadron lost 20-year-old Pilot Officer RFG Miller; of this incident, in *Spitfire Pilot*, Crook wrote:-

'I was flying just behind Mick and he turned slightly left to attack an Me 110 which was coming towards him. But the German was as determined as Mick, and refused to give way or alter course to avoid this head-on attack. Their aggregate speed of closing was at least 600 mph and an instant later they collided. There was a terrific explosion and a sheet of flame and black smoke seemed to hang in the air like a great ball of fire. Many little shattered fragments fluttered down, that was all. Mick was killed instantly and so were his two German opponents. Poor old Mick! I had known him for a year as he was at Flying Training School with me. His brother, also in the RAF, was killed only two months before on a raid on Germany.'

Miller's Spitfire, X4107, fell at Doles Ash, Dorset. The Me 110, of 9/ZG 26, came down nearby at Piddletrenthide. Gefreiter Liedtke was killed, but Gefreiter Jackstadt baled out wounded and was captured. The overall engagement was a great success for 609 Squadron who claimed six enemy aircraft destroyed and several probables. Crook, however, commented further upon Miller's loss:-

'I remember walking into the mess for lunch and sitting down and suddenly recollecting that at breakfast, only a few hours before, I had sat next to Mick at this very table and we had chatted together. And now, here we were at the next meal, everything quite normal,

but he was dead.

'That was the one thing that I could never get accustomed to; seeing one's friends gay and full of life as they always were, and then, a few hours later, seeing the batman start packing their kit, their shaving brush still damp from being used that morning.'

Others were able to cope with the losses. Norman Ramsey flew Spitfires with 222 Squadron in 1940 and recalls:-

'People missing or killed meant little to me by September, 1940. I had joined 222 from 610 at Biggin Hill after we had lost ten, yes ten, pilots, so I was well used to the disappearing faces.'

Despite the casualties, it must be stressed that Fighter Command's morale generally was extremely high. During the Battle of Britain, Wing Commander George Unwin DSO DFM RAF Retd was a Flight Sergeant and flying Spitfires with 12 Group's 19 Squadron:-

'At the time I felt nothing out of the ordinary. I had been trained for the job and luckily had a lot of experience. I was always most disappointed if the squadron got into a scrap when I was off duty, and this applied to all of the pilots I knew. It was only after the event that I began to realise how serious defeat would have been - but then, without being big-headed, we never ever considered being beaten, it was just not possible so far as we were concerned.'

Sadly, however, Flight Lieutenant David Crook DFC also perished, in 1944, when his Spitfire inexplicably dived from 22,000' into the sea near Aberdeen. He remains missing and is remembered on the Runnymede Memorial to British and Commonwealth airmen who have no known grave.

A 609 Squadron survivor, now 81, is Flight Lieutenant Michael Appleby AE, who was a Pilot Officer with David Crook during the Battle of Britain. Over 50 years later, he also vividly remembers the summer of 1940:-

'Towards the end of July Dowding ruled that all pilots should have at least eight hours stand down time in any 24, and at least a 24 hour continuous time off once a week. To enable us to do this we had a further intake of fairly newly qualified pilots, including a second from the Volunteer Reserve stable, John Bisdee. Being Orderly Officer one evening I took a telephone call from a newly posted pilot, who wanted to know if it would be possible for him to postpone his arrival until the next day as he would like to see his parents in London on his way down from training school. To this I agreed. Next day arrived the "Green eyed Monster" - Noel Agazarian, of French and Armenian ancestry, who had been

Pilot Officer Michael Appleby of 609 Squadron.

Author's Collection via Hessling.

sent down from Oxford having intended to read for the Bar. He was by nature a cosmopolitan and a brilliant linguist, but the English education had discovered that he was more of an athlete and his flying was typical of his slapdash but brilliant improvisations. He did survive the Battle of Britain but was then posted to the Middle East where he was killed.

'*On July 18th, I did five sorties, on one of which, a patrol of Lyme Regis, Swanage and Weymouth, I acted as a section leader, that is the leading aircraft of a set of three, but nothing of any event occurred so as the weather closed in we returned and patrolled base for half an hour before landing. I see from my log book that in August 1940, between 1st and 17th, I flew every day except on the 12th & 15th, and sometimes, for example on the 8th, four times, and it was on this sortie that I was flying No 2 to the Squadron Leader when he put me in such a position over some Me 110s attacking a convoy that I had nothing to do but press the firing button, and both the engine cowlings and the cockpit came off as the aircraft was seen to dive into the sea, much to the delight, we subsequently heard, of the Royal Navy. Then on August 13th there was a big raid which was intercepted by various squadrons, but 609 were able to claim many Ju 87s, Me 110s or 109s shot down without loss to ourselves. I did not personally claim any aircraft destroyed, but was credited with a Ju 87 and an Me 110 damaged. This was I think a great success for our CO, George Darley, because of the tactics he had adopted, getting us in the right position at the right time, providing the information from our radar people was reliable.*

'*Here I should mention that the groundcrew, the fitter and rigger looking after the aircraft, were naturally keenly interested in the success of our flying, and after this sortie they came up very delighted and asked me to come and look at the aircraft, which had three bullet holes in it, one in the wing tip, one in the wing root, and one in the propeller blade. What really was most extraordinary was that with a three bladed propeller going round, a bullet could go through the middle of a blade and just made a round hole, it did not even seem to me to be torn or oval. However, it shows the bravery of the rear gunner of an Me 110 who must have continued firing up until the last minute.*

David Crook's Spitfire, PR-L, being re-armed following combat over Weymouth, 1940.

Author's Collection via Hessling

'*Throughout August we were usually patrolling Brooklands, Guildford and other areas west of London to support No 11 Group and harry the stragglers who had possibly already dropped their bombs and were on the way home. Things do happen so fast at 20,000' in the air, collision speeds at well over 600 mph, that it is not surprising that with all that space around you it was not always possible to locate the enemy aircraft. Even if you did they might be so far away that by the time you caught them up something else had happened in between. Nonetheless if we did catch them we attacked, and the squadron had quite a lot of success.*

'*At dispersal points these not only split the aircraft up, but enabled them to take off a little more easily from three separate taxying points. The strain of waiting at dispersal was greatly emphasised by the field telephone; every time the 'phone rang everybody just stopped until the operator answering could call out "Sergeant so and so required in sick quarters", at which point we all promptly relaxed. On the other hand, when it was a scramble, we all rushed to our aircraft, preceded by the fitter and rigger, popped into the aircraft, set our parachute harness and did up our safety harness, quite tight too, and having got the throttle mixture control and airscrew pitch controls set, the fitter operated the starter battery and the engine started. Whilst taxying out to the take off point down wind, we adopted our position in the formation as previously decided. As I have mentioned we did give back up to 11 Group over London, but we also patrolled Portsmouth, intercepting raids coming across the Channel. In this way we managed to intercept six Do 215 bomber aircraft intending to cause damage in Portsmouth and we chased them back across the Channel. Since they were unprotected by fighters I led my section off to one side, intending to do a beam attack, which would probably be safer than attacking from the rear where the rear gunners could concentrate their fire. It was therefore somewhat galling to find that, having pressed on to get into the best position, the two aircraft which should have been with me had already turned and were attacking the Dorniers. I managed to get into position and join them. We managed to get two of them down, one of which turned back to land in England, realising that without his engines he was not going to get across the Channel. On this occasion I was credited with 1/6th of an aircraft, the other section also being involved and it was not quite possible to sort out which pilot did what.*

'*Also, I must not forget the time when the invasion was supposed to be imminent, church bells ringing, and we were all sitting in our aircraft awaiting a massed attack. Nothing happened!*'

To the west of Lyme Bay lies Exeter, and the small airfield there was opened by Sir Kingsley Wood on July 30th, 1938. The main users of the airport were Jersey Airways and Railway Air Services, although further activity was stimulated by the introduction of the Civil Air Guard Scheme. RAF Station Exeter, however, was not officially opened until July 6th, 1940. During the Battle of Britain, the airfield was attacked by a lone raider on August 21st, and two servicemen were killed in addition to a number of others injured. On September 12th, the Station Commander, Wing Commander John Dewar DSO DFC, took off in a Hurricane to visit Tangmere. He never arrived and also remains missing.

Having fought in France during the hopeless attempt to stem the German blitzkrieg, 87 Squadron arrived at Exeter on July 5th, 1940. Although on occasions flights were detached to both Hullavington and Bibury, Exeter remained the Squadron's home until November 1940 when it moved to Colerne for night-fighter duties. Flying from Exeter the squadron was heavily engaged in the Battle of Britain as it affected the West Country, and frequently its *LK* coded Hurricanes found themselves in action over Lyme Bay and Dorset.

Sgt LA 'Rubber' Thorogood with his 87 Squadron Hurricane at Exeter. Note the 'Pluto' Disney character and streamlined rearview mirror.

Author's Collection via Sqn Ldr LA Thorogood.

Amongst the squadron's personnel were several personalities and successful fighter pilots. Ian Richard Gleed, a doctor's son, had learned to fly privately with the London Aeroplane Club at Hatfield before joining the RAF in 1936. He joined 87 Squadron as 'A' flight's commander on May 14th, 1940, and during the next week destroyed seven enemy aircraft and damaged several others. During August he destroyed four more, and in September received the DFC. Short of stature, Flight Lieutenant Gleed was known as the *Wizard Midget*, or *Widge* for short. Eventually his luck also ran out, however, on April 16th, 1943, when leading 244 Wing in the Middle East. Shot down by Leutnant Reinert of JG 77, his empty Spitfire was discovered on sand dunes near the western coastline of Cap Bon. Although his final moments remain a mystery, Gleed's body is known to have been buried at Tazoghrane. Like David Crook, Gleed left behind testimony of his Battle of Britain experiences in his book, *Arise to Conquer*, also published in 1942.

Flying Officer John Cock, an Australian, also flew with 87 Squadron in France and similarly received the DFC for his courage during 1940. On August 11th he claimed a Ju 88 destroyed and an Me 109 damaged, but was himself shot down off Portland Bill. He baled out, slightly injured, and was machine-gunned by Me 109s during his descent into the sea. His Hurricane, V7233, however, was to remain submerged until recovered by enthusiasts in 1983. Cock returned to England to watch the spectacle and was later presented with the gunsight through which he had last taken aim over 40 years before.

No mention of 87 Squadron in 1940 would be complete without reference to Roland Beamont, who, during the Battles of both France and Britain served as a Pilot Officer. A successful Hurricane pilot who had also received the DFC, Beamont became a test pilot with Hawker Aircraft in late 1941. When he later returned to operational flying it was on the Hawker Typhoon and he did much to establish this machine as the excellent ground attack aircraft it eventually became after many initial problems. During the Flying Bomb attacks Beamont himself destroyed 32 V1s whilst flying Tempests. In October 1944, however, he was shot down and taken prisoner. After the war Beamont returned to test flying, and established several records in the Canberra and P1 jet aircraft. His immense experience in aviation was also absorbed into the Panavia Tornado programme.

601 *County of London* Squadron, known as the *'Millionaires' Squadron'*, was another Auxiliary unit and shared Exeter with 87 Squadron. The unit's Hurricanes were emblazoned with the squadron's badge, a winged sword, and were coded *UF*. 601's radio call sign was *Weapon*. At the outbreak of war, however, the squadron was equipped with twin-engined Blenheim Mk IFs, and in company with aircraft from 25 Squadron actually flew the first intruder mission of the war when Borkum seaplane base was strafed. In December 1939 the squadron moved to Tangmere, and there, in February 1940, received its Hurricanes. During the Battle of France its aircraft operated from Merville and St Valery, but returned to England on June 1st. The squadron arrived at Exeter on September 7th. Whilst previously flying from Tangmere, Pilot Officer *Billy* Fiske had been killed in action. Fiske was a wealthy stockbroker, film producer and international sportsman from Chicago. Officially he is the only American killed during the Battle of Britain and is remembered on a memorial plaque in St Paul's Cathedral which was unveiled by Sir Archibald Sinclair, the Secretary of State for Air, on American Independence Day, 1941. Other notables amongst the 14 pilots lost by 601 that summer included Flying Officer Richard Demetriadi, son of Sir Stephen Demetriadi, and Flight Lieutenant William Henry Rhodes Moorhouse DFC whose father had won a Victoria Cross in the Great War whilst flying with the Royal Flying Corps.

Amongst the survivors were The Hon. John William Maxwell Aitkin, son of Lord Beaverbrook, the Minister for Aircraft Production. Aitkin had scored well in France, and received his DFC in July, but that same month was posted away and did not return to operations until February 1941 when he subsequently became a successful night-fighter pilot. Another 601 Squadron pilot who survived the Battle of Britain was Flying Officer Whitney Straight, the post-war Managing Director of BOAC.

The pitiful remains of Flg Off Topolnicki's Hurricane which crashed at Exeter whilst taking off on September 21st 1940. The 601 Squadron Polish pilot was killed. The Hurricanes in the background belong to 87 Squadron.

Chris Goss Collection.

At Filton, near Bristol, was 504 *City of Nottingham* Squadron, yet another Hurricane unit of the Auxiliary Air Force. 504 had been formed at Hucknall as a Special Reserve Squadron in 1928, and exchanged its biplanes for Hurricanes in May 1939. On September 6th, 1940, the squadron flew from Castletown in Scotland to Hendon from where the squadron was engaged in the defence of London. The following day, Sergeant Mike Bush was shot up by an Me 109 over Eastchurch in Hurricane P3021, *TM-N*. A cannon shell passed through his instrument panel and into the reserve petrol tank behind. Mike managed to forced land at Eastchurch airfield. There he got the main tanks refuelled and eventually flew back to Hendon. He recalls that *'I was damned lucky not to catch fire as when hit petrol splashed all over me.'* 504 Squadron was also involved on September 15th, *Battle of Britain Day.* Having been attacked by many British fighters over the capital that day, Oberleutnant Robert Zehbe's Do 17 was finally brought down by Sergeant Ray Holmes of 504 Squadron who rammed the enemy bomber and was forced to bale out himself. The Dornier crashed on Victoria station and thus became the Battle's most famous German casualty. Having arrived at Filton on September 26th, 504 was in action on the 27th against the Yate raid, during which its pilots claimed a number of aircraft destroyed.

504 Squadron await a 'scramble' at 'dispersal' Filton, 1940. Seated with forage cap is the CO, Sqn Ldr John Sample, behind him in tunic is Flt Lt Tony Rook, with record player is Flg Off Michael 'Scruffy' Royce, and the seated NCO is Sgt 'Wag' Haw.

Author's Collection via Allan White

Taxying accident involving two of 504 Squadron's Hurricanes at Filton.

Author's Collection via Allan White

213 *Ceylon* Squadron had also fought in France before flying first from Exeter and then Tangmere. The squadron's Hurricanes were coded *AK* and its call sign was *Bearskin*. 213 lost a total of 15 pilots killed during the Battle of Britain. On August 28th, Squadron Leader Duncan MacDonald was posted to command 213 Squadron. On September 11th, Flight Lieutenant JEJ Sing was shot down in combat over Portland Bill. Although now 82 years old, Group Captain MacDonald DSO DFC RAF Retd remembers those events clearly:-

'Jackie Sing was shot down over the sea and rescued by an American oil tanker. You can imagine his feelings when informed by the Captain that the cargo consisted of 100 octane aviation fuel for Fighter Command! The tanker made landfall at Shoreham, Sussex, and I motored down from Tangmere in the early evening to recover this valuable member of my squadron who was a bit shaken but fortunately uninjured. He was in the air again the next day and none the worse for this most frightening experience.'

Fear must have been a constant companion, but pilots learned to control their feelings. Jurek Poplawski, a Polish Hurricane pilot with 229 Squadron at Northolt during the Battle of Britain, commented on the subject whilst recollecting his friend, Flying Officer Franciszek Surma, a Polish fighter *ace* killed in action during 1941:-

'He was a rather quiet person, a bit reserved really. Perhaps we were all like that,

trying not to think of tomorrow. It would be wrong to say that we were not afraid, after all we were just human beings and as such we all knew what fear was. But we also had a code of conduct, a sense of duty, that made us control our fear. That code was possibly the most important influence in our young lives.'

Of his Battle of Britain sorties generally, 54 years later Leslie Gordon Batt, at the time a Hurricane pilot with 238 Squadron, remarked *'they were all quite frightening and fraught with danger.'*

56 Squadron, based at Boscombe Down, was a regular air force unit and one of the most outstanding Great War fighter squadrons. 56 had been the first to fly the fabled SE5 scout. Its pilots included such legends as Ball and McCudden. Disbanded in January 1920, a week later No 80 Squadron at Aboukir, equipped with the Snipe, renumbered and became 56. By 1937 the Squadron was based at North Weald, in Essex, and flying Gloster Gladiators. Wing Commander Frederick *Taffy* Higginson OBE DFC DFM RAF Retd, now 83, joined 56 at that time as a Sergeant Pilot. He found the traditions of the Great War 56 Squadron very much alive: *'In a room was displayed McCudden's uniform and Victoria Cross, and every new pilot was made to study the exhibition and salute upon leaving the room.'* In April 1938 the squadron received Hawker Hurricanes, and in May 1940 was one of those squadrons fighting in France. By the end of May 56 was withdrawn to Digby. The following month, however, the squadron returned to North Weald, in 11 Group, and from there was heavily involved in the first and second phases of the Battle of Britain. One of the squadron's casualties during this time was Pilot Officer Geoffrey Page. On August 12th, Flight Lieutenant *Jumbo* Gracie led his section of three Hurricanes, numbers two and three being Pilot Officers Sutton and Page, into action against a large formation of KG 2's Do 17s some 10 miles north of Margate. Page's Hurricane, *US-X*, was hit, and the reserve petrol tank, situated directly behind the pilot's instrument panel, exploded.

Sutton saw Page's Hurricane plummet earthwards in a sheet of flame, and returned to base convinced that his friend was dead. But Page, who was flying with his canopy open, managed to bale out into the sea. Page was terribly burnt but, after convincing its crew using choice Anglo-Saxon that he was British and not a *Jerry*, he was rescued by the Margate lifeboat. 20-year-old Geoffrey Page was amongst those horribly disfigured young pilots whose faces and lives were eventually rebuilt by Sir Archibald McIndoe at East Grinstead's famous Burns Unit.

A quartet of 56 Squadron's NCO pilots. At left is Sgt Peter Hillwood who was to claim a 'Do17' as damaged during the Yeovil raid, and second right is the indomitable 'Taffy' Higginson.
Author's Collection via Wg Cdr FW Higginson

Taffy Higginson recalls that whilst flying from North Weald during that period 56 Squadron *'received a bit of a beating.'* There the squadron had lost five of its eight pilots killed during the battle, in addition to Page and several others having been badly wounded. Fighter Command had by this time introduced the Stabilising Scheme which categorised squadrons either 'A', 'B' or 'C' units. 'A' squadrons were those up to strength and in the front line, 'B' were those being rested due to previous losses but which could be called upon if necessary, and 'C' squadrons those unlikely to be recalled to action but being used as an extension of the training process by providing tactical instruction to new pilots prior to passing them on to either 'A' or 'B' units.

56 Squadron's pilots meet Sir Kingsley Wood, Minister for Air. The Minister is shaking hands with Sgt Jim Elliot, 'Taffy' Higginson's brother-in-law who was shot down in flames over Dunkirk. To Elliot's left is Sgt C Whitehead who claimed a damaged German bomber on the Yeovil raid. Sgt 'Taffy' Higginson, one of the unsung but most successful fighter pilots during the Battle of France, is at extreme right.

Author's Collection via Wg Cdr FW Higginson

So it was that on September 1st, 56 Squadron was categorised a 'B' unit and withdrawn from 11 Group's front line to Boscome Down in 10 Group. There the squadron began to receive replacement pilots and commenced, in addition to its operational duties, a training programme for them. On September 17th, Sergeants Dennis Nichols and Peter Fox reported for flying duties with 56 Squadron. Both were 19 years old and *sprog* pilots from 5 Operational Training Unit at Aston Down. In training too, however, losses occurred, and the day after their arrival Sergeants Nichols and Fox found themselves coffin bearers at the funeral of Sergeant Tweed, killed in a dogfight practice on September 15th. According to Dennis Nichols's log book, the training largely consisted of dogfight practice, practice air fighting and aerobatics, although his flights are punctuated with *X Raids*, being patrols in response to unidentified or hostile plots. Sergeant Fox flew an interesting exercise on September 20th - a height test to 32,800': *'I remember well the way I had to fight in nursing my Hurricane up the last few hundred feet and I kept falling out of the sky in stalls.'* Dennis remembers that Higginson, who was already a very experienced and successful fighter pilot commissioned on September 18th, tried hard to teach the replacements a little of what they needed to know to stay alive. *Taffy* Higginson: *'The main recollection I have of that period at Boscombe and Warmwell was that we were a somewhat disorganised lot. As a result of the action that we had seen we needed to re-equip and receive replacement pilots. The Station Commander at Boscombe was a Group Captain who, I believe, later took a unit to Russia and was killed. He was a first class chap, good rugger player and liked by us all. During the early part of the Boscombe sojourn, I remember thinking that morale would perhaps be boosted if we had a squadron mascot, so I went out to the local town and bought a small monkey which we named "109". He was a great success and kept in a cage and on a lead. Anyway, the Group Captain gave a cocktail party for the squadron and suggested that "109" should be present. "109" went down very well, until, that is, he started to undertake enthusiastic sexual self-gratification! Morals being what they were in those days, we had to remove him quickly!'*

In addition to Fighter Command, we must not forget that Britain was also defended in 1940 by gunners, searchlight and barrage balloon crews who grafted both day and night, for little recognition. During the first year of the war, the anti-aircraft gunners claimed the destruction of 444 German aircraft, although in reality the true total was but a fraction of that figure. The gunners made a very real contribution during the defence of the airfields in August and indeed throughout the battle, however, by forcing the German bombers to fly higher and thus bomb less accurately. Anti-Aircraft Command was a branch of the British Army that had been placed under Dowding's direction and given its Headquarters in the grounds of Bentley Priory. The Command's Commander-in-Chief, General Sir Frederick Pile, was a great friend of Dowding's and during the Battle of Britain the pair worked in total accord.

Most of the heavy 4.5" and 3.7" guns were deployed around key towns and factories in batteries of four which were linked to a local Gun Operations Room. Yeovil was protected by a four 3.7" gun battery of the 5th Anti-Aircraft Division during the Battle of Britain. However, Worcester, a city also featured in this book, possessed no guns at all. With guns at a premium, Pile was only able to defend key targets, and guns could not be spared for locations such as Worcester in the Midlands which had no particular strategic or industrial importance.

In addition to the guns, Britain's key centres were also defended from air attack by barrage balloons, or more correctly, the LZ (Low Zone) Kite Balloons which were hydrogen/air filled envelopes. These were designed to fly tethered from a fixed point at 5,000', but were in fact flown operationally at around 6,500'. Somerset had two barrages, each comprising 24 balloons protecting the aircraft factories at Yeovil and Weston-super-Mare. The balloons were controlled by No 32 (Barrage Balloon) Group at No 11 Balloon Centre, Bristol. The barrage, however, sometimes caused problems for our own aircraft; one night in May 1941, the Hurricane intruders of Sergeant *Rubber* Thorogood and Squadron Leader *Widge* Gleed flew into the Yeovil balloons whilst returning from an operation over France. Squadron Leader Laurence Thorogood now recalls that *'we were very lucky to get out intact!'*

Barrage balloon over a Yeovil suburb. Museum of South Somerset.

The Observer Corps was also an essential link in Britain's defences, being responsible for tracking enemy aircraft which had crossed the coast, and passing, via Observer Centres, this important information to Fighter Command. In Somerset there were 29 Observer Posts, part of a national network completed just in time for the Battle of Britain. Those posts in southern Somerset formed a part of No 22 Group whose headquarters were at Yeovil. At first the Observer Corps possessed no uniforms but a striped armband on which *Observer Corps* was overprinted in bright red. There were normally just two on duty at each post, No 1, who was in charge, and No 2 who acted as both telephonist and plotter. We should remember that the Observer Corps was a volunteer organisation and its members performed duty, sometimes as much as 24 hours a week, in addition to their often demanding full time occupations.

A Stadium Type Observer Post at Fordingbridge, Observer Storer on duty.

ROC Museum/Henry Willis.

The inside of the Bodenham Observer Post indicating the all-important kettle!

ROC Museum/Henry Willis.

The Air Raid Precautions service had been formed in 1937, when the ARP Act had designated local responsibility to county councils. The Service's intention was to provide *leaders and advisors* to supervise air raid shelters, issue gas masks and check black-out precautions. Most wardens were middle-aged or elderly men, although one in six was a woman. The Service was controlled by 12 Regional Commissioners answerable to the Ministry of Home Security, and did much valuable rescue and warning work during the blitz. Somerset was covered by eight ARP areas, Yeovil being No 6. On occasions the County Controller had to decide whether to send reinforcements to other badly bombed areas either within or outside the county. Therefore Yeovil's ARP members also helped in London, Bristol, Exeter, Plymouth, and, more significantly for the purposes of this book, at nearby Sherborne in Dorset.

The nation's police forces continued with their normal peacetime duties in addition to those many extra tasks that the war imposed upon them. They were assisted by temporary full-time constables of the Police War Reserve, and the part-time volunteers of the Special Constabulary. Just like the Special Constabulary of today, duties were performed largely at night and weekends in addition to full-time civilian employment. In country areas the local bobby assumed much extra responsibility and often found himself called upon to guard captured German airmen, direct rescues from bombed buildings, or even find transport for shot down British pilots trying to return to their stations. In 1940 the police stations of southern England became clearing houses for all manner of victims and survivors.

In the last years before the war, the call also went out for volunteers to join the Auxiliary Fire Service, and some 60,000 subsequently augmented the 6,000 professional firemen of the National Fire Service. However, numbers of the AFS dwindled throughout the winter of 1939/40 as its members were called up for service in the armed forces. When the bombing of Britain began in earnest, the critical importance of the fire service became recognised. With poor equipment and little training, the Auxiliaries worked long hours under appalling conditions throughout the autumn and winter of 1940. Eventually they therefore won even the respect of sceptical professional firemen. The National Fire Service was, as its name suggests, organised on a nationwide basis and had a great advantage in being able to move reinforcements quickly to wherever they were needed most.

A Bristol Police Constable, resplendent in steel helmet, carrying wreckage from the Me110C-4 of 2/ZG26's Oberfeldwebel Hans Tiepelt, shot down at Fishponds during the Yate raid of September 27th, 1940.

Author's Collection via Allan White

Also worthy of note are Somerset's 39 rescue parties which had a strength of seven and an establishment of 21 personnel. Rescue Squads were each allocated an ambulance, of which Somerset had 108. It was intended that a first aid party should not only move as a cohesive unit, but should also work and train as a team. Each ambulance was crewed by a driver and an attendant.

In May 1940 the British Government had appealed for civilians to come forward and create a force of Local Defence Volunteers in every town and village. Within a week 250,000 men had joined and a million by August, overwhelming the ability of the authorities to both organise and arm them. There were rifles for just a fraction of the men, the remainder being armed with shotguns, swords, clubs and staves. The

LDV was soon renamed the *Home Guard*, and has perhaps in more recent times found immortality through the long-standing hit television comedy series, *Dad's Army*. With hindsight it is easy to be scornful about the value of this army of untrained and feebly equipped old men and invalids. But they were invaluable in taking over endless local guard duties that would otherwise have overburdened the British Army. Perhaps most of all, however, they gave every community a sense of direct involvement in the defence of Britain without precedent in the nation's entire history. The LDV Battalion at Yeovil, a town that is in many ways this book's focal point, was formed upon the Government's call and was commanded by Lieutenant Colonel G.H.A. Ing. The Battalion, which later become No 3, covered a large area in Somerset's south-east corner which bordered both Wiltshire and Dorset.

Finally, we should remember the work of the BDU, or Bomb Disposal Units, whose daunting task was to make safe unexploded bombs -known as UXBs. The BDU teams were all volunteers, and mostly skilled men of the Royal Engineers. At the beginning of hostilities, UXBs actually posed few problems as the bombs in use were designed to explode upon impact, although some malfunctioned and were made harmless by removal of their fuses. A deadly game of cat and mouse soon began, however, when the Germans began building in anti-handling devices.

Thus, then did Britain, and in particular the West Country, stand to defy the invader and withstand his aerial onslaught in 1940. A fitting tribute to the bravery of Dowding's pilots is a remark recorded in Fighter Command Intelligence Summary No 182, and made by an anonymous Me 110 pilot of ZG76 who had been shot down and captured; this vanquished foe stated that the RAF pilots fought with *Kolossalen Verbissenheit* - or with tremendous stubbornness.

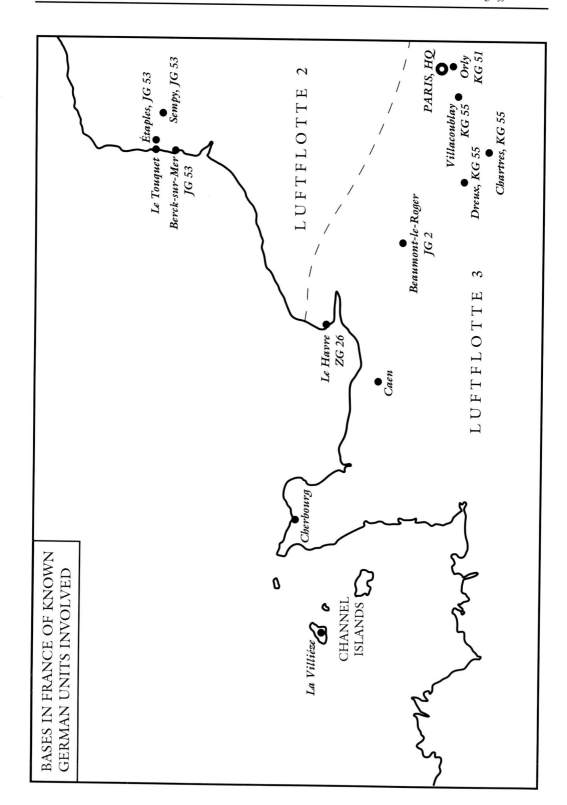

BASES IN FRANCE OF KNOWN
GERMAN UNITS INVOLVED

LUFTFLOTTE 2

LUFTFLOTTE 3

PARIS, HQ

Orly
KG 51

Villacoublay
KG 55

Dreux, KG 55

Chartres, KG 55

Beaumont-le-Roger
JG 2

Étaples, JG 53

Sempy, JG 53

Le Touquet

Berck-sur-Mer
JG 53

Le Havre
ZG 26

Caen

Cherbourg

La Villièze

CHANNEL
ISLANDS

The Attackers

In the wake of the First World War, the victorious Allies intended that Germany would never again rise to pose a military threat. Consequently the Treaty of Versailles in 1919, which was signed by Germany, significantly reduced the sizes of both its army and navy in addition to prohibiting the manufacture and possession of submarines, and banned the air corps entirely. Restrictions were even placed on the engine size and weight of civil aircraft. Despite this, however, the German aviation industry later produced many designs which though ostensibly civil, revealed many military characteristics to the keen observer. Whilst such machines became the backbone of the new Luftwaffe, the training of personnel, without arousing the suspicions of watchful nations, presented considerable difficulties. In 1923 the Reichswehr-Ministerium, or Defence Ministry, made an agreement with the Soviet Government which provided training facilities for both German air and ground crews. Adolf Hitler and the Nazis came to power in 1933, and the indoctrination process for young people became even more pronounced as many swelled the ranks of the Hitler Jugend, or Hitler Youth. Aviation minded youngsters were encouraged to join the Deutscher Luftsportverband (DLV), a pseudo sporting club, which trained them as glider pilots to ultimately form the basis of the clandestine air force.

The new Luftwaffe was revealed to a disbelieving world in 1935. Just one year later, the German *volunteers* of the Condor Legion fought for General Franco in the Spanish Civil War, and in order to distribute as much combat experience as possible throughout the Luftwaffe, units and personnel were frequently rotated. The Germans perfected their ground-attack and fighter techniques in Spain, and blooded both the Me 109 and new He 111 bomber. The He 111 was actually found to be faster than the Republicans' biplane fighters, so this was rashly regarded as proof that German air superiority would easily be obtained in any theatre, especially as at the same time the RAF was still equipped with similarly obsolete biplanes. Unfortunately for Germany, the Munich Agreement of 1938 would give Fighter Command the invaluable time needed to re-equip with the modern Spitfire and Hurricane. Spain nevertheless produced invaluable experience for the Luftwaffe's first generation of experten.

Reichsmarschall Hermann Goering, Air Minister and Commander-in-Chief of the Luftwaffe, was amongst Hitler's closest confidants and his designated successor. He had been one of Imperial Germany's most famous fighter pilots during the Great War, winning the coveted Pour le Merite, and actually succeeded Manfred von Richthofen in command of his celebrated *flying circus*. As a war hero with the credentials of a gentleman, Goering was a powerful asset to the Nazi Party when he joined in 1922. The *fat man* gained great support from the middle-classes, who had previously treated Hitler with caution, and, as the Nazis climbed to power, Goering became President of the Reichstag and Prime Minister of Prussia. In the early 1930s, it was Goering who organised stormtroopers, formed the Gestapo and even set up the first so-called concentration camps. Office and large-scale embezzlement gave Goering a life-style rarely equalled this century. The pink, girlish complexion, overweight body and many childish indulgences masked a personality, however, capable of superhuman self-control. The Luftwaffe's triumphs in Poland and the West had greatly increased both his prestige and lust for power. By the Battle of Britain, Hermann Goering was at his zenith.

On the Channel coast the Luftwaffe was organised into two Air Fleets which were each a self-contained air force. Luftflotte 2 covered north-eastern France and the Low Countries, commanded by Generalfeldmarschall Albrecht Kesselring whose Headquarters were at Brussels, and Generalfeldmarschall Hugo Sperrle's Luftflotte 3 embraced north-western France. Each Luftflotte also exercised responsibility for operations over a specific area of the British Isles.

The forbidding, scowling Sperrle was the most experienced air force officer in Germany. Also a pilot in the Great War, he had commanded the Condor Legion in Spain. He was 50 in 1940, a huge slow-moving, bear-like figure with a passion for luxury to match Goering's: his Headquarters were at the fabulous Palais du Luxembourg. In many ways he was the archetypal monocled German officer.

Generalfeldmarschall Hugo Sperrle, Commander of Luftflotte 3.

The Luftflotten commanders took their orders direct from Goering. Each of the specialized elements within the Luftflotte was controlled by a Fliegerkorps HQ. The new post of *Jagdfliegerführer*, or fighter leader (Jafü), had been created to centralize control of the fighters under one man answerable to the Luftflotte commander. In reality, however, the bomber Fliegerkorps HQ, responsible for many more men, always outweighed the Jafü in policy arguments. Thus the Jafü became little more than a liaison officer informing the fighters what the bombers expected from them. This was to have a serious negative implication on German tactics throughout the Battle of Britain.

At operational level, the Luftflotten fighters, heavy fighters, and bombers were organised by Groups - *Jagd, Zerstörer,* and *Kampfgeschwadern*. A *Geschwader* consisted of some 100 aircraft, commanded by the *Geschwaderkommodore*, an officer usually of Oberstleutnant rank. The Geschwader had its own staff flight, the *Geschwaderstab*, led by the *Kommodore*, which could be of *Staffel* strength, depending on how many staff officers were involved, such as the Adjutant, Technical and Operations Officers. The Geschwader was then subdivided into three *Gruppen*, I-III, each commanded by a *Gruppenkommandeur*, usually a Major. Each *Gruppe* also had its own *Stab*, and was further divided into three *Staffeln*, each commanded by a *Staffelkapitän*, and possessed its own communications, vehicles and staff. The Staffeln were numbered 1=12, thus 6/KG55 = the II Gruppe's 6th Staffel of Kampfgeschwader 55. A Staffel equated to an RAF squadron, so a Gruppe of three Staffeln compared to a Fighter Command Wing formation. A Geschwader, therefore, represented the equivalent of an RAF Bomber Group.

Air-to-air and air-to-ground communications were a problem for the Luftwaffe in 1940. For example, fighters could talk to each other in the air, but neither to the ground or the bombers. Therefore the system of colour coding identifying Geschwader, Gruppe, Staffel and individual aircraft became even more important in the air. For example, white indicated the first staffel in each gruppe, red the second, and yellow the third. The Geschwader and Gruppenstab used blue and green. Each bomber's fuselage bore the German black cross, either side of which were two characters. To the left a particular number and letter identified a specific Geschwader, for example KG55 was *G1*. Those two to the right indicated both the individual aircraft and its Staffel. The individual letter was either painted in, or outlined in, the particular Staffel colour.

In this book the two bomber types with which we are concerned are the Heinkel 111 and Junkers 88. The former was designed by the brothers Siegfried and Walter Gunter, and with a top speed of around 247 mph was one of the most outstanding warplanes of the 1930s. However, by the Second World War, and the advent of the Spitfire and Hurricane (113 and 81 mph faster respectively than the He 111), the twin DB601A powered He 111 had lost much of its potency. Against the British fighters' eight machine-guns, the He 111 was poorly armed with just three 7.9 mm MG15s situated singly in the nose, dorsal and ventral positions. The Heinkel's nose was virtually fully glazed, but, contrary to popular belief, caused various visibility problems for the pilot. During periods of sunlight the curved perspex panels emulated mirrors, whilst in bad weather conditions, with rivulets of water streaming down the nose, the pilot's visibility was further impaired, although the ability was built in to elevate the pilot's seat and controls for landing and taxying which allowed his head to emerge through a sliding panel, his face being protected from slipstream by a retractable windscreen. The glazed nose, in which was located the pilot, navigator/bombardier, and radio operator/air gunner, also gave a feeling of vulnerability during action. The He 111 handled excellently, however, being very stable around all axes, and offered good harmony of control. Leutnant Peter Wulff flew He 111s with III/KG53 *Legion Kondor* against the Russians. During the 16 operational flights that he made over the

Soviet Union before transferring to fly fighters in the west, Peter was impressed by the He 111: *'We felt very safe in our bomber as although it was slow most of the systems were mechanical, as opposed to hydraulic like the more modern Ju 88, and were therefore not so easily prone to serious damage.'*

Above Left: A Luftwaffe 'Black Man' prepares an He 111 for a sortie. Note the aircraft's glazed nose and cockpit area, and that the machine gun is missing from the Ikaria universal mounting, no doubt receiving an armourer's attention.

Chris Goss Collection

Above Right: An He 111 in flight, the bombardier in his prone position and manning a machine gun whilst maintaining a keen watch for British fighters.

Bundesarchiv

Left: An He 111 forced down in France having been damaged in combat over England. The crew are all wearing the tan coloured lightweight flying overall and lined flying boots. The original snapshot was found in the possession of one of these men, later taken POW in England

Author's Collection via Hessling

The Junkers 88 was the backbone of the German bomber force during the Second World War. It was a remarkable aeroplane which fulfilled multifarious roles from dive-bomber to nightfighter duties and was directly comparable with the legendary de Havilland Mosquito. The Ju 88 was originally designed by Professor Hugo Junkers as a high-speed or *Schnellbomber*, no other roles being perceived at that stage. The Ju 88's top speed, at just under 300 mph, was even comparable to that of the Hurricane's 328 mph. Again, during the Battle of Britain, the Ju 88's shortcoming was in its lack of defensive armament, being armed by three MG 15s, one each mounted in the front and rear cockpits, and in a ventral gondola. The four-man Ju 88, however, was recognised by the RAF during 1940 as the most formidable warplane in its category.

In 1940 the German bombers used a variety of bombs against the English mainland, but the principal high explosive (HE) types came in three categories: the *Sprengbombe-Cylindrisch* (SC), a thin-cased general purpose bomb, the *Sprengbombe-Dickwandig* (SD), a thick-cased Semi-Armour-Piercing Fragmentation Bomb, and the *Panzerbombe-Cylindrisch* (PC), an Armour-Piercing Bomb. Our story is concerned largely with the

SC family of bombs, also called *Minenbomben*. These had a high charge ratio for blast effect, contained 55 per cent explosive, and were used primarily for general demolition. In fact, eight out of ten bombs dropped on Great Britain were from the SC range, usually between 50 and 2,000kg. They were of three piece steel construction with a thick nose welded to a thin-walled tubular body. A sheet steel or alloy tail unit was then riveted to the bomb. When carried inside the fuselage

Ju88s of 4/KG51 lined up at Orly. Note that many of the aircraft have their canopies protected by tarpaulin.

Chris Goss Collection

An SC500 bomb on its wooden tow-sled. The He111 would appear to be undergoing an engine test as a panel is missing from the right hand engine

Chris Goss Collection

An SC250 bomb in foreground, and SC50's behind, all waiting to be loaded up into a Ju 88

Chris Goss Collection

bomb-bay, the bombs were stowed either vertically or horizontally. When carried beneath the fuselage or wings, the bombs were held by suspension brackets or bands. Often a *Kopfring*, a triangular steel ring, was fitted to the bomb's nose to prevent excessive penetration of the ground, thus obtaining maximum effect of blast. The *Trumpets of Jericho* were also sometimes fitted to SC 50 and 250 tail units, consisting of cardboard tubes shaped like organ pipes through which, as the bomb descended,

the wind blew causing them to shriek. Used
against either troops or civilians this banshee
howl was an effective morale breaker.

Civil Defence reports often refer to the *oil
bomb*; more accurately, this was the
Flammenbombe, an incendiary which
contained an oil mixture and an HE bursting
charge. The incendiary oil consisted of 70 per
cent petroleum and 30 per cent TNT.
Flammenbomben came in two sizes, 250 and
500kg. Bombs such as these were used to start
large fires and were far more dangerous than
the 1kg *Brandbombe* incendiary that fell upon
England in thousands.

For aiming these bombs, each aircraft was
fitted with the Lofte 7c tachometric sight,
similar in operation to the American Norden.
On a typical bombing run, the target was
sighted through a gyro-stabilized telescope
which was moved by an electric motor. As
the bomb aimer held the telescope on the

*An He 111 bombardier peers through his
Lofte 7c bombsight at the target below.*

Bundesarchiv

target, information on the aircraft's flight path was fed into a sighting computer which
had previously been programmed with details of the bombs used and altitude from
which the attack would be made. The computer gave course corrections which were
displayed in front of the pilot. As the target was approached, the sighting telescope
moved to coincide with the angle dictated by the computer and an electric circuit
released the bombs automatically. A run of some 40 seconds was needed for a standard
level flight attack with the Lofte sight, but low-level attacks required the bombs to be
dropped manually.

With medium-range bombers such as the Ju 88 and He 111, designed for the
tactical role in support of fast moving ground forces, however, the Luftwaffe in 1940
was not actually equipped to wage a strategic bombing campaign such as the RAF and
USAAF were later to launch against Germany with four-engined, long-range heavy
bombers like the Lancaster and Flying Fortress. The He 111's maximum bombload
was 2,000kg (4,400 lbs), and the Ju 88's 1,500kg (3,300 lbs). By comparison, the
Avro Lancaster carried 14,000 - 22,000 lbs of bombs, five times more than the
He 111.

All German aircrew spent six months in basic training. Pilots experienced ab initio
flight at elementary flying schools. There they also studied aerodynamics, navigation,
radio procedures, aviation law and other related subjects. Successful completion of
the course meant the next instalment of flying training in respect of more advanced

aircraft types. Bomber pilots then went to another training school and received a further 60 hours flying, and from there to a specialist school to learn instrument flying. The final stage in training brought a bomber crew together and they then flew operational aircraft on simulated sorties until ready to join an operational unit. As opposed to the RAF, the captain of a German bomber was usually the observer, and not the pilot.

Luftwaffe uniforms were field blue in colour and bore the eagle insignia on the right breast, in silver bullion for officers and embroidered for other ranks. The metal pilot's qualification badge was worn on the left breast. Collar patches and shoulder straps denoted rank, the background colour indicating the wearer's particular branch of the service, aircrew *Waffenfarbe* being golden yellow. Wings, borders and oak leaves were in silver. Bomber crews often flew in one-piece light brown flying overalls which carried simple rank badges on the sleeves. The life jacket was either the heavy kapok-filled waistcoat or the superior *Schwimmweste* which could be inflated either manually or by activation of a pressurised cartridge. Summer issue flying helmets were fawn in colour and featured both radio earpieces and a throat microphone. Flying goggles were either ordinary or of the shatterproof Nitsche & Gunter type with dark lenses.

A German 'Kampflieger' wearing the lightweight summer issue flying helmet, shatterproof goggles, oxygen mask and 'Schwimmweste'.

Bundesarchiv

Much has been written over the years regarding German fighter tactics and formations, which admittedly revolutionised fighter versus fighter combat, but by comparison little has been published regarding tactics and formations adopted by the Kampfgeschwadern. To understand fully the events related in later chapters of this book, however, it is imperative to examine this neglected subject.

The basic cohesive battle formation around which the entire Geschwader was built was the *Kette* of three aircraft flying in an arrowhead formation similar to the RAF vic of three. In daylight Gruppen formations disposed their aircraft in three principal variations (*see Figs 1-3*). These formations could constitute those for both cruising and attacking, or alternatively, depending on the size of target, could easily be changed in the air upon command. For example, during the raid on Yeovil of October 7th 1940, as studied in this book, the whole formation went into Gruppe, Ketten astern, in order to attack (*see Fig 4*).

GERMAN BOMBER FORMATIONS (*not to scale*)

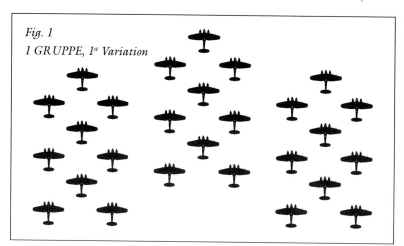

Fig. 1
1 GRUPPE, 1ˢᵗ Variation

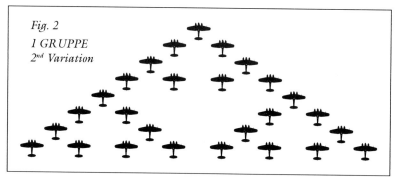

Fig. 2
1 GRUPPE
2ⁿᵈ Variation

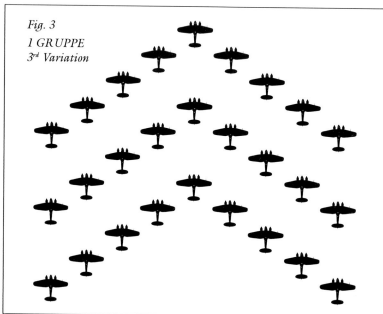

Fig. 3
1 GRUPPE
3ʳᵈ Variation

Fig. 4
GRUPPE in
Ketten Astern.

When more than one Gruppe was operating, the bombers flew, as a rule, in Gruppe line astern. Each Gruppe was then 500' above the one in front and a distance of from between a quarter up to three miles separated them. On occasions the raiders operated in shallow vics giving the impression of abreast formations in three waves *(see Fig 2)*. All formations in both line astern and abreast were generally flown well *stepped up*. Bomber formations largely operated at heights varying between 10,000' and 20,000', but the favoured optimum operational height was between 13,000' and 17,000'. British Intelligence, who monitored the Kampfgeschwadern's battle tactics, noted that *'it has been observed that the various units forming the main formation fly very close together and often succeed in maintaining their cohesion when attacked.'* When intercepted by fighters, the bomber formations would not adopt evasive tactics but would instead rely upon the mutual fire support that their close formation flying provided, and assistance from their fighter escorts. This applied to large formations which could only operate in fine weather. When RAF fighters encountered smaller formations, or when the main formation had been broken up, the bombers, either individually or in sections, adopted several evasive tactics by:-

i) Seeking the nearest available cloud cover.

ii) Descending to ground or sea level at high speed and making a *jinking* low level escape at full throttle.

iii Using dive brakes, when fitted, to enable execution of a steep dive, combined with turns, thus causing attacking fighters to overshoot.

Also according to British Intelligence, bombers sometimes *'simulated damage by emitting smoke from an apparatus fitted either in the tail or behind the engine nacelles.'*

Mass formations sometimes split into sub-groups on crossing the English coastline, each bound for different targets. Also small groups of aircraft sometimes flew independently towards the same objective, but often it was only one group that penetrated to the target with any degree of determination. This led British Intelligence to assume that *'the subsequent behaviour of the remaining groups has given the impression that their role has been to confuse our defence and divert our fighters from the main intention. These subsidiary formations have either dropped bombs on what has been an unidentifiable target short of the objective or turned for home without taking any offensive action. These tactics have been successful in that our fighter control has experienced difficulty in anticipating the development of the operation in its early stages and this has sometimes increased the difficulties of bringing about a successful interception.'* The German formations would also frequently approach their objectives on a *dog-leg* course. For example, on September 25th, 1940, the raiders flew straight to Weston-super-Mare where the formation turned for Bristol, thus only revealing the actual target at the last possible moment.

On September 30th, 1940, it was I and II Gruppen of KG55 which attacked the West Country. KG55 had been formed in 1937 with I Gruppe based at Langendiebach and II Gruppe at Giessen. It was its association with Giessen which led to the unit adopting the town's coat of arms as its badge, a red and black griffin on a white shield, after which KG55 became known as the *Greifen* Geschwader. KG55 saw action in the Polish campaign during September 1939. Three months later its III Gruppe was formed and based at Neudorf/Oppeln. All three Gruppen were deployed for the attack on the West in May 1940, and subsequently took over bases in France formerly occupied by the Armée de l'Air at Chartres, Dreux and Villacoublay, all within Luftflotte 3. The Geschwaderkommodore was Oberstleutnant Hans Korte. His Stabstaffel was based at Villacoublay, ironically near Versailles, and was commanded by Hauptman Heinz Hofer. There the Operations HQ, or *Gruppengefechstand*, of III Gruppe was also located. Korte's *Geschwadergefechstand* was at the nearby Chateau Monteclin. An important Geschwaderstab officer at the HQ was Major Doktor Ernst

Kühl, the Staff Operations Officer, who was not only responsible for the planning of KG55's operations but also flew on many himself. The Geschwaderkommodore also flew operationally, and indeed KG55 had already lost one Kommodore in action. I Gruppe was commanded by Major Joachim Roeber and based at Dreux with Major Friedrich Kless's II Gruppe. Kless had led the successful attack against the Bristol Aeroplane Company at Filton on September 25th, and had consequently received the Knights Cross. Flying with I Gruppe, having made his first operational flight against England on August 16th, was a somewhat less distinguished *Bördschutze*, or air gunner, an 18-year-old youth named Robert Götz. Amongst the youngest in his Geschwader, Flieger Götz flew on a total of 39 operations against England before adding some 300 more to that list on the Russian Front.

* Major Friedrich Kless, Kommandeur of II/KG55.
Kenneth Wakefield Collection

The Luftwaffe had already commenced a nocturnal assault on England by this time, and on the night of September 29th, 1940, III/KG55 had participated in a night raid on Liverpool. Consequently they were not involved in the daylight operation of the following day. The involvement in night attacks was reflected by KG55's He 111s. For day bombing the aircraft had been painted two shades of dark green in a splinter pattern on the upper surfaces, and light blue beneath. To help conceal the aircraft over Britain's night skies, however, a black distemper had hurriedly been applied to the aircraft, blacking out not only the pale blue but also even the white edging of numerals and national cross markings. For day operations this night finish could be washed off, but due to pressure of work this was seldom, if ever, undertaken by the *Flughafenbetriebskompanien* (FBK), the aircraft maintenance companies attached to KG55. With KG55 having been so committed to action over such a protracted period,

* Major Kless died in 1994.

the FBK had a busy enough time as it was repairing and maintaining their bombers. When the campaign in the West had commenced, for example, KG55 was equipped with 108 aircraft. Due to losses, despite receiving replacement aircraft, by September 7th, 1940, its strength was down to 68. Whilst the RAF's essential groundcrew were known affectionately as *erks*, the Luftwaffe's were called *Black Men* owing to the black overalls they wore.

An impressive 'Tail-Art' found on a 3/KG55 He 111, Werk Nummer 2145.

Chris Goss Collection

On October 7th 1940, the German attack against Westlands was made by the Ju 88s of II/KG51 *Edelweiss*. KG51 was a long-range bomber unit of V Fliegerkorps with Headquarters at Paris-Orly airfield. Like KG55, the unit had already lost a Geschwaderkommodore, Oberst Doktor Hans Fisser, whose Ju 88 had been shot down on August 12th by 152 Squadron's Spitfires during an attack on the Ventnor RDF station. Fisser was succeeded by Major Hans Bruno Schulz-Heyn. The Geschwaderstab and I Gruppe, the latter's Gruppenkommandeur being Hauptmann Kurt von Greiff, were also based at Paris-Orly until August 1st when they moved to Melun-Villaroche. On August 24th, II Gruppe, commanded by Major Winkler, moved from Étampes-Mondesir, where III Gruppe, commanded by Major Marieufeld, was also located, to Paris-Orly. KG51's unit code was *9K*, and during the Battle of Britain it was heavily committed as a part of Luftflotte 3. The *Edelweiss* Geschwader lost over 100 aircrew killed in action during the battle. One crew of the 5th Staffel that had failed to return from operations over England was that of Ju 88 *9K+GN*. On July 25th, Unteroffiziers Friedel Dörner, Wilhelm Hügelschäfer and Walter Theiner, and Gefreiter Gottfried Treue, were briefed to undertake a *Störflug*, or harrassing attack, to the Gloster Aircraft Factory at Hucclecote in Gloucestershire. However, near the target the Ju 88 was intercepted by two Hurricanes from No 4 Ferry Pilots' Pool at Kemble. Pilot

The crash site of KG51's '9K+GN' at Oakridge, Gloucestershire.

Author's Collection via Allan White.

Officer Alec Bird pursued the raider into cloud where it is believed a collision occurred. Bird crashed and was killed, but as the Ju 88 emerged from the cumulus it was attacked again, this time by a Spitfire flown by Flight Lieutenant Peter Prosser Hanks DFC, an instructor at the nearby training unit at Aston Down. However, the Germans' fate had already been sealed by that time and the crew were in the process of baling out. *9K+GN* crashed at Oakridge, Gloucestershire. All of the crew were captured except Theiner who had been killed as his parachute had failed to open.

In addition to such lone aircraft attacks, KG51 were also used to mass formation operations, having frequently been engaged upon such raids against targets in southern England. On August 12th, for example, the raid on which the Geschwaderkommodore had been lost, 100 Ju 88s of KG51, with a large fighter escort, slipped through the balloon barrage and successfully dive-bombed Portsmouth, causing widespread damage. Like KG55's He 111s, KG51's Ju 88s would also have appeared over the West Country during autumn 1940 painted with the black distemper. Two pilots of II Gruppe were both blind flying instructors, Oberleutnant Sigurd Hey and Oberfeldwebel Ludwig Piller, the latter of the Gruppenstab, and as such were generally retained for specialist night flying. Both, however, would find themselves flying Ju 88s bound for Yeovil on October 7th.

A stunning snapshot of a Ju88 crew ready to go, their aircraft bristling with machine guns. KG51's 'Edelweiss' badge is shown to maximum effect. The pilot is the 4th Staffel's Unteroffizier Robert Ciuraj who flew this aircraft, '9K+GN' on the Yeovil raid

Chris Goss Collection

Oberfeldwebel Robert Ciuraj (in shorts) pictured in Sicily during 1941 with his crew, Leutnant Sartor, Feldwebel Mittlemann and an unknown member. It is believed that this is the crew with whom Ciuraj flew on the Yeovil raid.

Chris Goss Collection

During the Battle of Britain, the German fighter units (Jagdgruppen) were, quite rightly, supremely confident in the use of their superior combat tactics which had been adopted during the Spanish Civil War. A firm belief in these tactics, and confidence in their aircraft and equipment, were both vital parts of the Luftwaffe pilots' training process which took over two years to complete. The single-engined German fighter type of the period was the legendary Me 109 *Emil*, comparable in performance to the Spitfire, but markedly superior to the Hurricane. One great disadvantage for the British fighters was that when pushed down into a steep dive, their engines would momentarily cut out as centrifugal force upset the float carburettor, whereas the direct fuel injected DB601A engine of the Me 109 was not affected by such manoeuvres. The Me 109E was armed with two 20 mm wing-mounted Oerlikon MGFF cannons, and two 7.9 mm MG17s mounted on top of the engine block and which fired through the propeller arc. Such a combination of fire power was far more devastating than the eight .303 machine-guns of the Spitfire and Hurricane. To sight his target, the Me 109 pilot had a Revi C/12C reflector gunsight. The cannon fired high explosive, armour-piercing, and incendiary ammunition at the rate of 520 rpm, and the machine-guns at 1,100 rpm. A thumb button on the control column fired the cannons, and a finger trigger the machine-guns. The jagflieger was also provided with excellent personal equipment, and generally they wore into action at this time the summer type lightweight flying helmet, either the one-piece fawn flying overall or normal uniform, the Schwimmweste life jacket and leather flying boots. With two crossings of the English Channel with which to contend per operational flight, the pilot was also equipped with a Mauser flare pistol, which was often attached to his life jacket, and a plentiful supply of cartridges strapped to the top of each flying boot. An inflatable life-raft was also stowed in the cockpit.

The Me 109E. This superb photograph was 'found' by a British soldier in a German house in 1945. It is believed to show a machine of III/JG52 following a landing accident at its German base in 1940. The numerals and III Gruppe wavy bar are probably black. The aircraft is painted in standard summer 1940 camouflage of pale blue under and side surfaces with a two-tone splinter pattern green upper.

Author's Collection

The Jagdwaffe was also built up around the Geschwader system, hence *Jagdgeschwader* which consisted of three Gruppen, again each of three Staffeln. The Geschwaderkommodore flew with his *Stabschwarm*, comprising the Geschwader Adjutant, Operations and Technical Officers. Each Gruppen also had its own *Gruppenstabschwarm*, led by the Gruppenkommandeur. Each Staffel, commanded by a Staffelkapitän, was then sub-divided into *Schwarm* of four aircraft, and further into pairs, or *Rotte*, each consisting of a leader and wingman. Individual aircraft within each Staffel were marked with numbers from 1 onwards, painted in the Staffel colour and (if looking at the left hand side of the aircraft) painted to the left of the fuselage's national cross. The marking to the right indicated the aircraft's Gruppe: no marking identified I Gruppe, a horizontal or vertical bar II Gruppe, and a wavy line III Gruppe. The Geschwaderstab and Gruppenstabschwarm used a system of chevron, horizontal bar and circle symbols indicating to which particular officer each aircraft belonged. Each Geschwader normally had its own emblem painted on its fighters, which may also have borne another badge particular to just one Gruppen or Staffeln. Engine cowlings, rudders and wing-tips were also often painted yellow or white to further assist with ease of identification in the air (post August 28th, 1940).

Following heavy losses suffered by the Kampfgeschwadern, Goering ordered that the fighters would, from mid-August onwards, provide a close escort to the bombers. Consequently practically all the Me 109s of Luftflotte 3 were transferred to Luftflotte 2 and based on airfields in the Pas de Calais. This gave Generalfeldmarschall Kesselring an overwhelming provision of escorts for the attacks against south-eastern England, but even so the Me 109 only had fuel enough for 20 minutes flying time over England. For those based within the Pas de Calais, London was at the extreme limit of their range, whilst Luftflotte 3's few remaining *Emils* in Normandy and Brittany were hard pushed to penetrate very far inland at all over Dorset and Hampshire.

As British Intelligence had reported on the German bomber tactics, so too had it studied the methods and effectiveness of fighter protection:-

'Escorting fighters are dispersed in various positions relative to the bomber formations they are protecting. During the early phase of attacks on this country it was usual for the fighter escort to fly behind and several thousand feet above the bomber formation. If our fighters attacked the bombers, the escort would descend and attack them providing that they (the German fighters) were not outnumbered. If our fighters attacked the enemy fighter escort, the latter would usually form a self-defensive circle, thus ceasing to afford protection to the bombers which they were supposedly escorting.

'Heavy casualties suffered by the bombers led to a change of tactics involving an increase in escorting fighters with new dispositions relative to the bomber formations. Fighters were encountered ahead and on both flanks as well as above and behind the bombers and usually flying in closer proximity to the latter. On occasions the individual bomber units were found to be more spaced out with the fighters weaving amongst them. Accompanying

formations of fighters have also been observed acting as remote escort or "freelance" patrols flying at a great height above, and in the vicinity of, the bomber formations, but they have rarely taken offensive action.'

On August 12th, 1940, Oberleutnant von Hofe was flying an Me 109 of JG53 protecting KG51's Ju 88s during the attack on Portsmouth. He later recorded his experiences flying with the fighter escort that day, and in particular a brief moment of hectic action:-

'Six Spitfires dived down from the left, turning towards us. We zoomed up very tightly and they flashed by behind us. We went into a diving turn to the right and the leading Messerschmitts of our Staffel got behind the Spitfires. All our guns were firing. Two Spitfires went down trailing smoke, one of them exploded after a 1000m dive, the other one flew away leaving white smoke behind it. The other Spitfires turned sharply to meet us and fired away at our Staffel's rearmost machines. We then got behind the enemy fighters. The Kommandeur set one of them on fire and the English pilot baled out immediately. His parachute blossomed beneath us. The rest of the "Tommies" dived away, showing us their blue bellies and "Peacock's eyes". Two of our aircraft reported that they were leaving the formation as both had been badly hit. The Kommandeur ordered two others to cover them and accompany them home.'

Von Hofe also wrote about a bomber that had been damaged:-

'Once again we were flying near the bombers, from which we had been separated in combat. One of them fell back about 200m behind the formation. A long white smoke cloud trailed from the right engine. A hit! Some of our fighters covered the machine. It lagged further and further behind; its right propeller was stationary but apparently the machine could maintain its altitude and was still protected by fighters. I hope it reached the French coast...'

The two Me 109 units that provided fighter escort for KG55 and KG51, during their West Country raids of September 30th and October 7th, were Jagdgeschwader 2 *Richthofen* and Jagdgeschwader 53 *Pik-As.*

JG2 was considered to be the Luftwaffe's senior fighter unit and had been the first to receive the Me 109. The Geschwader was named after Germany's most famous Great War fighter pilot, Rittmeister Manfred Freiherr von Richthofen, better known as the *Red Baron*, and its pilots wore a prestigious cuff-title indicating their unit. In July 1940 JG2 became based at Beaumont-le-Roger, an area of huge cornfields (in Luftflotte 3). The Geschwader also operated from other airfields throughout the Battle of Britain, including

JG2's luxury HQ at the Chateau in Beaumont-le-Roger

Michael Payne

Le Havre (where III Gruppe became based), Théville, Mardyk-Dunkirk and Oye-Plage.

The aircraft of 1 Staffel carried a white Bonzo Dog badge, and 3 Staffel a blue pennant bearing a dagger and the word *Horrido*, the hunters' victory cry. This emblem also became the personal badge of Hauptmann Helmut Wick, Gruppenkommandeur of I Gruppe from September 9th, 1940. Also, during our period of interest, II Gruppenkommandeur was Hauptmann Griesert, and III Gruppenkommandeur Hauptmann Otto Bertram. The Geschwaderkommodore was Major Wolfgang Schellman. All of JG2's Me 109Es bore the Geschwader emblem, a silver or white shield on which the letter *R* was painted in red.

Above: This is the Me 109E that Helmut Wick flew throughout the summer of 1940. It was coded Yellow '2' when he led the 3rd Staffel. Here it carries his markings as Kommandeur of I/JG2. Later it bore the Kommodore's Winkel and Bars after Wick's promotion to command the Geschwader. Contrary to popular opinion, the pennant badge was blue with yellow sword and lettering. Note also the 'Richthofen' Geschwader 'R' shield.

Below left: The Gruppenkommandeur of I&II/JG2, Oberleutnants Wick and Schellmann at Cherbourg-Maupertus.

Below right: Helmut Wick briefing his pilots at Beaumont-le-Roger whilst Staffelkapitän of 3/JG2. The pilot on Wick's right is another experte, Kurt Buhligen.

Michael Payne

22-year-old Helmut Wick was one of the Luftwaffe's leading experten, and without doubt the most famous jagdflieger participating in the actions covered in this book. When war broke out he was a Leutnant with 1/JG53, but during the Polish campaign transferred to I/JG2. However, although Wick scored his first kill on November 22nd, 1939, the unit saw virtually no action at this time due to having been assigned the defence of Berlin. Wick's next victories came during the blitzkrieg against the West in May 1940. By June 1940 he had been promoted to Staffelkapitän of 3/JG2 and also received the *Eisernes Kreuz I*, or Iron Cross First Class. On August 18th, 1940, 3/JG2 was amongst the fighters escorting the Kampfgeschwardern on a maximum effort attack against various airfield targets in southern England. He later wrote about a traumatic moment over England:-

'Three Englishmen flew towards me, very close together. I pulled the stick full backwards and positioned myself behind them. A fast look to both the right and left - for the next few seconds the sky was clear. I dived faster, got the leader in my gunsight, depressed the buttons - he plunged down, and the two others were gone. I zoomed upwards. Something was going on to the right. I could hardly believe my eyes. The sky was filled with Spitfires and amongst them a few poor Messerschmitts. Into the gaggle to get the chaps out! Immediately a Spitfire was sitting behind me. I got away, with full throttle - in front of me another Spitfire, and behind? Dammit, another was sitting on my tail so I dived and made a climbing turn. To the right, just beside my cockpit, strange white lines appeared. More and more - but they stayed to the right hand side. I checked behind quickly. Another Spitfire was sitting there and spraying his tracer around my ears, tracer which we call corpse-fingers. I looked left - Holy terror! Behind me to the left hung three more Spitfires! I was surrounded and in a bad spot. Throttle fully open I made a sharp left turn and the tracers flashed past above me. I would certainly thank the gods if my mother's son got away from this mess unhurt.

'The climb had given me some room to manoeuvre but still my few comrades were outnumbered. Whenever I tried to intervene I got Spitfires on my tail and had to take evasive action. Then an Me 109 flashed by at an incredible speed, and behind it a Spitfire. It was sent by heaven - I got behind the Tommy, got him in my gunsight and after a few volleys he nosed down.

'We had more room now, so I could watch the Englishman. He splashed down into the water and even from my altitude I could see the white foam. Then no more - nothing betrayed the fact that a gallant pilot had died an heroic death at that spot.'

On August 25th, Oberleutnant Wick claimed his 19th and 20th victories to bring JG2's overall tally to 250 enemy aircraft destroyed. During this period of the war, to receive the coveted *Ritterkreuz des Eisernen Kreuzes*, or Knights Cross of the Iron Cross, Germany's highest gallantry award, a jagdflieger had to destroy 20 enemy aircraft; Wick's *throat-ache* was therefore relieved that day when the Ritterkreuz was hung around his neck on its red, white and black ribbon. By October 6th, he had personally accounted for 41 enemy aircraft, and thus became just the fourth experten to receive the *Eichenlaubs*, or Oak Leaves, to add to his Ritterkreuz. Wick became the Kommodore of JG2 on October 20th. His Headquarters were located at the luxurious Chateau at Beaumont-le-Roger, home of the Duchesse de Magenta whose husband spied on JG2's activities. Major Wick, however, lost his life on November 28th 1940, when shot down by 609 Squadron's Flight Lieutenant John Dundas off the Isle of Wight. Dundas was himself killed seconds later by a member of Wick's Geschwaderstabschwarm, Hauptmann Rudi Pflanz. No trace of either Wick or Dundas has ever been found. Wick's final score was 56 victories.

There were actually many experten amongst JG2's pilots during 1940, so undoubtedly some of those men also flew on the Yeovil escort missions, jagdfliegern who had either already received the Ritterkreuz or would do so in due

The coveted Knights Cross with Oak Leaves. Swords and Diamonds, or the 'Ritterkreuz des Eisernen Kreuzes mit Schwerten und Brillanten', to which but a select few German fighting men aspired.

course, such as Oberfeldwebels Seigfried Schnell (RK 09.11.40) and Werner Machold (RK 05.09.40), and Oberleutnant Erich Leie (RK 01.08.41) and Leutnant Julius Meimberg (RK 24.10.44).

During the early part of the Battle of Britain, JG53, the *Ace of Spades* Gechswader, was part of Luftflotte 3, based to the west of the Seine, and operating extensively against south-west England. Some aircraft even flew from La Villiaze on Guernsey. On August 28th, however, when Goering transferred the majority of his jagdgruppen to Luftflotte 2,

4/JG2's Julius Meimberg with his 'Emil' during the autumn of 1940. The rudder was painted yellow, note the victory bars in white.

JG53 moved to the Pas de Calais with I & II Gruppe at Sempy, and III Gruppe at Berck-sur-Mer. JG53's Me 109s bore the famous *Pik As*, or ace of spades, badge, but for some unknown reason this was suppressed by Goering who ordered that it would be replaced by a red ring around the cowling. However, after the Battle of Britain the *Pik As* marking reappeared. It is interesting to note that Hauptmann Wolf-Dietrich Wilcke, Gruppenkommandeur of III Gruppe, ensured that the swastika emblem, painted as standard on the Me 109s' tails, was removed from his Gruppe's fighters as a political gesture.

A victorious pilot of JG53 'Pik As' recounts his adventures over England.

Bundesarchiv.

German records indicate that on September 30th, 1940, JG53 supplied five Me 109s to join the fighter escort to Yeovil, and on October 7th, seven machines. As a Schwarm usually consisted of four fighters, five and seven were therefore unusual numbers. The documents do not identify, however, exactly which Staffeln were involved. However, a photograph taken at Cherbourg of Hauptmann Wick's famous Me 109, shows 32 victory bars on the aircraft's rudder; his 32nd victory was scored over Lyme Bay on September 30th, thus identifying the photograph as having probably been taken between then and October 2nd when Wick scored again. Behind Wick's aircraft is an aircraft of JG53 bearing the red ring around its cowling, its fuselage marking '−+−' identifying it as from a II Gruppe Stabschwarm. Michael Payne, an authority on the Me 109E, suggests that the JG53 contingent might have either been led by a *Stabsoffizier* or been accompanied by him, although this officer could have been supernumerary and not have flown on the operation, perhaps merely overseeing the administration. It is known that during

A close-up of victory bars on the tail of Wick's 'Emil'. Of more interest, however, is the Me 109E of 5/JG53 in the background. Note the red ring around the aircraft's engine cowling, and the horizontal bar indicating the IInd Gruppe. This photograph was taken at Beaumont-le-Roger in late September 1940 and could be at the time of the Sherborne raid.

Michael Payne.

the September 30th escort operation, II/JG53 claimed two British fighters destroyed. One must assume, therefore, that on that occasion the five JG53 aircraft known to have been involved belonged to either the II Gruppenstabschwarm or one of the II Gruppe Staffeln (4,5 or 6).

Accepting that II/JG53 were involved on at least one of the escort sorties with which we are concerned, this Gruppe also included some notable experten. The Gruppenkommandeur was Hauptmann Gunther Freiherr (Baron) von Maltzahn who was one of the jagdwaffe's leading personalities. On October 10th, 30-year-old von Maltzahn was promoted to Major and became JG53's Kommodore, subsequently leading the Geschwader in the West, Russia and the Mediterranean until October 1943 when he became *Jafü Italy*. His Ritterkreuz was awarded in December 1940, and the Eichenlaubs in July 1941. He survived some 500 wartime combat missions with a total of 68 victories, but died in 1953 at the young age of 43. In September 1940, another member of II Gruppe was Leutnant Gerhard Michalski, who would ultimately be similarly decorated to von Maltzhan; having flown 652 combat missions with 73 victories, Michalski was ironically killed in a car accident during 1946.

Gunther Freiherr von Maltzahn, 'Kommandeur' of II/JG53 during the period in question.

The final unit contributing to the fighter escort was *Zerstörergeschwader 26 Horst Wessel*, which was named after a young Nazi storm-trooper killed in Berlin by the communists during the 1930s. At the outbreak of war, all three Gruppen were equipped with the Me 109, but by 1940 the Geschwader had converted to the Me 110, seeing action in France. By 1939, the Luftwaffe was the only air force in the world which had considered the possibility of producing an escort fighter to accompany bombers, and so the twin DB601A powered Me 110 was born. The aircraft was much vaunted by Goering, who had total confidence in the machine and consequently posted many of his best pilots to the *destroyer* units. Again, like the He 111, when first conceived the Me 110 was markedly superior in performance to the fighters of other air forces. During the Battle of Britain, however, its poor acceleration and wide turning circle made the *Zerstörer* no match for the Spitfire, but it was around 40 mph faster than the Hurricane. This deficiency gave the overworked Me 109 escort pilots an even greater burden as often the Me 110 escorts had to be protected themselves. However, the aircraft's nose was formidably armed with two 20 mm MG FF cannon and four 7.9 mm MG 17 machine-guns, the combined fire-power of which were devastating providing the Me 110 pilot could outmanoeuvre his opponent and bring his guns to bear. The machine was double-crewed, however, and the *Bordfunker* (wireless operator/

air gunner) had a rearwards firing MG 15. The Me 110 units were used as long-range escort fighters, although British Intelligence noted that *'it has become customary tactics for the escorting Me 110s to avoid combat until after the bombing attack, when the Me 109 escorts have more or less lined the route home, and the Me 110s have endeavoured, by such manoeuvres as circling, to delay our fighters and so cover the retreat of the bombers.'* This *Abwehrkreis*, or defensive circle, at least afforded the Me 110 crews some mutual cover in combat.

ZG26 fought the majority of the Battle of Britain over south-eastern England under the control of *Jafü 2*, but in September the Geschwader was transferred to *Jafü 3* for operations with V Fliegerkorps and operations over the West Country. This move helped to compensate for Goering having passed the majority of Sperrle's Me 109s to Kesselring's Luftflotte 2; the longer range of the Me 110 was required to fly the greater distance across the sea from Cherbourg to Dorset, whereas the shorter crossing between the Pas de Calais and south-eastern England was at least manageable for the shorter range Me 109s. Subsequently, therefore, ZG26 operated from the Luftflotte 3 airfields at Cherbourg, Le Havre and Thiberville. The *Zerstörergeschwadern's* system of fuselage identification letters and numbers was identical to that of the Kampfgeschwadern. However, the ZG26 Geschwader code was originally *U8* but later changed for *3U*. The change was not immediately implemented en bloc, so during the Battle of Britain I/ZG26 were *U8*, and II and III Gruppen *3U*. The noses of III Gruppe's aircraft were painted white.

This is an Me 110C-3, 'U8+HL', of 3/ZG26 'Horst Wessel'. Note the white nose indicating III Gruppe. This machine was shot down at Lenham, Kent, on September 11th, 1940.

ZG26's Geschwaderkommodore was a remarkable man, Oberstleutnant Joachim-Friedrich Huth, who had been born in 1896 and flew fighters during the Great War, in which he lost a leg. On September 11th, 1940, Huth had been awarded the Ritterkreuz for ZG26's success in the fighting to date, particularly during the French campaign. The Kommandeur of I Gruppe was Hauptmann Wilhelm Mackroki who received his Ritterkreuz on October 6th, 1940. Mackrocki has been missing since May 21st, 1941, when he made a flight over Crete. II Gruppenkommandeur was 29-year-old Hauptmann Ralph von Rettburg who had served with ZG26 since 1937 and had fought during the Battle of France. Von Rettburg's *throat-ache* was cured in June 1941. During the war he flew about 200 missions, destroyed eight enemy aircraft in the air and a further 12 on the ground. He is still alive and living in Germany, aged 83. The Kommandeur of III Gruppe was an *Alte Adler* (Old Eagle), 37-year-old

Hauptmann Johann Schalk whose Ritterkreuz had been awarded on September 5th, 1940. Later a nightfighter pilot defending the Reich, Schalke also survived the war.

Oberstleutnant Joachim-Friedrich Huth, 'Geschwaderkommodore' of ZG26.

Hauptmann Ralph von Rettburg, 'Kommandeur' of II/ZG26.

Hauptmann Hans Schalk, 'Kommandeur' of III/ZG26.

Again, contemporary Luftflotte 3 records do not identify the exact Gruppen or Staffeln of ZG26 that were involved on either September 30th, or October 7th, 1940. However, we do know that on the former occasion 40 Me 110s of ZG26 took part, so it was not an operation at Geschwader strength. Certainly II/ZG26 participated, as one of the Gruppe's aircraft returned to base damaged after combat over England. The same is the case for October 7th, although II/ZG26 made combat claims that day, and ZG26's losses were from 4, 6 and 9 Staffeln in addition to Stab III/ZG26, indicating therefore that both II and III Gruppen participated.

Unteroffizier Johann Schmidt, in the wireless operator/air gunner's position of Leutnant Joachim Koepsell's Me 110. This 3/ZG26 crew were brought down over the West Country on September 27th, 1940. Schmidt died as his parachute failed to open.

Kenneth Wakefield Collection.

The amusing emblem of I/ZG26 showing the German 'shark' chasing a British 'fish'. The photograph shows to excellent effect the Me 110's terrific forward-firing armament (four machine-guns and two 20mm cannons).

Bundesarchiv.

A snapshot taken at Cherbourg-Théville in October 1940 showing ZG26's Me 110s and Me 109 pilots of II/JG2, Rudi Rothenfelder and Peter Neumann-Merkel (both 9/JG2), and Bruno Stolle (8/JG2).

Chris Goss Collection.

An oft neglected contribution during 1940 was that made by the air-sea rescue organisations. Fighter Command, in fact, had no proper ASR system, just 18 high speed launches to search for downed aircrew along the entire south coast. Frequently pilots were saved by chance encounters with passing trawlers, or by a civilian lifeboat. British pilots had no dinghies at this time, without which the survival rate, even in summer, was just 1-2 hours. German aircrew, however, wore bright yellow skullcaps and carried flare pistols, sea-dye and one-man dinghies. At strategic positions in the Channel were located rescue buoys, known as *Lobster Pots* by the RAF, which contained four bunks with bedding and anything else a downed airman might need. Better still were the He 59 floatplanes of the *Seenotflugkommando*, or air-sea rescue unit, which were capable of landing to rescue a ditched airman. One crew of a ZG26 Me 110 that had ditched in the sea after escorting bombers to an airfield in south-east England were certainly grateful for the He 59, as the pilot, an anonymous Oberleutnant, later described:-

'The coast was some way off and the water was cold. The current was carrying us away from land. My wireless operator had a good idea - he fired a flare. That saved us. German fighters saw us in the water and four Messerschmitts circled above us. Despite the cold we two smiled at each other - even if we were exhausted and injured. The fighters fortunately signalled a Seenotmaschine which came and took us aboard a short time later.'

So disposed, then, was the Luftwaffe during the summer and autumn of 1940 to wage war over England, its aircrews fighting bravely to bring to reality Reichsmarshall Goering's dream of invasion.

Target Westlands

The ancient kingdom of Wessex comprised what are now Somerset, Wiltshire Hampshire, Dorset, Devon and Cornwall. This book is mainly concerned with that part of the *West Country* composed of Somerset and Dorset. Wessex, its northern shores eroded by both the Bristol Channel and Atlantic Ocean, and by the English Channel in the south, has never been stranger to the threat of invasion. It was extensively occupied in Roman times, and again later by the Saxons. During the reign of Ethelred II, the bloodthirsty Vikings posed a dangerous threat to this heartland between the Severn and the Solent. It was in Somerset that the great King Alfred, *Founder of the English Nation*, sought refuge after a surprise attack in Wiltshire by the Danes, and there dozed in a peasant's cottage whilst the cakes burnt. Wessex also has strong associations with the enigmatic King Arthur of romantic myth, legend and indeed some truth, for the fabled Camelot might actually be Cadbury Castle in South Somerset. In the 19th century, fear of an invasion by Napoleon caused Dorset folk to build beacons on the downs, ready to flash news inland of his coming. Although the Cherbourg peninsula lay just 60 miles off Dorset's coastline, the panic was ill-founded, as the French Emperor never landed.

In southern Dorset a narrow, broken ridge of chalky hills roughly follows the coast, the easterly heights known as the Purbeck Hills. In the north a region of sandy heathland extends from the Hampshire border to the county's centre, and another range of chalk downs runs east-west towards Wiltshire's Salisbury Plain. Central Dorset is traversed by the wide, rolling expanse of Blackmore Vale, and in the north is the densely wooded Cranborne Chase. Portland Bill is a rocky peninsula extending south into the Channel, connected to the mainland by the long pebble ridge known as Chesil Bank. For centuries Portland has been an important Royal Naval installation, which it remains today. To Dorset's eastern coastal county border lies the busy harbour at Poole.

Dorset is a rather tranquil backdrop of rural and coastal contentment, punctuated not by busy industrial or commercial centres but by such quaint, *olde worlde* country towns as Sherborne, tucked away in the peaceful valley of the river Yeo and on the county's north-western border with neighbouring Somerset. Thomas Hardy, himself a Wessex man, based his *Sherton Abbas* on picturesque Sherborne with its medieval biscuit-coloured buildings. In the centre of the town, proud and mighty, stands Sherborne's famous Abbey, originally a Saxon cathedral as early as 706 AD.

In roughly the middle of Wessex, the county of Somerset is an area of rich variety. Within its borders can be found a microcosm of British landscape and geography. The Moors or Levels of Central Somerset comprise a defined region, the eastern side of that plain being flanked by the Mendip Hills, and the west by the Quantock Ridge. To the south lies fertile agricultural land so characteristic of this county. Taunton is now Somerset's administrative centre, with Yeovil and Bridgewater the principal industrial towns.

Situated in the southernmost part of Somerset on the Dorset borders, the historic market town of Yeovil was located on one of the main routes from London to the West. Yeovil, cradled by gentle hills and with golden-coloured buildings made from local limestone, is recorded in both Saxon times and the Domesday book. By the Middle Ages its market had been confirmed by a Royal Charter and was one of the foremost in the area. Glove making gradually developed into Yeovil's staple industry, though for a considerable period linen cloth, sail making and rope and twine provided employment for many townsfolk. With the gradually improving network of roads from the eighteenth century, and railways during the mid-nineteenth, the town rapidly expanded and Yeovil's prosperity was enhanced. Leather dressing, gloving and woollen industries flourished. Its agricultural importance continued concurrently with other industries and the establishment of the *Western Gazette*, an important regional newspaper. Towards the end of the nineteenth century, however, began what would ultimately provoke young German airmen to strike against Yeovil during the summer of 1940.

In 1868, James Bazeley Petter married, and, as a wedding present from his father, received the long established ironmongery business of Haman & Gillett. Both the marriage and business prospered, the Petters having 15 children in total, and by 1870 a partner had been added to the company, now known as *Petters & Edgar*. The business's horizons had also extended beyond ironmongery to the production of agricultural equipment. Petter acquired the Yeovil Foundry and Engineering Works where he produced the castings for the Nautilus patented fire-grate which Queen Victoria later chose for use at both Osborne House and Balmoral Castle. It was to this foundry that the third Petter child, Percival Waddams, came after leaving Yeovil Grammar School. By 1893 he had become manager.

Percy became interested in the *horseless carriage* being developed on the continent and consequently designed and built a single-cylinder oil engine to provide the power for such a vehicle. When installed in a chassis built by the local carriage builder, Yeovillians were able to see one of the first motor cars built in this country. Although the design failed to gain any recognition at a Crystal Palace competition, Percy Petter, joined by his brother, Ernest Willoughby, realised that there was great business potential in marketing the oil engine for agricultural use. This line of development was so successful that by 1901 the independent company of *James B Petter & Sons* had been established which produced and marketed a range of oil engines. The following year the company produced an agricultural tractor powered by an oil engine. By 1910, Petters Limited was a public company and had outgrown its existing premises. To resolve this, an area of meadowland was purchased on the western side of Yeovil, the new foundry being ready for use by 1914. The site was known as *Westlands*.

By this time the Great War had consumed the World in conflict, but, so far as the manufacture of arms and munitions were concerned, Britain was ill-prepared for war. This prompted Sir Ernest Petter, as he was by then, to place the entire manufacturing resources of JB Petter & Sons Ltd at the government's disposal in 1915. The offer was accepted by the Admiralty and the Petter brothers attended a meeting in London at which it was stated that the Navy was in urgent need of seaplanes for spotting beyond the visual range of vessels at sea. Despite the fact that the Petters had no experience in aircraft production, the Navy had no misgivings: *'You are the fellows we want; we will send you the drawings and give you all the help we can. Get on with it.'* Sir Ernest and Percy Petter did indeed *'get on with it.'* Between receiving their first order for 184 Short float-planes, and by Armistice in 1918, some 1,100 aircraft had been produced at Yeovil. The early days were not easy, however, as the company had no airfield from which to test its aircraft. Instead, these had to be crated and conveyed via a horse-drawn vehicle to Yeovil Junction railway station, thence by freight train to Short Brothers at Rochester where the production test flights took place. Consequently, farmland adjoining the Westland site was acquired from the Yeovil & District Hospital Board and made into an airfield, although this was not actually ready until 1917.

During the First World War, in addition to the Short seaplane, Westland also manufactured Sopwith fighters, de Havilland DH4, DH9 and DH9A bombers, and the Vickers Vimy FB27 bomber. Westlands also produced three prototypes of their own designs, the Scout, Wagtail, and Weasel, but with the war at an end none ever saw service.

In the wake of the Great War, amongst many other aircraft manufacturers, Westlands entered the civil aviation arena by producing a pilot and three passenger aircraft called the *Limousine*. The Limousine III won its class in the 1920 Department of Civil Aviation aircraft production competition. The company received an outstanding boost in 1927 when it introduced the Westland Wapiti, a two-seat general purpose military aircraft of which it sold 563. During the 1930s the company experimented with the development of rotary wing aircraft, but these projects were shelved when war seemed imminent.

The production of fixed wing machines continued, however, and amongst those built under sub-contract was the Hawker Audax, a two-seat army co-operation biplane that had entered service in 1932. In contrast to the radical thinking in Germany between the wars that by 1939 would redefine the laws of military science, the British battlefield mentality had remained as stagnant as the trench warfare of 1918. Whilst in Britain the fighter aircraft was neglected therefore, the role of army co-operation flying was considered essential. Air Ministry Specification A39/34 sought a successor to the Audax, and Westland's P8 was the first design to enter production. *Teddy* Petter's team had spared no effort to meet the Air Ministry's requirement of wide speed range, good low-speed control, short field take-off and landing capability. The P8 prototype,

K6127, was rolled out at Yeovil on June 10th, 1936. On June 15th, it was flown by the company's test pilot, Harald Penrose, for the first time. Subsequently the Air Ministry ordered 144 of this new aircraft that was to make Westlands a household name - the Lysander, of which 1,400 were ultimately built. The Lysander, or *Lizzie* as it became affectionately known, was amongst the RAF aircraft sent to France, and the last to see action over Dunkirk. Lysanders later flew over virtually every theatre of war in addition to rendering invaluable service to the Special Duties units. More mundane tasks were also within the range of the machine's capabilities, such as air-sea rescue and target towing work.

Westland Lysander V9287 wearing SOE markings for clandestine operations, and photographed at the Yeovil factory.
Westland Helicopters Publicity Department.

Lysander production line at the Westland aircraft factory, 1940.
Westland Helicopters Publicity Department.

During the mid-1930s, however, the Air Ministry had become concerned with increasing the firepower of its fighter aircraft. With both the Me 109 and Me 110 armed with quick-firing large calibre cannons, in addition to rapid-firing machine-guns, there was growing concern that even the eight .303 Brownings of the new Spitfire and Hurricane would be insufficient when faced with such formidable European firepower. The Air Ministry therefore spawned Specification F37/35 for a single-seat day/night fighter armed with four 20 mm cannons. Westland's design team produced the P9, later known as the Whirlwind. Harald Penrose tested the prototype, L6844, on October 11th, 1938. The *Crikey* was powered by twin Rolls-Royce Peregrine engines of 885 hp, had coolant radiators within the wing centre section which therefore offered minimal drag, the four 20 mm Hispano-Suiza cannons were grouped together in the nose, and the tailplane was mounted very high on the tail fin to keep it clear of the wake created by the powerful Fowler-type flaps. Despite these flaps, however, the Whirlwind maintained a high landing speed which made it difficult to operate from grass runways which thus reduced the number of aerodromes from which it was able to operate. On July 6th, 1940, 263 Squadron received the first of the 112 Whirlwinds built. The machine was found to be very fast at low level, which, coupled with its long-range capability, meant that the Whirlwind found its niche in the ground-attack role, instead of as the interceptor it was actually meant to be. As the war progressed, however, the Whirlwind's shortcoming at high altitude, due to it being underpowered, became more pronounced. Unfortunately Rolls-Royce was too committed to the development of the Merlin engine to spend further time on the Peregrine, so the Whirlwind was replaced by the Hawker Typhoon in 1943. 263 Squadron's pilots, however, had formed a great respect for the Whirlwind by this time, as the squadron diary recorded: *'All pilots who flew the Whirlwind on operations against the enemy had absolute confidence in and affection for their aircraft.'*

A Westland Whirlwind fighter-bomber, flaps and wheels down. Note the four 20mm cannons protruding from the aircraft's nose.

Westland Helicopters Publicity Department.

In 1935, the Yeovil company had become known as *Westland Aircraft*, and as Lysander production commenced a new erecting shop was built. By 1940, therefore, *Lizzie* production was in full swing alongside that of the Whirlwind. Furthermore, as of June 1936, the Supermarine factory at Woolston had found itself ill-equipped to mass produce the Spitfire. Sub-contracting was the obvious answer, so Supermarines employed other aircraft manufacturers to produce the detail parts whilst they handled final assembly of the airframe. Amongst those companies involved in the sub-contract work was Westlands, who produced wing ribs for the Spitfire. In August 1940, however, Westlands received a contract for 300 complete Spitfire Mk 1A fighters (later updated to include 140 Mk VBs and 110 Mk VCs). Deliveries from this contract commenced on July 18th, 1941, and the second aircraft concerned was Spitfire Mk 1A, AR213. This machine is extant, operated by Tony Bianchi, and continues to delight crowds at air-shows throughout each summer (one of the Mk VCs, AR501, is also still flying with the Shuttleworth Trust).

Westland-built Supermarine Spitfires at the Yeovil factory. Note the camouflaged hangar.
Westland Helicopters Publicity Department.

Near to Yeovil was the Fleet Air Arm (FAA) training aerodrome at Yeovilton. Realising that the programme for new aircraft and carriers would rapidly outgrow existing training facilities, the land on which the new airfield, or *HMS Heron*, would be built was purchased in July 1939. The first hangars were erected there early in 1940 but on completion were handed over to Westlands as a sub-site for their Yeovil factory. The Yeovilton site was the intended home of the Naval Air Fighting School, which opened in April 1940, and during the early days Blackburn Rocs, Skuas and Sea Gladiators were amongst the aircraft on charge. Some of the FAA pilots trained at Yeovilton actually flew with Fighter Command during the Battle of Britain, when the call for replacement pilots was extended not only to other commands but also the senior service.

In July 1940, both Westlands and Yeovilton were occasionally harrassed by the Luftwaffe. During one instance, Westlands' flight shed was hit and its grass runway pitted, although mercifully the new Whirlwinds, dispersed around the airfield, were spared. The recent building carried out at the works had left large patches of lightish

The Westland aircraft factory at Yeovil pictured in 1938. Preston Grove is the long row of houses at extreme right.

Westland Helicopters Publicity Department.

Westlands as presented on a Luftwaffe target document. This photograph was not, as one might assume, taken by a spy or fifth columnist, but was in fact a between the wars postcard!

Imperial War Museum.

coloured concrete, which, it was feared, would be highly visible from the air; in the event of an air raid warning, the workers each collected a corrugated sheet which was laid down on the new concrete to break up the symmetry of the ground near the hangars. The main factory building and aerodrome were marked with a paint and sawdust mix to represent fields bounded by hedges and trees. So effective was this camouflage, apparently, that on a dull November day in 1939, the pilot of a Short L17 four-engined transport aircraft actually landed within one of the *fields,* much to the delight of Westland employees!

Luftwaffe Intelligence, commanded by Generaloberst Hans Jeschonnek, had not surprisingly spied on Westland Aircraft which had been allocated the target file reference number: GB 74 60. According to the file, prepared by the Luftwaffe's 5 Abteilung, which contained aerial photographs and maps pinpointing the factory in relation to Yeovil and other landmarks, the *Flugzeugfabrik Yeovil Works* had a workforce of around 3,500. The production of both the Lysander and Whirlwind *Zerstörer* is clearly recorded, although no mention is made of the Spitfire sub-contract work. The report coldly concludes that Westlands must be dealt with by October 7th, 1940.

In late September 1940, the Luftwaffe intensified its attacks against the British aircraft industry, the intention being to prevent Fighter Command making good its losses. Logically factories producing fighter aircraft were a priority target. As part of an overall strategy, however, plants concerned with the manufacture of aero-engines, ancillary equipment and aircraft other than fighters were also included in a list of 30 major targets. Some raids against these locations did little more than add to the Luftwaffe's ever mounting losses, whilst others inflicted serious damage upon British industry. On September 25th, 1940, a carefully planned and well executed attack against the Bristol Aeroplane Company at Filton caused serious damage. Yeovil was actually thought to be the target, so when KG55 turned for Bristol the defenders were caught off-balance. The following day KG55 attacked the Supermarine factory at Woolston, still the main centre of Spitfire manufacture, causing such damage that production was brought to a standstill. Although this was to create a reduction in Spitfire deliveries during the weeks ahead, in isolation and at such a late stage in the battle, this Luftwaffe success would not affect Fighter Command's ability to continue the fight. A day later the Me 110s of Erprobungsgruppe 210, a daring low-level bombing unit, made an unsuccessful attack against the Parnall Aircraft factory at Yate, which produced gun-turrets for bombers. On September 28th, the fast bomb-carrying Me 110s and Ju 88s escorted by hundreds of high flying Me 109s threatened to overwhelm the penny-packet forces of Spitfires and Hurricanes sent to intercept them. Targets were mainly London, Portsmouth and Southampton. Ominously, as if the lull before a great storm, September 29th was a day of reduced activity on which Fighter Command's pilots were able to draw a welcome respite from the heavy demands imposed upon them over recent days. The storm broke just a few hours later on Monday, 30th September, 1940.

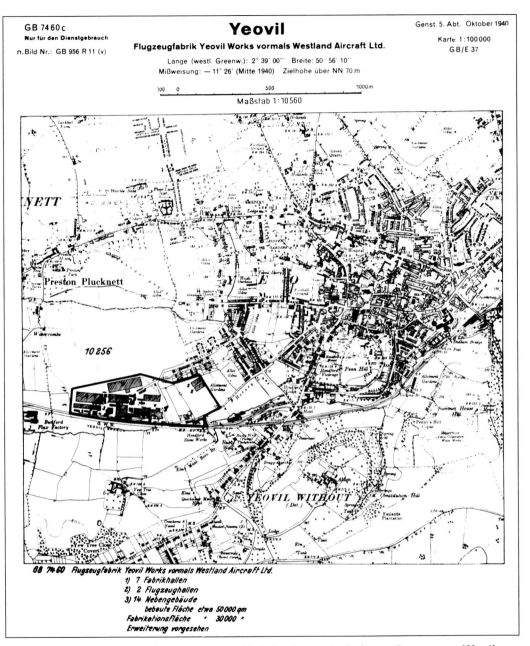

GB 7460c
Nur für den Dienstgebrauch

n.Bild Nr.: GB 956 R 11 (v)

Yeovil

Flugzeugfabrik Yeovil Works vormals Westland Aircraft Ltd.

Länge (westl. Greenw.): 2° 39' 00''   Breite: 50° 56' 10''
Mißweisung: — 11° 26' (Mitte 1940)   Zielhöhe über NN 70 m

Genst. 5. Abt. Oktober 1940

Karte 1:100000
GB/E 37

Maßstab 1:10560

GB 74 60 Flugzeugfabrik Yeovil Works vormals Westland Aircraft Ltd.
1) 7 Fabrikhallen
2) 2 Flugzeughallen
3) 14 Nebengebäude
    bebaute Fläche etwa 50000 qm
Fabrikationsfläche   " 30000 "
Erweiterung vorgesehen

*This document from the 'GB 74 60' target file is based upon the Ordnance Survey map of Yeovil.
Westlands is clearly indicated.*

Imperial War Museum.

An aerial photograph of Yeovil brought back by a German reconnaissance aircraft. Westlands is at the bottom, and slightly to left of centre. By this time the airfield itself had been cleverly disguised as several agricultural fields with hedgerows.

Imperial War Museum.

Black Monday

At dawn on Monday, 30th September 1940, most of England was shrouded in low-lying mist and swept by a light, generally north-easterly wind. The day was cool, and at 1030 hrs the Air Ministry's Meteorological Office predicted the further outlook to be *'Quiet and dry except in the extreme north.'* Given such weather conditions, one could also predict with some certainty that during the day Britain's and Germany's air forces would continue their duel for aerial supremacy.

Such thoughts were certainly uppermost in the mind of 609 Squadron's Pilot Officer David Crook when he woke at Middle Wallop that morning:-

'The weather was brilliantly clear, and when we got up we shook our heads dismally as we knew there would be a lot of trouble. As Mac used to remark, "We should have quite a job to keep the Grim Reaper at bay".'

609 Squadron were scrambled at 1030 hrs that morning to patrol London, the 11 Group Controller having called upon 10 Group for assistance, but was recalled half an hour later. The enemy had been active over the south-east coast since 0635 hrs, when lone reconnaissance aircraft probed inland as far as Farnborough and Worthing. At 0900 hrs came the first attack on Kent when 12 bombers and 50 fighters from Generalfeldmarschall Kesselring's Luftflotte 2 crossed the coast east and west of Dungeness respectively. Met by 12 British fighter squadrons, the raiders penetrated as far as the airfields at Biggin Hill and Kenley. Meanwhile, more German fighters patrolled Dungeness and others remained offshore at Dover. During the ensuing action, Northolt's 229 Squadron received rough treatment by the enemy; within eight minutes of combat four Hurricanes had been shot down, with three pilots wounded and one killed, and three other aircraft damaged. At 1010 hrs, a further 75 enemy bombers and fighters crossed the coast at Dungeness and again made it to Biggin Hill and Kenley where the defenders broke up and scattered the enemy formations. By 1030 hrs all raids were returning to France, so thus 609 Squadron was ultimately not required by 11 Group that morning.

The next attack was to be launched against the West Country and undertaken by Luftflotte 3, involving the Me 109s of I and II Gruppen of JG2 *Richthofen*, with further *Emils* of II/JG53 *Pik As*, and Me 110s of I and II Gruppen of ZG26 *Horst Wessel*. Together the raid comprised 100 enemy aircraft on a Freie Jagd which crossed the Dorset coast at St Alban's Head and penetrated to the Somerset border.

504 Squadron at Filton was scrambled to patrol Bristol, it being feared that the Bristol Aeroplane Works might again be the raiders' target. 238 Squadron's Hurricanes patrolled Bournemouth, meanwhile, but although they did not meet the enemy two Hurricanes collided and were lost. Pilot Officers Simmonds and King each baled out safely, although the latter was severely shaken as his parachute had ripped when it

came into contact with his aircraft's tail. Pilot Officer Richard Covington landed his Hurricane in a field adjacent to where King landed, but later returned safely to base.

At 1100 hrs, 56 Squadron, which had earlier that morning flown down from Boscombe to operate out of Warmwell, was scrambled to intercept the enemy raid. At the same time, 609 Squadron was also ordered into the air, as David Crook later described:-

'I threw this diary into a chair, the card players dropped their hands, and everybody sprinted out of the door towards their machines. All the airmen were running hard too, and by the time I got to my Spitfire two men were already there to help me on with my parachute and then fasten it when I was in the cockpit. I put on the starter and ignition switches, turned on the R.T., gave the priming pump a couple of strokes, and pressed the starter button. The engine started immediately, and I put on my helmet and oxygen mask. Within ninety seconds of the alarm coming through we were all taxying out on the aerodrome. I was leading Green Section with Pilot Officers "Novi" Nowierski and Johnny Curchin behind me, and we got to our taking-off point and turned into wind. I looked round at "Novi" and he gave me the "thumbs up", meaning everything okay, and Johnny did likewise. I dropped my hand, opened the throttle and we all accelerated rapidly over the aerodrome and took off. The rest of the squadron were either taking off or already in the air, and we all joined up and started to climb towards Swanage, nearly fifty miles away.'

56 Squadron's Hurricanes had been ordered to climb to 22,000' and patrol their airfield at Warmwell, but when at just 16,000' and still climbing, the enemy was sighted approaching from the SE and out of the sun - Me 110s flying at 22,000' and the Me 109s higher still. Pilot Officer *Taffy* Higginson was *Baffin Leader* and he led the Hurricanes straight for the Me 110s in a head-on attack. As he later recorded in his log book, there were *'Fouzens of 'em.'* At 1125 hrs, Higginson opened fire at the leading zerstörer of Hauptmann Ralph von Rettburg's II/ZG26. As the two aircraft flashed by at a terrific closing speed, *Baffin Leader* immediately delivered a six second burst at an Me 109, but from 400 yards range his fire appeared ineffective. Red 3, Sergeant George Smythe, saw the Me 110 that Higginson had attacked break off and head for France with its port engine streaming smoke. Both crew members were in fact wounded, and the aircraft was subsequently written off when it crash landed in France.

Hauptmann Helmut Wick, Kommandeur of I/JG2, and his Stabschwarm then pounced on 56 Squadron. Within seconds the German ace had added numbers 32 and 33 to his score. Oberleutnant Fiby, I/JG2's adjutant, also claimed a British fighter destroyed. Certainly at 1130 hrs two of 56 Squadron's Hurricanes were despatched from the fight: Flying Officer Ken Marston who crash landed near Longcutts Farm, East Knighton, and Sergeant Ray who suffered a broken arm when his aircraft was also shot down.

Fortunately for 56 Squadron, 609's Spitfires were just about to intervene. The squadron was led on this occasion by Flight Lieutenant Frank Howell, who, upon sighting the enemy, had cleverly led his Spitfires out and up-sun over Weymouth Bay. *Sorbo Leader* ordered sections line astern; just in the nick of time for the hopelessly outnumbered Hurricanes, 609 Squadron *bounced* the Germans from above and out of the sun. The sky immediately became an arena of cutting, thrusting fighters which wove a crazy pattern of condensation trails high over Weymouth.

Howell led 'A' Flight off to attack from starboard, whilst Pilot Officer Michael Appleby led 'B' Flight, consisting of his Blue Section and Crook's Green, off to port. Three Me 109s in line astern, and at the same height, passed Appleby's port side travelling in the same direction. At first the Spitfire pilot thought that the fighters were Hurricanes, and swung round to protect their rear, but soon realised his mistake; 'B' Flight then dived out of the sun, guns blazing. Appleby fired six 2 second bursts onto the rearward Me 109, noting hits around the cockpit area, and flashes from within as the enemy aircraft dived down. Having followed the Me 109, Appleby broke off when another fighter appeared in his rear view mirror, although fortunately this proved to be a Spitfire. Michael Appleby remembers that after breaking away, *'I looked for more Me 109s or our own aircraft, but as so often happened in this kind of scrap could not see anyone else anywhere, a strange phenomenon peculiar to air fighting.'*

David Crook was about one hundred yards behind Blue Section, and after Blue 1 broke away, saw Appleby's victim *'more or less break up in mid-air - some very nice shooting on Michael's part. I distinctly remember him saying on the R.T., "That's got you, you bastard!"'*

In his dive after an Me 109, Crook's speed built up to 500 mph, the sea rushing up at him. As he gingerly eased out of the dive, the strain was terrific and a black mist formed in front of his eyes. Upon levelling out, however, Crook attacked the Me 109 from below and astern as it too pulled out. The enemy fighter rolled over onto its back, burst into flames and dived straight into the sea off Swanage. Crook watched fascinated as the aircraft hit the water in a great cloud of white foam. The pilot did not get out. Sergeant Alan Feary had stuck with Crook and witnessed the German's demise. Crook took stock: *'a few of our Spitfires were chasing Me 109s all over the place and obviously a very nice little massacre was in progress as a few minutes later I saw another Hun go into the sea.'* Green 1 then spotted a lone Me 109 going flat out for France. Crook dived again and easily caught the Me 109, at which he fired a *'good burst.'* The cockpit canopy broke off, flashing by dangerously close to the pursuing Spitfire, and the Me 109 plunged towards the sea. To Crook's amazement, however, at sea-level the aircraft flattened out and climbed, streaming glycol. The Me 109 was still travelling at full speed for France, although badly hit. *For the first time in this war I felt a certain pity for this German pilot and was rather reluctant to finish him off. The last few moments must have been absolute hell for him, I could almost feel his desperation as he made this last attempt to get away.'* Crook made no mistake, though, as he lined up the stricken enemy and poured the remainder of his ammunition into the enemy fighter from very close range. The Me 109 hurtled into the sea at great speed. Crook circled the spot but there was no trace of anything, just the waves of a neutral sea. The chase had actually taken him to just 15 miles off Cherbourg, a very dangerous place indeed for a lone Spitfire to be. Having hastily returned to the English coast, elated at having destroyed two enemy aircraft in one sortie, Pilot Officer Crook approached the cliffs in Weymouth Bay at 300 mph, just above the wave tops. At the last minute he pulled back on the stick, rocketing over the top *'to the very considerable amazement of some soldiers!'*

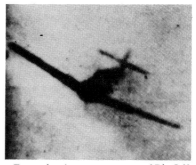

From the cine gun camera of Plt Off David Crook and showing one of the Me 109s attacked by him during the morning combat, 'fast turning over, on fire, before diving into the sea.'

Author's Collection via Hessling.

Meanwhile, Howell's 'A' Flight were also getting stuck into the enemy. Pilot Officer John Bisdee, Yellow 1, was flying in line astern on *Sorbo Leader* when three Me 109s made a beam attack on Yellow Section. Bisdee shouted *'Break Left!'*, and the enemy fire was avoided by a narrow margin. The *Bish* then saw a lone Me 109 some 300' below him and diving south. The Spitfire pilot rolled over inverted, so as to prevent his engine from cutting, and in the process fired all his ammunition at the enemy aircraft. Pieces of tail unit broke off, and thick black smoke poured from the engine. Bisdee was then attacked from behind and immediately broke off. Red 3, Pilot Officer Michael Staples, got in a quick deflection shot at a fleeting Me 109 which emitted glycol as it dived seawards. Pilot Officer Keith Ogilvie: *'We ran into a swarm of Me 109s. I paired off with one and we commenced turning. I was pleased that the Spitfire was able to turn inside of the 109, but he suddenly flipped over and disappeared before I had fired a shot - a moral victory only!'*

'Nothing on the clock but the maker's name!' *Sqn Ldr Michael Robinson (2nd right) and Plt Off Keith Ogilvie (Canadian), both of 609 Squadron, listen as Count Rodolpha de Grunne (Belgian) explains how it should be done at Biggin Hill, 1941. On September 30th, 1940, Robinson was a flight commander in 238 (Hurricane) Squadron.*

Chris Goss Collection.

As quickly as it had begun the fight was over, the Germans heading back to France, and the Spitfires and Hurricanes retiring to their bases. Thanks to 609 Squadron's timely intervention, although still heavily outnumbered, for the loss of just two Hurricanes with both pilots safe, the RAF pilots had definitely destroyed four Me 109s in addition to Higginson's Me 110. Feldwebel Wilhelm Hermes of 2/JG2, and Gefreiter Fritz Schumacher of 5 Staffel, were both missing. An unidentified pilot of II/JG53 was more fortunate, however, and is believed to have been rescued from the sea by the Seenotdienst.

Thus was the scene set for a major battle over Wessex.

At 1300 hrs the Meteorological Office recorded various weather data at numerous locations throughout the British Isles. At Portland Bill a force 4 NNE wind was noted, and the sky was by then *'generally cloudy.'* The cloud was low, and at 4,000' recorded as 10/10ths, being a complete covering of cloud. At the same time, cloud in the Bristol area was reported as being 8/10ths at 3,000'. The West Country was virtually hidden, from those heights, beneath an almost unbroken blanket of cloud.

Earlier in the day KG55's Operations Officer, Major Dr Ernst Kühl, had liaised with the *Wetterstelle* (meteorological office), and in the *Kartenstelle* (map room) had prepared an operational order for an attack on the Westland aircraft factory at Yeovil. Kühl was an artillery officer during the Great War, and had not learned to fly until he was 44. At the age of 52, a veteran of many bombing missions during the Battle of Britain, he now proposed to participate in the attack on Westlands. His plan was transmitted from the Gefechsstand by teleprinter to the I and II Gruppenkommandeur, Major Joachim Roeber and Major Friedrich Kless. Four He 111s of the Geschwaderstabstaffel were to lead the attack, each carrying 15 SC250 HE bombs. I Gruppe was to supply 16 bombers carrying a total of 76 SC250s. II Gruppe's 23 He 111s were to be the fire-raisers with 8 SC500s, 131 SC250s, and 15 Flamm SC250s. In total, therefore, the formation was to carry 245 bombs.

The airfields at Dreux and Chartres, homes of I and II Gruppe respectively, were hives of activity. The *Black Men* of the *Flughafen-Betreibs-Kompanie* swarmed like ants over the blackened bombers: *Flugzeugmechanikern* (aircraft mechanics), *Motorenschlossern* (engine mechanics), *Feinmechanikern* (instrument fitters), *Waffenwarte* (armourers), *Bombenwarten* (bomb armourers), and *Funkwarten* (wireless mechanics) all worked to prepare the He 111s for the battle ahead. The *Fallschirmwart* (parachute packers) also took care of every parachute.

The bombers were to assemble over Normandy before proceeding to Cherbourg where the 43 He 111s would rendezvous with their fighter escort provided by Jafü 3, 47 Me 109s of JG2, 5 of JG53, and 40 Me 110s of ZG26. The entire formation was then to set course for Portland Bill before forging its way inland just over 20 miles to Yeovil. By this time, KG55, its pilots experienced all, most being *old hands* from peacetime days and some even veterans of the Spanish Civil War, was familiar with the

West Country, although the Geschwader had not attacked Yeovil before. The attack leaders would have therefore studied carefully the landmarks between the English coast and their target, crews also being shown aerial photographs of Westlands from the target file. They would also have received appropriate advice from the *Funk-und Navigationsoffizier* (wireless and navigation officer). During each Gruppe's briefing, pilots were also allocated their precise positions in the formation. Most important too was the *Bodenleitstelle* (ground control centre) which was constantly in touch with the aircraft's wireless operators advising of any important matters, such as changing weather conditions. In turn the Bodenleitstelle was kept constantly informed regarding the course of the air battle which enabled the Gefechsstand to issue new orders if necessary. As part of the afternoon's overall plan, 11 Ju 88s of KG51 were to raid Southampton in a diversionary attack. Take-off time for KG55 was scheduled at 1524 hrs.

Having donned their flying gear, the crews sat in groups around their aircraft, awaiting the start time. These moments of waiting must be the worst for all fighting men. Soon the Gruppenkommandeurs climbed aboard their Heinkels, indicating that the waiting was over. Inside each bomber the crews went through their pre-flight checks of instruments and controls. Gunners swung their weapons around, ensuring that ammunition drums and belts were correctly fitted. Navigators stowed their maps and charts, and prepared to set course for Yeovil. As the twin-engines of each bomber roared into life, before settling down to the distinctive, unsynchronised throb peculiar to some German wartime aircraft, the flight engineers busied themselves with final checks of oil pressure and engine revs. To the right of the pilot's seat were two yellow throttle levers which controlled each engine's 1,150 hp. These the pilot would ease forward after releasing the brakes, causing the bomber to move slowly forwards across the grass to its take-off point.

Above: An He 111 lifts off from its French base bound for action over England.

Chris Goss Collection.

Left: Superb snapshot of an He 111 navigator and pilot. Both are wearing yellow skullcaps over their flying helmets as an aid to identification if shot down into the sea. The black rubber tube protruding from the navigator's 'Schwimmweste' is for manual inflation of the lifejacket. Note also the hot drinks flask strapped to the bulkhead on the navigator's right.

Chris Goss Collection.

The *Start-und Landeaufsichtsoffizier* was responsible for orderly take-offs and landings, so in a carefully choreographed sequence each aircraft in turn taxied to its take-off point, usually to form threes which in the air would form a Kette within the formation. With engines roaring, watched by the Black Men waving off their crews, the Heinkels rushed across the airfield, leaving great dustclouds in their wake. Once airborne, the landing gear was retracted and the warning signal within the cockpit went quiet. With the hangars slipping by just feet below, the heavily laden bombers started climbing, each pilot concentrating on holding formation. The sight of an entire Gruppe taking to the air must have been an impressive sight, not least perhaps for 18-year-old Flieger Robert Götz, a bombardier and air gunner in a I Gruppe aircraft. Despite his youth, the Yeovil attack was Götz's ninth operational flight against England, his first being on August 16th 1940. As the Heinkels climbed into the French sky and became specks in the distance, each of the aircrew became immersed in his own thoughts.

He 111s of 9/KG55 in Gruppenkeil formation. This photograph is believed to have been taken over the West Country as the raiders headed for Filton on September 25th, 1940.

Kenneth Wakefield Collection.

Having flown north-west for some 120 miles, the He 111s, in *Gruppenkeil*, sighted their fighter escort orbiting over Cherbourg. As the bombers slipped across the French coast, the Me 110s and Me 109s took up their stations around the Heinkels. The bomber crews, however, were not necessarily confident in their escorts, appreciating the general inadequacy of the Me 110 and short endurance of the Me 109s, which would again be operating at their maximum range. Shortly, beams detected the *Beehive* heading towards Portland, and radar

He 111s of KG55 en route for England, autumn 1940. Note that the national cross and identification letters are painted over in hurriedly applied black distemper indicating the aircraft's new role as night bombers. Undoubtedly KG55's aircraft would have appeared like this over Wessex on September 30th, 1940.

Bundesarchiv.

stations on England's south coast activated the early warning system. The raid of '100+' was seen as two distinct plots and given the numeric designations '163' and '165'.

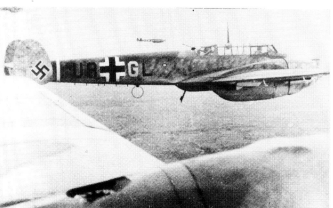

Above: Fighter escort, Yellow '8' with insect badge on cowling. Note also the 'R' shield. The yellow markings indicate the third Staffel, and the wavy bar the IIIrd Gruppe, hence 9/ JG2. Due to their limited range, the Me 109s were to play little part on 'Black Monday.'

Michael Payne.

Right: Me 110 long-range fighter escorts of ZG26.

Kenneth Wakefield Collection.

The first 10 Group fighter squadron to be scrambled was 238 at 1600 hrs from Chilbolton. The nine Hurricanes of Blue, Green and Yellow Sections, led by Flight Lieutenant Michael Robinson, were ordered to patrol the Worth Matravers line. *Blue Leader* led his aircraft on course but below the cloud, which he reported as being *'10/10ths at 4,000'*, before climbing up through it. The Ground Controller informed Robinson that the enemy were approaching from the south-east, so the Hurricanes turned westwards gaining height. When 15-20 miles south of Portland, suddenly, Blue Leader sighted the enemy formation 3,000' below, at 15,000', and heading north. 238 Squadron had the sun behind them, and were in an ideal tactical position. Blue Leader shouted *'Sections echelon port, go!'*, and *'Tally Ho!'* as he led his nine Hurricanes into a head-on attack. With gun button turned to *Fire*, Robinson delivered a continuous burst of fire as his fighter plunged through the leading Kette of Heinkels. Immediately the staccato chatter of machine-gun fire, and flashes of tracer ammunition, abruptly shattered the autumn sky. After the initial charge, Yellow 1, Flying Officer Bob Doe, attacked an He 111 from below and behind from 150 yards. Its starboard engine caught fire and its undercarriage dropped. However, Doe was forced to break off when the fighter escort intervened. Losing his assailants, Doe found another Heinkel, swiftly setting its port engine alight. The KG55 pilot dived down towards the thick clouds before turning back towards England when just above them. Yellow

1 pursued his quarry, the rear gunner still desperately firing at the attacking Hurricane. After emptying his remaining ammunition into the crippled bomber, Doe noted with satisfaction his victim crash into the sea some 15 miles off Portland. Doe's aircraft had not escaped unscathed, however, and during the return flight to Middle Wallop his Hurricane vibrated strangely. Upon landing it was discovered that a bullet had split one of the Hurricane's three wooden propeller blades.

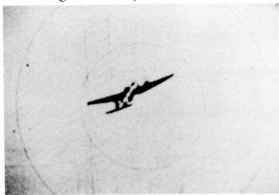

An He 111 firmly in the gunsight of a British fighter.
Author's Collection.

238 Squadron's Yellow 3, Sergeant Kucera, had also fired at an He 111 on the squadron's first pass, but took evasive action himself when attacked by an Me 110. He then selected another Heinkel which he attacked from astern, closing from 300 - 100 yards. Smoke poured from one engine and that bomber also plunged into the sea. There were no parachutes. Green 3, Sergeant Jeka, attacked an Me 110 from the rear, but a schwarm of Me 109s soon singled him out. When Jeka broke away, the 110 was in a gentle glide southwards with smoke pouring from its starboard engine.

As the Germans battled northwards across the sea towards England, Warmwell airfield became another scene of frantic activity. At 1608 hrs, 12 Spitfires of Squadron Leader Peter Devitt's 152 Squadron were scrambled, followed two minutes later by six Hurricanes of 56 Squadron led by Squadron Leader Herbert Pinfold. Both units arrived, over Portland and Lyme Bay respectively, at 1630 hrs.

Baffin Leader had climbed 56 Squadron slightly to the west of Portland Bill to gain the advantage offered by the sun. When at 16,000' and flying due south, he sighted *'God knows how many Do 215s and Me 110s'*, the bombers being reported at 19,000' with the fighters 5,000' above and behind. As the Heinkel crews spotted the fighters curving down to attack them, up went the cry *'Achtung, Geschwader, Indianer!'* All of the Heinkels appeared to open fire simultaneously on 56 Squadron. Red 1 climbed the squadron up to 19,000' and as the Hurricanes attacked the bombers from behind, the enemy fighters rained down on them. Squadron Leader Pinfold attacked a Heinkel, but a bullet from the *Gruppenkeil's* combined firepower hit Hurricane P2910 and glycol fumes filled the cockpit. Red 1 broke off the engagement, and over 50 years later remembered:-

'With the cockpit full of glycol fumes do I bale out over the sea or land on it? I then saw a small "hole" in the cloud to the north. I throttled right back, opened the cockpit hood and glided towards it, keeping an eye on the engine temperature which was slowly going up due to loss of coolant. When over the "hole" I was delighted to see land, and even more so to see Warmwell airfield where I executed a "dead-stick" landing. Subsequent inspection revealed no damage to the aircraft or engine other than a few bullet holes in the fuselage and glycol tank which was just in front of the cockpit. Lucky me!'

Pilot Officer Higginson last saw Pinfold's target 'going downwards with both engines streaming black smoke.'

Red 2, Sergeant Robinson, attacked an He 111 and saw smoke coming from its starboard engine as tracer suddenly whipped around him from behind. He broke right and saw another bomber heading south, streaming glycol from one engine. As Robinson approached, another Hurricane attacked the raider, which was losing height, so Red 2 delivered an attack after the first British fighter had broken away. His ammunition exhausted, Robinson noted the other Hurricane return and make a second attack before the Heinkel reached the safety of nearby cloud.

Flight Lieutenant Brooker was leading 'B' Flight's Green Section. As Pinfold's fighters attacked the enemy from out of the sun, the section flying in front of Green attacked some Me 110s, but Brooker successfully led his fighters to the bombers' rear. Green 1 selected a target and fired in one long, overtaking burst. A large section of cowling broke away, and the Heinkel throttled right back so that the Hurricane overshot. The rear gunner, however, put a bullet through Brooker's petrol tank, which thankfully did not ignite.

Sergeant Peter Fox was in action with 56 Squadron for the first time:-

'I was 19 years of age, had flown Hurricanes for 20 hours but just couldn't believe it when I saw the enemy which I understood to be a 60+ raid of Heinkels and their fighter escort. I had never seen so many aircraft together before. As far as I knew, we of 56 Squadron would be attacking the bombers whilst a Spitfire squadron engaged the enemy fighters. Tally Ho! My mouth felt very dirty tasting with apprehension. We gained height going out to sea, and then curved down and round into attack the Heinkels which were going towards the English coastline. One or more of ours went to attack the enemy leaders, and others the rear. I selected one of the latter, aimed firstly at one engine, pressed the gun button and sprayed across to the other. I did not see any return fire, but suddenly the Heinkel started to slow down and slowly peel off to port. I started to follow him down, still firing, when there was an explosion and I saw there was very little left of my instrument panel. I had been advised by an "old-timer" to fly with my hood open when in action as bullets could damage it and prevent it sliding back. Luckily I had followed this advice otherwise my head would have been blown off as the shell hit the canopy. I broke to starboard, pulling upwards and away, with all controls seemingly working correctly. I got over land at about 3,000' and was wondering whether I would make Warmwell when I saw flames coming *up between my legs. I don't think I even thought of my next action, but I had turned the kite upside down, released my harness and saw my feet way above me and the 'plane above my feet, presumably stalled. Where was the ripcord? I told myself to calm down, as I remembered a film where a German was shown dead on the ground with fingernail marks where he had clawed at his ripcord when his parachute had not opened. I also recall remembering that someone had told me that 3 or 6, or some number, should be counted before pulling the cord. My hand went to the metal "D" ring, all was forgotten about counting and I pulled! I had never pulled a ripcord before, never seen one pulled, never seen a parachute packed, and never had any instruction. The "D" ring was flung into the air followed by some wire. Obviously I'd broken it. Whether my hands moved towards the parachute strapped to my backside or not I'll never know, but my thoughts were that I had to open the pack somehow,*

Sergeant Peter Fox of 56 Squadron. Author's Collection via Mr P H Fox.

when I felt the small tug of the pilot chute, followed almost immediately by the full wrench of the main parachute. I was safe! The next second I was aware of an "enemy" racing down to shoot me, a pilot over his homeland who, if he survived, could fight again. A flaming 'plane - my Hurricane - then missed me literally by inches. The kite slowly screwed round, going into a steeper and steeper dive until almost vertical, aimed directly at the cross hedges of four fields to the NE of a wood towards which I was drifting. It hit the cross hedges spot on. A short, but noticeable pause and then a huge explosion followed by another pause before flames shot up to a great height. I'm glad that I wasn't in it! I was safe again, although I didn't feel so as the sea looked rather close and I didn't want to end up swimming. I then recalled the film about the German parachutist which had shown how, if you pulled the parachute cords on one side or the other, the direction was slipped off accordingly. I tried, but which side, as I could not see which way I was drifting. I certainly could not think aerodynamically at that moment. Leave well alone, I thought. I was safe again. Blood! Trickling down my right leg. I tried to lift my leg to see, but couldn't. I'd met aircrew who had lost limbs but told me how they could still feel extremities which were no longer there. My leg had been shot off and would crumble under me when I landed. I was getting close to the ground, worried about my "shot off leg", when I remembered the tale of a pilot being shot in the foot by the Home Guard. "British!" I shouted at the top if my voice for the last few hundred feet. Oh Lord, I'm going straight into that wood. I grabbed the harness above my head to ease the bump of landing on my "shot off leg" and pulled hard as my 'chute clipped a tree on the edge of the wood. I only fell over gently, when the wind pulled the 'chute sideways. I shouted "British!" again, but as no-one came, started to roll up my parachute when a farm labourer climbed over a fence requesting confirmation that I was okay. My "shot off leg" was not shot off. In fact it was a tiny wound about half an inch long on my knee where a small piece of shrapnel had entered, and another the same size also half an inch away where it had come out. A lady with a horse then came along and I draped my parachute over the animal, and off we went on foot until a van took me to Lyme Regis Police Station. I was entertained in a local pub to await squadron transport back to Warmwell. Someone from Air Sea-Rescue came in and I told him that I was pretty sure the Heinkel I had engaged with had gone down into the "drink".'

Although Peter Fox was safe, his Hurricane having exploded into a thousand fragments at Wootton Fitzpaine, the air battle was gaining in ferocity. Other 56 Squadron Hurricanes were also despatched from the fight: Pilot Officer Wicks had forced landed at Warmwell with a damaged aircraft, and Pilot Officer Constable-Maxwell crash landed safely in a mined area on Chesil Beach opposite the Abbotsbury Swannery. Flight Lieutenant Edwards was also shot down and forced to bale out.

Flieger Robert Götz searches for British fighters over England.

Author's Collection via Herr Robert Götz.

Lying in the bombardier's prone position within the glazed nose of his Heinkel, Flieger Götz frantically fired his single machine-gun situated in its Ikaria universal mounting. The teenager from Würzburg knew that things were going to be tough when the *Tommies* intercepted the raiding force even earlier than on his previous eight operational flights.

152 Squadron's Spitfires had also attacked from the west and out of the sun at roughly the same time as the Warmwell Hurricanes. To reach the enemy the squadron had flown for 25 minutes through the cloud *'on instruments'*, as later recorded in the logbook of Flight Lieutenant Thomas, who flew as Blue 1 that afternoon. Pilot Officer Dudley Williams sighted the enemy whilst still over the sea, heading for Lyme Regis, and gave the *'Tally Ho!'* Squadron Leader Devitt led his cavalry charge down on to the enemy fighter escort, after which the squadron broke up and individual dog-fights ensued.

Plt Off W D Williams (left), and Plt Off E S 'Boy' Marrs (right), at Warmwell during the Battle of Britain. On 'Black Monday', Williams claimed an Me 110 destroyed and shared a second with 'Taffy' Higginson of 56 Squadron. Marrs damaged an He 111.

Author's Collection via Allan White.

Williams, Green 1, attacked an Me 110 which dived into the cloud-mass below with smoke pouring from both engines. He climbed again, and found another 110, flying SE, with one engine emitting white smoke. The Spitfire pilot finished off his ammunition, and when expended Pilot Officer Higginson, of 56 Squadron, continued his attack against the same target. The two pilots last saw their quarry streaming smoke from both engines and going down west of Portland.

Devitt's Red 2, Pilot Officer *Cocky* Cox, fired at one of 40 Me 110s during the squadron attack, and watched fascinated as *'bits flew off it.'* Nine Me 109s then surrounded Cox, who managed a short burst at one of them, before half rolling and diving into cloud.

Green 2 and 3, Sergeants Kearsey and Reddington, had been weaving behind the squadron as *tail-end Charlies,* but also attacked with the squadron. Kearsey surprised an Me 110 and closed to 50 yards. The zerstörer flipped on to its back and dived vertically over Chesil Bank. An enemy fighter turned the tables on Green 3, however, and Leslie Reddington, a family man from Coventry, plunged into the sea and no trace of him has ever been found.

152 Squadron's Sergeant A W Kearsey at Warmwell with 'UN-N'. *Note the outsize* 'N' *codeletter. Kearsey claimed an Me 110 destroyed on* 'Black Monday'.

Author's Collection via Ray Johnson.

Pilot Officer *'Boy'* Marrs, Blue 3, managed to attack the Heinkels from the beam and got in a short burst before an enemy bullet smashed into the 2" thick windscreen in front of his face, shattering the armoured glass. Another bullet from KG55's murderous cross-fire hit his petrol tank, situated directly in front of the young pilot, but this did not explode. Marrs wrote: *'Crash! and the whole world seemed to be tumbling in on me. I pushed the stick forward hard and went into a vertical dive which I held until I was below cloud. I had a look around. The chief trouble was that petrol was gushing into the cockpit. My knee and leg were tingling all over as if I had pushed them into a bed of nettles. There was a bullet hole in the windscreen where a bullet had come in and entered the dashboard, knocking away the starter button. Another shell, I think an explosive one, had knocked away one of the petrol taps in front of my joystick, spattering my leg with little splinters and sending a chunk of something through the backside of my petrol tank near the bottom. I made for home at top speed to get there before my petrol ran out. I was about 15 miles from the aerodrome and it was a heart-rending business with all that petrol gushing over my legs and the constant danger of fire. About five miles from the drome smoke started to come from under the dashboard. I thought the whole thing might go up at any minute, so I switched off the engine. The smoke stopped. I glided down towards the 'drome and tried putting my wheels down. One came down but the other remained stuck up. I tried to get the one that was down up again. It was stuck down. There was nothing for it but to make a one-wheel landing. I switched on my engine again to make the aerodrome. It took me some way and then began to smoke again so I hastily switched it off. I was now near enough and made a normal approach and held off. I made a good landing, touching down lightly. The unsupported wing slowly began to drop. I was able to hold it up for some time and then down came the wing tip to the ground. I began to slew round and counteracted as much as possible with the brake on the wheel which was down. I ended up going sideways on one wheel, a tail-wheel and a wing tip. Luckily the good tyre held out and the only damage to the aeroplane, apart from that done by the bullets is a wing tip which is easily replaceable.'*

At 1620 hrs, several pilots of 87 Squadron's 'B' Flight also scrambled from Exeter towards the enemy. Although 'A' Flight was detached to Bibury, Flight Lieutenant *Widge* Gleed DFC had flown down to Exeter that afternoon and so joined the

Flt Lt 'Widge' Gleed of 87 Squadron flying Hurricane P2798 and leading a flight of 87 Squadron from Exeter to Bibury. Nevertheless, having 'scrambled', this is very much as the Hurricanes would have appeared as they headed for Portland in vics of three on 'Black Monday'.

Author's Collection via Allan White.

Hurricanes in their dash to Portland. The rest of 'A', led by Flying Officer Rayner and comprising Pilot Officer Watson and Sergeants Thorogood and Howell, took off from their Gloucestershire base and patrolled Bristol as a precautionary measure. Pilot Officer Andrew McLure and Sergeant Herbert Walton were first of 'B' Flight on the scene, and sighted the enemy still over the sea just before crossing the English coastline over Lyme Bay. The two Hurricanes attacked from out of the sun, but as McLure approached the bombers an Me 110 was soon on his tail. Turning steeply into a left hand turn, the position was reversed, McLure attacking the Me 110 from 200 yards. The enemy fighter's starboard engine caught fire and it dived into the cloud some 14,000' below. McLure again climbed up-sun and executed a quarter attack on a group of bombers. Selecting one of these and firing a long burst, he noted the Heinkel *'go out of control and divert slightly, but resumed its course again.'* A further burst of fire saw the bomber dive steeply, but, ammunition exhausted and with enemy fighters closing around him, Pilot Officer McLure broke off the engagement and headed home.

87 Squadron's Plt Off Andrew McLure who claimed an Me 110 destroyed on 'Black Monday.'

Author's Collection via Allan White.

By this time the raid was crossing the coast over Lyme Bay and heading northwards. Flight Lieutenant Gleed and Pilot Officer John Cock were the next of 87 Squadron to arrive, just as the enemy passed over Bridport. Whilst still climbing at 8,000', just above the clouds, Cock was attacked by an Me 109 which overshot, itself then becoming a target. Cock fired from astern, the 109 flipped on to its right side and disappeared into cloud. The Hurricane gave chase, but over Dorchester encountered a lone Ju 88. Having fired at the enemy aircraft immediately, from the beam, Cock swung round to attack from the rear, setting alight the starboard engine and fuselage, the Ju 88 then commencing a right-handed dive into cloud. Almost certainly this was Ju 88A-1 4U + MH of 1st Staffel Aufklärunsgruppe 123, a reconnaissance Gruppe operating from Buc and Bordeaux, and on this occasion briefed to photograph the damage at Yeovil immediately after KG55's attack. The enemy aircraft later crashed into the Solent off the Isle of Wight. Its crew of four were killed, the bodies of

87 Squadron's Flg Off John Cock (Australian), pictured at Exeter, who destroyed a Ju 88 and damaged an Me 109 on 'Black Monday.'

Chris Goss Collection.

three being washed up on the south coast a few days later. Leutnant Frenzel, however, remains missing.

Flt Lt 'Widge' Gleed (in cockpit) of 87 Squadron, who found himself alone amongst KG55's He 111s on 'Black Monday'. The other pilot is Flg Off R Watson. Note the Squadron Leader's rank pennant on the Hurricane.

Author's Collection via Sqn Ldr L A Thorogood.

Flight Lieutenant Gleed suddenly found himself alone amongst *'70 Ju 88s'*, which in reality were KG55's He 111s. He attacked the right-hand bomber which broke away and spiralled down through the clouds. Lying in the bombardier's prone position within the glazed nose of his Heinkel, it appeared to Flieger Götz that at first the Hurricane was trying to formate on the bombers. Momentarily stunned by the close proximity of the British fighter, Götz and the Geschwader's other gunners soon recovered and opened fire. As the Hurricane pitched into a dive, Götz's Staffelkapitän instructed the Bordfunker to broadcast their position to the Seenotdienst, hoping that if he went down in the sea then the British pilot could be rescued. Gleed's Hurricane had been hit several times, but fortunately no serious damage was caused and he was able to return safely to Exeter.

At 1615 hrs, Flight Lieutenant Frank Howell had led 12 Spitfires of 609 Squadron from Middle Wallop towards the action, on what the squadron diary called *'the now customary tea-time scramble.'* When the Spitfires arrived the enemy had already crossed over Lyme Bay and was heading inland. The Observer Corps now took over responsibility for tracking the raid's progress and landlines immediately became busy between them and the Observer Centre as this vital information was relayed.

As 609 Squadron tailed the enemy from the south, having swung round and approached from a direction of Swanage and also out of the sun, a formation of fighters was sighted below and to the Spitfires' left. Suspecting them to be Hurricanes, Howell ordered Pilot Officer David Crook to take Green Section down to investigate. Accordingly, Crook, Nowierski and Curchin broke away and dived. As Green Section got closer, Crook realised that they were in fact Me 109s! The Spitfires had the elements of both surprise and sun in their favour, and their approach was undetected. Flying Officer Nowierski fired a short burst at the rearwards 109, followed by another of 3 seconds. White, then *'very thick black smoke'* came from the enemy aircraft which dived away. Green 2 then made after another Me 109 on his right, which he attacked from astern. After just one 2 second burst white and black smoke also emitted from that aircraft. As the Polish Spitfire pilot broke left, he saw the jagdflieger bale out of the stricken *Emil*, but his parachute failed to deploy sufficiently as a cord had fouled half-way up the canopy. Unteroffizier Alois Dollinger of 5/JG2 subsequently fell dead at Grimstone with an unopened parachute. His Me 109 crashed and exploded on the Dorset Downs at 100 Acre Field, Spriggs Farm, Sydling St Nicholas.

As the Me 109s broke up, Crook went after one which took *'the most violent evasive tactics'* for nearly two minutes. The 109 dived, zoomed and turned madly all over the sky, but was unable to shake off the Spitfire, its pilot desperately trying to line up a shot: *'After a dive even faster than before, he zoomed up almost vertically for 2,000', going straight into the sun in an effort to shake me off that way. Almost completely dazzled, I managed nevertheless to follow him up and when he did a stall turn at the top I got another quick burst at him but without any apparent effect. At the top of the zoom I rolled*

Two Polish pilots of 609 Squadron, Flg Off Z Olenski (left), and Flg Off T Nowierski who shot down Unteroffizier Alois Dollinger of 5/JG2 at Sydling St Nicholas.

Chris Goss Collection.

over on to my back, but the recoil of my guns practically stalled me and I hung there for a second upside down and then fell away in a very drunken dive after the 109. He streaked away in front of me, going hard for a layer of cloud. I went down vertically after him, gathering speed like a bullet and doing a quick aileron turn to get into line again. Outside the cockpit I could see the earth and clouds and sky all apparently revolving crazily around my head, but they did so in a curiously detached way because I was conscious only of the small racing object in front. He managed to reach the cloud below and I chased after him, missed him with another burst, and then hunted him through this cloud for some miles, dodging in and out, seeing him just for a fleeting instance every now and then. He wasn't very clever about this, and he never changed course in the cloud, and thus, if I lost him, I had only to keep straight on to pick him up again. We tore over Weymouth, going very fast indeed, and passed out to sea. This was his undoing, as he probably thought he had shaken me off and he made the bad mistake of climbing out of the cloud. I climbed up behind, came into very close range, and then absolutely blasted him. He turned over and spun down into the cloud, streaming glycol smoke, which meant that his radiator had been hit. I dived below cloud but could see no trace of him at all, and I think there can be very little doubt that he crashed into the sea as he was badly hit and could not have reached France with a radiator leaking like that.'

54 years later, 609 Squadron's Pilot Officer Keith Ogilvie remembered this particular action:-

'During the afternoon things happened on a much larger scale. We arrived in time to engage the He 111s. I did not see any results but I found an He 111 and fired from his rear. The rear gunner returned my fire but then stopped. I began to pull in for a better target when there was an almighty bang behind me which destroyed my radio. A hole in the port wing told me that I had company! I was quick to break off, but never did see my attacker, nor indeed any other aircraft after that time. I made for home and landed

gingerly but without incident with a flat tyre. As I recall we were so short of aircraft that I had to fly my plane to the Spitfire plant for repairs and returned to Middle Wallop with a serviceable example. September 30th, 1940, was an exciting day, but all I could claim in both engagements was experience.'

By now the raid was approaching the Yeovil area, only to find that the sea of cloud had extended inland like a thick shroud. KG55's crews were frustrated that having fought their way inland at such cost, the target could not be seen. The formation leader, hoping to find a break in the cloud through which the target could be identified, swung around in desperation to the south-west, then leading the formation in a south-easterly direction. In roughly the right place such a *hole* appeared, through which could be seen a town, roughly the same size as Yeovil according to their briefing and also straddling a railway line. With more British fighters bearing down, a quick decision was made - attack! As the order was received, the Heinkels changed formation into Ketten in line astern so as to concentrate the bombing pattern. The bombers approached the town travelling from north-east to south-west. Lying in the nose of the lead Heinkel, the bombardier peered through his Lofte 7c bombsight; as the buildings below slid into the lens, he allowed slight adjustment for wind and drift, shouted *'Bomben Los!'* and pressed the bomb release button. At that moment, 1640 hrs, the real carnage began.

152 Squadron was poised to attack the bombers again, when Squadron Leader Devitt saw *'their bombs falling away from their bellies. On looking down to see what the target was to my horror I saw the old Sherborne School Courts, which I knew so well. I was*

Right: Sqn Ldr Peter Devitt, CO of 152 Squadron during 1940. Incredibly he was an 'Old Boy' of Sherborne School and was fighting over the town in his Spitfire during the attack.

Author's Collection via Allan White.

Below: Plt Off Roger Hall of 152 Squadron at Warmwell, 1940. Note the Spitfire's black port wing with its very 'weathered' leading edge.

Author's Collection via Flt Lt R M D Hall.

Sherborne
Barackenlager

Länge (westl. Greenw.): 2° 30´   Nördl. Breite: 50° 57´
Zielhöhe über NN: 91 - 122 m

LfL Kdo. 3   Februar 1943

Karte 1:100 000
GB: E 37

Maßstab: 1:15 000

Teil I etwa 35 Unterkunfts- und Wirtschaftsbaracken
Bebaute Fläche   etwa   16 000 qm
Gesamtfläche   etwa   125 000 qm
Teil II etwa 45 Unterkunfts- und Wirtschaftsbaracken
Bebaute Fläche   etwa   18 000 qm
Gesamtfläche   etwa   290 000 qm
Bebaute Fläche von Teil I u. II zusammen   etwa   34 000 qm
Gesamtfläche von Teil I u. II   etwa   415 000 qm
Gleisanschluß nicht vorhanden

Sherborne as it appeared to the Germans in early 1943. The town is to mid-left of centre, at centre is Sherborne Castle and Lake, and the target indicated at bottom right is an American army barracks. The non-industrial and rural nature of the area is clearly indicated by this photograph.

Via Mr Gerald Pitman.

at that time just about to attack, which I did, but was molested by a pack of Me 109s. After that I could not see much of where the bombs fell, as I was too intent upon what was happening in my immediate vicinity, but I did see a great deal of smoke around my old school's buildings, and so knew that there were some hits and possibly casualties.' Pilot Officer Roger Hall remembers that *'we intercepted the raid over what we now know was Sherborne, but at the time, due to the poor weather with lots of cloud, it could have been anywhere.'* It must have been quite a shock to Red 1, therefore, to suddenly identify Sherborne below. Flight Lieutenant Thomas, commander of 'B' Flight, also remembers *'seeing some fires in Sherborne.'*

High up, over 800' above sea-level, near the Chalk Pit on Pond Farm, 18-year-old Leslie Griffin was thatching a corn rick. Over the hill from a direction of Cerne Abbas the German formation appeared, travelling towards Yeovil:-

'On spotting me they loosed off a burst of machine-gun fire. I slid off the roof as fast as possible. A few minutes later I returned to my work, watching those planes making their way, by which time the Yeovil barrage balloons had appeared and the Germans turned away. I could see everything. The Germans were en route for Sherborne, suddenly I heard and felt the shock of bombs as they were dropped on what had been, until then, a peaceful market town. A few minutes passed, then a pall of dust rose into the cloudy sky, and the sun shone through.'

Clinton Trewlany of the Observer Corps at Yetminster, saw the bombs fall: *'Then the whole sky was filled with dust, and suddenly the sun came out and the dust was gold; it was a lovely sight.'*

With the crash of the first bomb, Sherborne's idyll was shattered as its townsfolk experienced at first hand the true horror of war. When the siren wailed, warning people to take cover, the majority took heed, but none in the country town could have remotely suspected that soon Sherborne would actually be the target for two Gruppen of He 111s. On what became known as *Black Monday* in Sherborne, the West Country was doing its best to enjoy the last of the summer sunshine. Monica Hutchings never expected anything to happen in the small town of 5,000, there being *'nothing worth bombing.'* Furthermore, the town lay on the bombers' route to Bristol, a city

'Bomben Los!'

Dr Alfred Price.

already subjected to heavy attack, so when the siren sounded the young accounts clerk took little notice. As she made her way to take shelter at the Swan Hotel, Monica was momentarily petrified by the crash of exploding bombs - she threw herself down on the ground and lay in the centre of the main road. All around her flew masonry, and thick dust gathered in a great cloud. Next to her a man lay dying; he had forgotten the oft repeated instruction to lie flat.

Frank Childe had been accepted as a Constable in the Dorset Constabulary in 1933, *'when to be so was considered an honour.'* Having served at various stations throughout the county as a single man, he had moved into married quarters on Sherborne's Lenthay housing estate in 1938. PC58 Childe remembers the raid:-

'During those times a policeman was on duty for 24 hours a day, and was expected to be available for each alert. On this day, when the alert sounded, I was off-duty and immediately dressed for the occasion and made for my designated post, which was at the Lenthay Post Office, about three doors away. There I met Ted Lemon, the Postman, who was collecting the mail, a resident of Nether Compton. We stood there outside the Post Office chatting and thinking "Oh, just another raid that would pass over heading elsewhere", when we were soon abused of this idea by the menacing roar of an extraordinary number of aircraft engines, the air vibrating from the concentrated noise. I looked westwards into the sky and saw what appeared to be a double handful of peas thrown towards the earth and breaking through the clouds. Ted and I dashed into the Post Office and threw ourselves on the floor. The time was 1640 hrs. All hell broke loose. It felt as though the whole world was a bouncing ball. For myself, it felt as though nothing could survive such an onslaught. Suddenly, dead silence, which after the bombs was uncanny on the hearing. Ted and I got up, both surprised that we were still alive. He took me by the hand and said "Thank you for saving my life", and after that moment we were lifelong friends.'

10-year-old Gerald Pitman was a pupil at the Abbey Junior School in Horsecastles:-

'When the siren went I ran as hard as I could along Trendle Street, up the steps in front of the Digby Memorial where a group of people were talking, and up Cheap Street. When I reached the Eldridge Pope & Co premises at the top of Cheap Street I could see my Grandmother at the door of our house and shop which was on the corner of Higher Cheap Street by the Milborne Port bus-stop. She called out to me to hurry, and I was soon inside the shop. Inside the little shop were two ladies waiting for my father, who ran a taxi, to drive them out into the country. They had just arrived from London to escape the raids.

'I showed my grandmother a lead soldier that I had either swapped or been given that afternoon and it was then that the noise of bombs became obvious. We hurried for shelter under the stairs which had been shorn up as a shelter. The front door seemed as though it was being continually thumped. The people from the bus queue had taken shelter on our stairs. The bird's cage, which was hanging in the window with "Joey" in it, went up and down. One of the ladies from London fainted but by that time the bombing had ended.'

Gwynne Douglas James was a 16-year-old pupil at Sherborne School: *'I was down at school when the siren went during English. We sighed - with relief or disappointment, and wandered, I'm afraid to say rather slowly, up to Lyon House. There was not the sound of an aeroplane to be heard, in fact it was just the same as many other raids we had been having and we were rather bored with them.'*

Another English pupil was an anonymous member of Lyon House who also committed his memory to paper just two days after the raid:-

'I was having an English lesson in the Lower Library, and, as that veritable hive of historical books is considered safe enough in an air raid, we stayed where we were and did not go to the Cloisters as people in the other classrooms do when the siren sounds.

'About a quarter of an hour later we heard the sound of aero engines, rather like the characteristic zoom-zoom of Boche planes. Then a minute or two later we heard a distant whistle and "crump", then some more ominous bangs nearer, so we all crawled under the massive oak tables and waited in suspense. Nearer and nearer came the explosions, the lights went out, thud followed thud in a hideous deafening roar, the big library above seemed as if it would fall down on us at any moment. Glass split and cracked. Then gradually it got further and further away and stopped altogether. We crawled out from under the tables, rather dazed, and looked out of the windows. The whole air was filled with like a thick fog.'

Charles Burgess (14):-

'Surely I cannot die at fourteen? Far too young. Gradually the detonations came nearer and nearer. Suddenly a terrific explosion rocked the Cloisters. The pressure on my eardrums was enormous. A piece of shrapnel whined over my head. That is my most vivid impression, that piece of sharapnel. A cloud of brown dust rolled over the lying figures. Then someone laughed and before I knew where I was, I was laughing too. We all laughed when Scott appeared with his face caked with dust. I think he must have escaped death by a hair's breadth.'

Anon:-

'They were the longest 86 seconds I have ever experienced and I wish to state that I hope never to experience them again.'

John Meredith Williams (14):-

'A silver Spitfire banked low over the Abbey and restored a great deal of my spirit.'

Denzil Kingston Freeth (16):-

'God, don't let me be buried under debris. I don't mind dying but don't let me lie there cold, bleeding, wounded, unable to move; perhaps buried alive. Why have I got to die? Please God don't let me die. Glass crashing around. My fingers in my ears. Oh God - and the noise dies away in the distance.'

Geoffrey Leonard Baker (16):-

'When the siren went, we being an industrious maths set, went on with our work. A few minutes later we heard bombs being dropped about a mile away and I gathered that some place was getting a rather sticky time, not guessing for a moment that it would be our turn soon. At the first sound of a bomb, work stopped and we all listened. Mr Randolph, who was taking us, told us to put our heads down under the desks while he, on the other hand, went outside to see if he could spot any planes, not yet having seen a German plane himself. As the bombs came nearer and everything started to shake, Mr Randolph wasn't so keen on looking for planes and came in with us pretty quickly!

'The noise was terrific, nothing but whistles, bumps, explosions and the roar of aeroplane engines in the background. The door shook like anything so that in the first lull Mr Randolph went and sat with his back to it. When the second lot of bombs started falling everyone's head darted under the desks again, and we lay there thinking that our last day had come, because it was then that the bombs in the Courts were dropped. I could see out of the window and when those dropped I saw a great pile of earth and stones thrown high into the air, and at the same time glass fell out of the windows.'

The boys of Sherborne's Foster's School were also ushered out of class when the siren went and up floated the Yeovil balloon barrage. Harold Osement was amongst them, and remembered that 'the western sky had the look of dull, mild oatmeal and it was from there that the drama unfolded. From somewhere out there, beyond the horizon of dark roofs and chimneys of The Avenue, out there in the oatmeal haze, came what sounded like heavy waggons crumping across hard, rough ground. Still nobody talked. The sound effects out there demanded to be heard in their own awful way. Into the muzzy off-yellow sky came what looked like strings of black sausages, and falling from them were flights of cloves. "Get Down!", the French master shouted. A great hiss scythed up through the sky, but then nothing more seemed likely to happen so we came up. I looked at a band of jagged, blackish metal at the edge of the trench. "Don't touch it", the French master shouted, "It's still hot!". It looked like the mane of a little sea-horse, and as I admired our trophy with almost affectionate contemplation, I noticed that the grass nearest to it was faintly steaming. Over to the left, in front of the school buildings, a two-storey house burned, flaming away in a business-like way as if it enjoyed doing what it had to, and the north-east wind bent the flames in long streams and continually brightened its red centre.'*

In Sherborne's shopping area, Mrs Minterne had taken cover within the building firm premises owned by her husband, known as *Minterne's* and opposite Parson's Butchers in Half Moon Street. Suddenly there was a loud bang as a bomb exploded nearby, and a lump of shrapnel 'as big as a dustbin lid' came hurtling through the shop's plate glass window. At the time *Minterne's* was being decorated, and the blast knocked all the paint over which splattered everywhere 'like a rainbow.'

---

* *reproduced from 'Wartime Sherborne' by kind permission of the author, Harold Osement*

The ground tremored even as far away as Yeovil. 11-year-old Norman Collard had taken shelter in Eastland Road, and remembers that *'the building shook all the time.'*

At Houndstone Camp, a Royal Artillery depot on the western edge of Yeovil and some seven miles from Sherborne, Private Martin, a cook in the Officers' Mess, clearly heard the bombs and saw the cloud of golden dust rising into the sky from Sherborne's direction. 14-year-old John Gaunt was standing on the roof of his parents' home at Charles Dairy, Yeovil, and after the siren went saw columns of smoke lifting over Babylon Hill. Suddenly the boy saw a parachute, and a fighter aircraft tumble out of the sky and crash near Yeovil Junction railway station.

Fred Denham was a member of Yeovil's St John Ambulance Brigade, and when the siren sounded he made haste to the Police Station to be deployed. Overhead he saw *'fifty bombers plus fighters which turned over Yeovil and bombed Sherborne. As I arrived at the Station, the Superintendent was running out to his car, strapping on a revolver. "Quick, man!", he said, "come with me, we'll capture him", and looking up I saw a parachutist descending in a direction of Yeovil Junction. Off we went and found that a Hurricane had crashed at Newton House, to the south-east of Yeovil, and we later found the pilot taking tea in a cottage at East Coker.'*

John Hall was cycling up Grove Avenue, Yeovil, when he saw the *'Hurricane attacking a great formation of enemy aircraft. There was no other sound, just the machine-guns of that lone fighter rattling away until it was hit and disappeared over towards Sherborne. It was undoubtedly an act of great courage.'*

At 10.30 hrs that morning, the Robinsons had emerged from Yeovil's Registry Office, a newly married couple, to an air raid warning, of which, *'as there had been so many'*, they took no heed. During the afternoon, the couple, Mr Robinson being a regular soldier in the RA, were having a cup of tea when the *Alert* sounded again. However, on that occasion they did take shelter as the bombers could be heard flying overhead. Anti-aircraft guns were firing, and as the newly-weds ran to their garden's surface shelter, Sybil saw a parachute drifting down. Next the loud thuds of bombs dropping on Sherborne could be heard.

Schoolboy Michael Trevett: *'I saw a Hurricane attack the wave of German aircraft, it was destroyed and dived to earth in flames. Its pilot baled out and parachuted to safety.'*

Certainly 87 Squadron's Sergeant Walton had pursued the enemy inland, and was himself shot down whilst attacking the raiders over Sherborne. Fortunately he baled out, and his parachute was seen by many boys of Sherborne School, amongst them John Ching (15): *'They've got one down, I think its a Jerry! Then a cheer, such as I've never heard before rent the air, or I should say the dust. This encouraged me, and I felt happier.'* Walton's Hurricane impacted at Burdon's Nurseries, Osborne Road, Sherborne, and Walton was taken to Sherborne Hospital slightly wounded. Peter Lane (15), another pupil at Sherborne School saw *'a parachute drifting down in Thornford direction. We cheered thinking it was a German, but later discovered it to have been a British pilot.'* Whether Lane saw Walton, or the parachutist who landed at East Coker (in roughly the same direction as Thorngrove, i.e. to the south-west of Sherborne), it cannot be said as neither the pilot or aircraft concerned in the latter instance have been identified, although there is no dispute that a Hurricane did indeed crash at Newton House, Yeovil, at this time.

The bombs extended along the length of Sherborne in a distinct triple line from Bedmill Copse to Crackmore. The formation of 43 Heinkels had been carrying 245 bombs in total. Although KG55 had suffered casualties by the time of the attack, the quantity of bombs dropped on Sherborne must be somewhere near that figure. Around 50 fell on the town itself. The bombs crashed down on Lenthay, through Horsecastles, Richmond Road, Acreman Street, Sherborne School Garden, Abbey Road, the School Courts, Half Moon Street, Cheap Street, Newland and North Road. At *Sydney Villa* in the Avenue, and at a

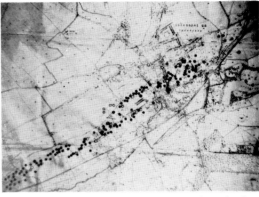

The map of Sherborne's bomb plots made up by the District ARP Controller, Mr Freeman.

Via Rodney Legg.

bungalow and garages in Tinney's Lane, two large fires burned. Several roads were blocked, but the main A30 was clear. Gas and water mains were seriously damaged

Photographed on October 1st, 1940, the crater at the centre of Cheap Street, Sherborne.

Via Rodney Legg.

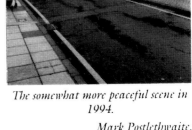

The somewhat more peaceful scene in 1994.

Mark Postlethwaite.

and the electricity supply had also failed. UXBs lay in the main road at Cheap Street, in a garden at Back Abbey, in St Swithin's Road, in a garden off the Avenue, and in a lawn at the back of Monks Barn, Newlands. Southern Railway reported the *Up* and *Down* lines damaged between Yeovil Junction and Sherborne, and all traffic stopped. There was also a direct hit to the cemetery where coffins were blown out of the ground. Incredibly, however, Sherborne Abbey, in the town centre and overlooking the scene of destruction, was undamaged.

Above: 1994 scene.

Mark Postlethwaite.

Left: Half Moon Street looking west from the junction with South Street.

Via Rodney Legg.

In Cheap Street was the Post Office, at which was located the Telephone Exchange. The telephone system was maintained throughout the raid due to the bravery and devotion to duty of the telephonist supervisor, Miss Maude Steel, a local girl, who remained at her post despite the devastation around her. By her action, and that of the temporary telephonist who remained with Miss Steele, the Emergency and ARP services were kept in constant touch with their headquarters until local landlines were put out of action. Even then, when a bomb exploded within the Post Office's precincts, Miss Steele proceeded from the Refuge Room to the Exchange in the hope that she could be of assistance. She was magnificent in the face of real danger, and by her action contributed greatly to the effective working of the ARP and other services. She had remained at the Exchange until the position became impossible, but even then she was reluctant to leave. For such selfless acts of courage, Miss Steel later received the George Medal which had only been instituted six days previously.

As the Heinkels' bomb doors closed and the raiders set course for France, the attack over, the stunned populace of Sherborne took stock.

The boys of Sherborne School have left us with a rich record of their feelings after the bombing.

Anthony Harbottle (15):-

'After the four bombs fell in the Courts we were dumbfounded. One or two gingerly stood up and peered out of the window. One of the masters then informed us that no-one had been hurt.

'We were then summoned to the Cloisters. Whilst walking across the Courts untold damage could be witnessed. Pieces of leaden window-frames were hanging despondently, as if suspended in mid-air, all twisted and shattered. Cruel scars were to be seen on the stone walls, craters twenty feet and more in diameter were gaping at us as we walked across the Courts that fateful afternoon. There was truly change and decay in all that we saw around, though the destruction wrought might have been a hundred times worse.

'When we arrived in the Cloisters many were talking and laughing cheerfully, none the worse for the providential escape from death. Suddenly there was a hush, the Headmaster was speaking to us. In an unemotional voice he told us to go back to our Houses and "Work, work, work!" Several had lost valuable possessions, but all were thankful to have been spared.

'On the way back, several Spitfires could be seen and heard circling round. Going up the hill I saw a workman with a gory bandage round his head, making his way to hospital but looking as cheerful as ever.

'Since there was neither gas, electricity, nor water, the "Raiders Passed" was never sounded, and thus it was we found ourselves eating a ham roll for tea, and two large kettles boiling on the coke fire. Later on, after much gossip, we vainly tried to do our Hall by candlelight, during which time we despatched brief postcards to our parents to confirm our escape.'

Frank Nicholls (15):-

'I went to see if I could be of any assistance to the neighbours. I was greeted in the yard by Mrs Palmer and her maid, shouting that there was a dead man in her garden. I handed her over to Mr Ross and ran down through the garden to Thorn's house to see if he was hurt. I climbed over a heap of debris, caused, I discovered later, by a time-bomb, and found both he and his wife uninjured, though busy having hysterics. I promised to come down and help him soon, and ran off up the road, negotiated a bomb crater in the road, a dead gardener, messy but not sickening, telegraph and power wires. The stench of explosives was everywhere, an aircraft did a victory roll over the school, and a man, one of ours, I saw coming down by parachute.'

John Maxwell Ward (18):-

'A fatal casualty in Mr Palmer's garden. I went there and found Jimmy Lintern in the garden approximately five yards from a crater. Thence I ran down to the First Aid Post and told them that there was no hope for the fellow and returned to poor Jimmy whose heart and eyes I inspected with the obvious negative result. Then Hamerseley appeared

with a sheet to cover the unfortunate fellow. Later on a stretcher party arrived and simultaneously an ambulance, but having seen their patient remarked that it would be a waste of time to do anything, and so left poor Jimmy to get colder and stiffer. A warden came up soon afterwards and later on an old van from a garage. The warden and the other two then asked me if I could find some sacking - I ran off and as I was passing through the House, Wilson asked me whether I had "cleared out" my study - not quite understanding quite what on earth he was on about I replied "No". To which he roared in response "Well go and do it then, and brace up!" Thinking that other things were more important, I hurried on without paying any attention to him.

'We four, the Warden, two others and myself then lifted the corpse on to the van and the latter moved off. I then moved off in search of Thorne, who was weeping in the back parlour, and tried to console him. Little did I know that I was standing directly over a 550lb unexploded bomb!'

Outside the Westminster Bank at the south end of Cheap Street, an unexploded bomb wedged itself in an old well shaft. The following day the UXB has been sandbagged to protect against blast.	*Phillips and Sons' outfitters from the north-east, the bottom of Cheap Street, looking along Half Moon Street, with the Half Moon Hotel set back from the debris in the centre of the picture.*
Via Rodney Legg.	*Via Rodney Legg.*

Anthony Harbottle describes the scene that night:-

'We had an early bed. Just before settling in our attention was riveted on a burning house, not far distant. The rafters could clearly be seen against the red glow.

'During the night we were called up no less than three times by police whistles. At about 2 o'clock there was a violent explosion -one of the time bombs dropped during the raid had gone off. This was followed a few minutes later by another, and the sound of falling masonry. Neither bomb did serious damage. The suspense while waiting for the explosion was ghastly. No more exploded, however, and the rest of the night was spent in comparative peace and calm.'

For other pupils sleep did not come so easily:-

John Maxwell Ward: *'When night came with more contemplation I felt physically sick and very unhappy.'*

Donald Moffat Wilson (17): *'My impressions of the bombing are these, cold fear as the bombs whistled down, immediate reaction of excitement and laughter, cheerfulness till nightfall which brought with it exhaustion and nervousness; and for the next few days cheerfulness but finding it very difficult to concentrate.'*

The boys had all come through their ordeal with flying colours. According to young Frank Nicholls, they could *'take it and take it again and again if necessary to beat the dastardly Hun.'*

Monica Hutchings, shocked at having discovered her friend, Miss Gartell, dead, the unfortunate woman's face a mask of shock and terror, waited for a kettle to boil on a fire made from the timber of bombed buildings.

Hampered by the UXBs, Mr Edward J Freeman, the District Air Raid Precautions Controller, and his men, assisted by an ARP detachment and a Rescue Party from Yeovil, soon commenced restoring the town's essential services and helping the injured. The dead ultimately numbered 18, including a youngster from London who had been evacuated to escape the bombing there only the day before. 32 people were injured and detained in hospital. Of the 1,700 properties in the town, 31 were demolished and 776 damaged. In true wartime spirit, a fund for the relief of victims was opened immediately, started by a lady resident with the generous gift of £200. Blankets were brought into the town by the Red Cross Society, and offers of assistance came from as far afield as Sherborne, Massachusetts. Surrounding villages sent tarpaulins for gaping roofs, and oil-stoves to combat the lack of power, and candles and bedding and food; many of them threw open their doors to the bombed townspeople until their homes were restored.

PC Childe remembers the aftermath:-

'After Ted Lemon and I had picked ourselves up, I ran the short distance home to check that my wife was alright. She was in a shelter that I had made in our garden against such an occasion. She had survived, so I ran back to my post and duties. I was obliged to pick my way back over tangled telephone and electricity cables. Work went on throughout the area and we found that all public services, water, electricity and telephones were completely cut off. It was a case of "make do and mend".

'I found myself in the Lenthay council housing estate at a premises which had sustained a direct hit. The complete roof had been blown off and came down again on the demolished house. Neighbours told us that the house had contained a mother and three children. We had no proper tools or equipment but started making a way through the roof and rubble. The mother was located by her fingers showing beneath the door of the under stairs cupboard. It was whilst we were working our way through the debris of this house with domestic tools that we were encouraged by the arrival of a small ARP squad from Yeovil, complete with more suitable tools and a doctor who crawled through the tunnel we had made and gave the trapped woman an injection.

'At this point I must give credit to the licensee of the "Traveller's Rest" in Horsecastles, for his gallant gesture, in spite of the law and regulations, of keeping his Pub open until midnight providing refreshments FREE to all those persons helping in the rescue operation. All public services, of course, were out of action.

'The path of the enemy planes was from Yeovil towards Templecombe, leaving a path of death and destruction in their wake. It was not until the following day, however, that we learned the true extent of damage and casualties. A friend of mine, Harry Ireland, had a saddlery business in Half Moon Street, next door to the "Phillips" drapery shop. His premises was demolished by a direct hit and poor Harry was later found, still in his chair, beneath the debris in the cellar.

'Percy Coaker, a well known local character, ran a furniture store in Cheap Street, opposite the Methodist Church. His premises were extensively damaged, but a large notice, typical of the spirit of the time, appeared on his shop: "WE HAVE BEEN BOMBED, BUGGERED & BEWILDERED, BUT BUSINESS IS AS USUAL!"

'Mr Harold Pitman, a taxi-cab owner of Cheap Street, was driving from Chetnole to Sherborne when he saw a parachute descending. This would have been the gallant pilot of a fighter plane who attacked the Germans but was himself shot down. This occurred immediately before the bombs fell.

'In spite of the fact that particularly all the roads in the centre of Sherborne were blocked with debris and essential services completely disrupted, the local services and authorities did a wonderful job in getting everything going again in the shortest time possible.'

As the raiders left Sherborne agonising beneath the pall of golden coloured dust, the German crews turned on a southerly course; it was still a long way home.

At 1630 hrs that afternoon, Squadron Leader Johnny Sample DFC had led 12 Hurricanes of 504 Squadron off from Filton with orders to patrol base at Angels 20. Red 1 was then vectored 205 degrees for 10 minutes and told to increase height to 25,000' and patrol Yeovil. Upon reaching the Yeovil area, the squadron saw two close formations of Heinkels, *'numbering 20 and 30 aircraft respectively, flying north @ 17,000'. The enemy aircraft were roughly 20 miles east of our squadron, each formation was a rough vic composed of smaller vics of three aicraft.'* As the Hurricanes manoeuvred into position for an attack, the enemy turned slowly to the right and flew on a south-westerly course. Shortly after that Sherborne was bombed, but due to the range involved the Hurricane pilots could not see this. As the squadron approached bent on assailing the enemy, the Germans turned south onto a course that would ultimately take them out over Weymouth.

When 87 Squadron's 'B' Flight had received the order to scramble from Exeter at 1650 hrs, Pilot Officers Beamont and Mitchell, and Sergeant Badger, had been left behind as their Hurricanes were being refuelled. *Bee* Beamont remembers: *'After take off (I was leading), the R/T told us to "Buster Portland Angels 20, very many bandits heading south". Over Dorchester we briefly saw some Me 110s diving fast towards the coast but we lost them in cloud. It was frustrating.'* An even more frustrated 87 Squadron pilot was Flight Lieutenant Ward who had dashed back to the airfield from the local cinema upon hearing the siren. Off too late, he failed to contact the enemy at all.

After 609 Squadron's first charge at the enemy, Pilot Officer Noel Agazarian, the squadron's *weaver*, had lost the other Spitfires and was thereafter unable to locate his comrades. Instead he decided to intercept the Heinkels during their return flight. Inland of Warmwell he attacked the rearmost bombers from the beam with a four second burst. As he broke away, however, he noted that his glycol tank had been hit. Attacking just once more, the *Green Eyed Monster* noted with satisfaction as he broke away that the Heinkel's starboard engine was streaming black smoke and apparently on fire. The bomber was not losing height, but Blue 4 was unable to do anything about this as he was losing coolant fast, so broke off and landed quickly at Warmwell. In his combat report, he later noted that *'the Heinkels, between 50 and 60 of them, bombed in "V" formation and as they turned south to go home changed into a thick solid echelon port. The return fire was terrific, highly concentrated.'*

609 Squadron: extreme left: Flt Lt THT Forshaw, in tunic; Flg Off T Nowierski, and at extreme right, Plt Off N leC Agazarian.

Chris Goss Collection.

At 1610 hrs, Squadron Leader Duncan MacDonald scrambled from the 11 Group Sector Station at Tangmere with 12 other 213 Squadron Hurricanes behind him. The squadron was initially vectored to intercept a 200+ raid which had crossed the Kent coast just two minutes previously. However, Sergeant Geoffrey Stevens, flying *AK-D*, clearly remembers an unexpected turn of events:-

'Quite abruptly and without warning we were ordered to turn 180 degrees and told "Buster". R/T talk between our "Bearskin Leader" and Ground Control elicited the information that it was a 60+ raid. We soon saw the enemy, first as dots which gradually developed into a mixture of He 111s and Me 110s, and some Me 109s which were, as usual, above us. We were at about the same height as the bombers and 110s. I initially went for one of the latter, but he evaded by executing a spiral dive. I did not follow as I wished to retain height, but then saw a formation of three He 111s below me, so I dived on them, selecting the left hand aircraft as my target. I got a fair amount of stick from all three gunners and opened with quite a long burst. However, I was travelling too fast and broke away left and downwards. I pulled back into a steep, almost vertical climb at full throttle, intending to come around again for another go, feeling quite sure that I had silenced the gunner in the aircraft I had fired at. At this point, near the top of the climb, the belly of an Me 110 slid into view going from right to left. I opened up and continued climbing. I saw strikes all along the underside, but I had reached the point of stall and at that moment ran out of ammunition. I fell

Taken during service flying training, Sgt Geoffrey Stevens on right (but who is the pilot with him?). On 'Black Monday', flying with 213 Squadron, Stevens damaged an Me 110.

Author's Collection
via Flt Lt G Stevens.

out of the skies, as the saying goes, and as there was no point in returning to the fray I let the aircraft dive. This was very nearly my undoing, as I had built up too much speed and had great difficulty in getting out of the dive. The airscrew over-revved and sprayed oil all over the windscreen, but thankfully I made it by about 100'. Later the airframe fitter told me that several wooden slats which ran underside and aft of the cockpit had been stove in by the pressure of my pull out.'

213 Squadron had intercepted the enemy at about 1700 hrs and over Portland. For no loss, Squadron Leader MacDonald and Flying Officer Kellow each claimed an Me 110 destroyed. Sub-Lieutenant Jeram, a Fleet Air Arm pilot seconded to Fighter Command, claimed a further 110 as probably destroyed, whilst Sergeants Stevens and Barrow each claimed one damaged. Pilot Officer Atkinson claimed an Me 109 destroyed.

Just south of Portland, 504 Squadron eventually caught the enemy formation and Squadron Leader Sample led his Hurricanes into a quarter astern attack in sections on the rearmost German bombers.

Following Sample's Red Section was Yellow 1, Flight Lieutenant Tony Rook. Attacking the port rear section of Heinkels, the starboard engine of one *'gave off lots of smoke and on my second attack, stopped.'* By the time Rook had broken away, this machine had left the formation and was flying very slowly on one engine, and even that was emitting black smoke. Yellow 1 then got into a spin, but by the time he recovered *'there was nothing in sight.'*

Tucked in behind Squadron Leader Sample was Red 2, Flying Officer Michael Royce. He noticed no effect from his first attack but then spotted two stragglers, firing several bursts at one of these. During this attack his Hurricane also became covered in oil from the enemy aircraft. As he broke away he *'noticed that both engines were smoking badly with the airscrews just ticking over. The aircraft was losing height gradually.'* Noting his own rapidly decreasing oil pressure, Royce then broke off and returned to Filton, landing at 1730 hrs.

Flight Lieutenant William Royce, Blue Leader, carried out a quarter astern attack on the Heinkels in company with Red 1, and his younger brother, Flying Officer Michael Royce. Blue Leader continued firing until he was *'dead astern, black smoke appeared from the port engine and oil covered my machine. I was then hit in the wing and front fuselage, so broke away. Whilst doing so I saw an He 111 fly above the formation, stall and spin down. Before entering cloud its port wing broke off and the aircraft burst into flames as it hit the sea.'*

Undoubtedly the latter Heinkel was one of those attacked by Green 2, Sergeant Herbert Jones:-

'We went into attack from astern and I picked the aircraft on the starboard side of the rear formation. I closed in to 250 yards and put a 5 second burst into the starboard engine causing pieces to fly off and black smoke to pour out of the enemy aircraft. It then broke away from the enemy formation upwards and across the top and eventually went into a spin. The starboard wing fell off and it crashed into the sea and burst into flames. I then noticed another enemy aircraft which had dropped out of the formation and was making for clouds. I closed to 250 yards and put a 5 second burst into the fuselage and engines. Pieces flew off and my windscreen became smothered in oil. I broke away at about 25 yards, there was no return fire. I went round and made a further astern attack of a 4 second burst. Both engines

Sgt HDB Jones of 504 Squadron who shot two He 111s down into the sea on 'Black Monday.'
Author's Collection via Allan White.

appeared to have stopped and the undercarriage dropped down as the enemy aircraft disappeared into the clouds. Green 1, Pilot Officer White, was watching this encounter, dived down through the clouds and saw the Heinkel crash into the sea. There was no sign of anyone getting out. I was then attacked by 7 Me 109s which came out of the sun, so I did a steep turn and sought refuge in the clouds.'

By the time 504 Squadron broke off its attack, it was very near to the French coast. Flying Officer John Reginald Hardacre, however, was missing over the sea in P3414, *TM-K*. His body was later washed up on the Isle of Wight. Mike Bush remembers that *'when pilots did not return, we were told not to dwell on it, their names were simply not mentioned again.'*

Three other 504 Squadron Hurricanes would not reach Filton. Pilot Officer Murray Frisby forced landed his damaged Hurricane near Whitcombe Church, east of Dorchester, at 1700 hrs. At around the same time, Sergeant Banks forced landed a damaged *TM-V* in the *Yeovil area*. Sergeant Mike Bush and *TM-N*, P3021, had quite an adventure, however:-

Flg Off John Reginald Hardacre of 504 Squadron, 'missing' over the sea on 'Black Monday', his body washed ashore at Yarmouth ten days later.

Author's Collection via Allan White.

504 Squadron Hurricanes at Filton, 1940. The foremost machine is P3021, TM-N, which was usually flown by Sgt Mike Bush. On 'Black Monday', Bush forced landed P3021 near Priddy, lost and short of fuel after damaging an He 111 over the sea.

Author's Collection via Flt Lt BM Bush.

Sgt BM 'Mike' Bush of 504 Squadron.

Author's Collection via Flt Lt BM Bush.

'*After the interception I was unable to obtain radio contact with Filton. As it was getting dusk and I was lost somewhere south of Bristol I was fearful of getting caught in balloon cables, so decided to land in a field. I picked what I thought to be a long landing run in a particular field which I had spotted, but on the approach I came in low over a hedge and landed, only to discover that it was in a much shorter field than the one I had selected, and ahead I saw a brick wall. Having landed I could do nothing but jam on my brakes and switch off the engine. The action of applying the brakes hard resulted in tipping my Hurricane up on its nose. It then flipped over on to its back and I was left hanging by my harness upside down and several feet from the ground. Thankfully I was soon released by men of the Observer Corps from nearby Priddy village.*'

In fact, as the last aircraft of each side touched down at their respective aerodromes that fateful afternoon, so ended the final great daylight air battle of Summer 1940. On September 30th, 1940, the Luftwaffe had lost a total of 46 aircraft destroyed, another 12 damaged, and two more written off in a flying accident. That afternoon, KG55 had lost four He 111s, all shot down over the sea, all but four men of their crews perishing. The body of one, Obergefreiter Willi Schocke, a gunner in the 4th Staffel's

G1 + CM, was washed ashore at Horsesand Fort some two weeks later. Amongst those rescued by the Seenotdienst, albeit after 36 uncomfortable hours afloat in a dinghy, was Major Doktor Ernst Kühl, the Geschwader Operations Officer who had planned much of the raid himself. The crew of the 1(F)123 Ju 88 attacked by Pilot Officer Cock similarly crashed into the sea, its crew also being killed. 5/JG2 had left Unteroffizier Alois Dollinger dead at Grimstone, his Me 109 burnt out at Sydling St Nicholas, Dorset. The reader may be surprised at the actual number of enemy aircraft lost when compared with that claimed by the British fighters. Over-claiming was common, and greater the more aircraft involved. It was simply a case of the speed of combat deceiving the eye, i.e. several pilots independently attacking the same aircraft and claiming accordingly. In several instances during the foregoing narrative, for example, one could suggest that a number of claims were for the same aircraft, the crippled He 111 which sprayed oil over two of 504 Squadron's Hurricanes being a prime example.

The grave at Gosport of Obergefreiter Willi Schocke, a 21-year-old gunner of 4/KG55 shot down over the sea in 'G1+CM'. His body was washed ashore at Horsesand Fort two weeks later. Note the incorrect date of death.

Miss Margaret Balfour.

Fighter Command lost a total of 20 aircraft on this particular day. Eight had been lost over the West Country with two pilots killed and three wounded. A further eight aircraft were damaged. During the afternoon raid against Yeovil, four British fighters were claimed as destroyed by II/JG2, four more by III/JG2, two by II/JG53 and four by ZG26. Unfortunately very few *Abschussmeldung*, or combat victory reports, survive, so it is impossible to say which individual German pilots made these claims. It is known, however, that II/JG53's Oberfeldwebel Patho claimed two Hurricanes destroyed on this day.

After September 30th, the German High Command at last accepted the folly of daylight operations by poorly equipped mass formations, and consequently the He 111 was withdrawn from the arena only to thereafter operate over England at night. Indeed, the main assault against the British mainland switched to nocturnal attacks, which at first posed further problems for both sides. Britain's night defences were in their infancy at that time, thus allowing the Kampfgeschwadern to operate over England with comparative impunity. In turn, the night sky presented the raiders with navigational and target location difficulties, although both were soon solved by the use of radio guiding beams, *Knickebein, X-Gerät* and *Y-Gerät*, which led the bombers to their targets, bomb release being automatic and upon receipt of a special signal.

With regard to the bombing of Sherborne, however, it must be remembered that the enemy formation was relying entirely upon dead reckoning navigation to locate their target, a hopeless task in view of the prevailing cloud conditions. Having been attacked by British fighters almost continually since first intercepted some 20 miles off Portland Bill, it is actually to the Germans' credit that they got anywhere near Yeovil. They were certainly not *'turned back'* by RAF fighters as some accounts have previously suggested, although in view of the navigational problems caused by the cloud and with further attacking fighters in sight, the appearance of Sherborne below was undoubtedly a Godsend for the Heinkels.

The Luftwaffe soon accepted that a mistake had been made. Opening with the familar phrase *'Germany calling, Germany calling'*, Lord Haw Haw broadcast an apology to Sherborne. However, the Irish traitor, William Joyce, who was ultimately executed by the British at Wandsworth in January 1946, ominously predicted that Yeovil's turn was yet to come.

Störflug to Worcester

On October 1st, 1940, the Battle of Britain moved into its fifth and final phase. In the main, the German bombing effort was shifted to nocturnal operations, chiefly to continue the progressive destruction of London, and secondly, and of much lower importance, to interfere with production in the great arms centres of the Midlands. During the day, Goering resorted mainly to using fighter-bombers at high altitude. As these *jabos* were mixed in with ordinary fighters, the British Ground Controllers were unable to identify which enemy formations contained bomb-carrying aircraft and so were unable to prioritise, meaning that all had to be met. The volume of these raids, the majority against south-east England, stretched Fighter Command, already weakened by two months of bitter fighting, to the limit by flying almost constant defensive patrols and interception sorties. The German High Command had also agreed that daylight bombing operations should continue to some extent, but only by either lone aircraft on occasions when weather conditions were suitable, or by Ju 88s of up to Gruppe strength escorted by many fighters. Such bombing was clearly not preliminary to an invasion, but was considered by the enemy as an investment showing small but growing damage to both industrial and domestic property. It was hoped that the proposed invasion would in the long term be assisted by such *Störflug*, or *harassing attacks*, by hampering production and distribution, in addition to lowering public morale. The aircraft industry was still the main objective for such daylight raids. During October, 30 hits were recorded on aircraft factories against just eight between September 7th and 30th.

Worcestershire, in the south-west Midlands, was to have little direct experience of war. The county is bordered by Shropshire and Staffordshire in the north, Warwickshire to the east and Herefordshire in the west, the Malvern Hills forming a natural boundary at that point. To the north of the central plain towards Birmingham, are the Clent and Lickey hills. The fertile Severn vale runs north to south, through the centre of the county, its orchards a blaze of blossom in springtime. Straddled across the River Severn, the *Corridor of the West*, is the Cathedral City of Worcester, the *Faithful City,* so called after having rallied to the Royalist cause during the English Civil War. Worcester's principal industries comprised pottery, light engineering and clothing manufacture. Like Yeovil, Worcester had also been scrutinized by the Luftwaffe reconnaissance aircraft. They brought back photographs and possible targets were coded accordingly: the Worcestershire Regimental barracks at Norton, petrol storage tanks at Diglis, government buildings at Whittington, and Worcester's *Zivilflugplatz,* or civilian airfield at Perdiswell.

On the west bank of the Severn lies the Worcester suburb of St John's. Situated in Bromyard Road, adjacent to the main western railway line, were the premises of the

Mining and Engineering Company Ltd., known locally as the *MECO*. The busy factory manufactured various equipment for the mining industry, but in 1940 was also sub-contracted by the Air Ministry to produce surge drums for barrage balloons. Early precautions against air attack had been taken, and included the construction of shelters, in conjunction with Worcester Corporation the establishment of an auxiliary fire station, and direct landline communication with the Guildhall in respect of air raid warnings. At a cost of £800, the works had also been camouflaged.

At 0700 hrs on Thursday, October 3rd, 1940, the Meteorological Office recorded at Birmingham a light NNE wind, and a low layer of stratus cloud at 5,700'. The weather generally was *'dull, rainy and rather cold.'* Throughout the day the cloud base would considerably decrease to just 500', being 10/10ths, and even visibility out of it was just 500 yards. In short, the conditions over England were perfect for Störflug by lone *hit and run* raiders.

After mid-day, a fairly continuous succession of such raids were crossing the coast. The enemy operated at 1,000-1,800'. Targets were generally either London or the Midlands. Fighter Command flew countless patrols but, due to the weather, failed to intercept. 10 Group alone flew 32 patrols, involving 52 fighters, in response to 32 individual enemy aircraft operating over the Group area. 12 Group noted that after 1330 hrs the weather became even worse, so no further fighter action was taken. During this period the Hun was very low and was often below 1,000' when dropping his bombs. The main objectives appear to have been aerodromes and industrial areas, although other places were visited. HMS Royal Arthur at Skegness was attacked, but most of the bombs fell in a potato field. In addition, bombs were dropped near Bedford, Kettering, Daventry, Stafford, Worcester, Banbury and Crewe. Aerodromes at Upwood, Cosford and Wyton were also attacked but no bombs fell on them.

Oberleutnant Siegward Fiebig and his crew of Stab I/KG77, based at Laon, were briefed to attack *Reading* aerodrome (more accurately Woodley, home of Phillips and Powis {Miles} Company aircraft factory). For Oberfeldwebel Erich Goebel, Fiebig's Bordfunker, it was his first operational flight. Due to the poor visibility over England, the Ju 88 crew failed to find their target, so turned eastwards seeking an alternative. Near St Albans they found the de Havilland works adjacent to Hatfield aerodrome. Fiebig's attack caused direct hits on both a large assembly shed and a Technical School, and a sheet metal shop was destroyed. The defences were alert, however, and both machine-guns and heavier Bofors anti-aircraft guns opened up on *Raid 30*. Both engines were hit and caught fire. At 1126 hrs, Oberleutnant Fiebig skilfully forced landed his aircraft at Eastend Green Farm, Hertingfordbury, and the crew managed to escape just before it became engulfed in flame. Fiebig and Goebel were joined by Feldwebel Ruthof and Unteroffizier Seifert, and all were captured. The only other Luftwaffe loss that day was a Do 17Z of 3/Küstenfliegergruppe 606 which inexplicably crashed into the sea during a sortie to bomb St Eval airfield in Cornwall, the crew all being killed.

The wreckage of Oberleutnant Fiebig's Ju 88, shot down on October 3rd, 1940, whilst making a solo attack on the de Havilland factory at Hatfield. Fiebig was of Stab I/KG77 based at Laon, and it is possible that this unit was responsible for the MECO raid later in the day.

From 0630-1230 hrs, nine single enemy aircraft crossed the east coast between Yorkshire and Harwich. According to the Fighter Command Intelligence Summary, *'In two cases aircraft penetrated far inland, one flying to Worcester, where bombs were dropped, to Birmingham and Wellingborough which were also bombed. The second crossed the coast at Bawdsey, flying to North Weald and Debden. Bombs were dropped near North Weald from 1,000'.'*

In Worcester, October 3rd, 1940, had started like any other day; it was to end recorded by history as the only occasion on which the enemy mounted an air attack against the *Faithful City.* Some of its inhabitants were certainly to receive a baptism of fire that autumn day.

Maurice Jones was being pushed in his pram along Castle Street, in the city of Worcester and across the river from St John's. As a German bomber passed over, *'people started to get excited and nurses came out of the infirmary to stare. My mother hurried us on down Castle Street and up Loves Grove. We got into the entrance of my grandmother's garden and I saw the bomber flying east over Moor Street.'*

The MECO's office staff had left for lunch at 1215 hrs. A few men were clocking out early. The main workforce was not scheduled for lunch until 1230 hrs. That lunchtime, a lone Ju 88 descended from cloud over Worcester and circled above the Cinderella Works and Alley & MacLellan factory in Bromyard Road. But neither of these were subjected to attack; it was the MECO that the raider sought.

Margaret Woodward was 16 and working at her first job as a shorthand typist in the office of the Quality Cleaners, in Bromwich Road, St John's. Hearing the aircraft passing very low overhead, the typists ran out of the office where they heard gunfire. Only a few yards from where they stood, bullets spattered into the ground. *'The markings of the plane were visible and it was very frightening - we rushed back indoors!'*

Aviation mad Frank Appleford was playing hide and seek in Swinton Lane woods with his friend, Len Appleby, when the Ju 88 suddenly shot over: *'there was a "whoosh", and then it was gone.'*

12-year-old Terry Hulme was playing with school friends in hopfields towards Bransford: *'We heard aero engines, very low, looked up and saw a Ju 88 approaching at 300' from a direction of Malvern. It whizzed over us pooping off a few rounds of machine-gun bullets, so we ran like hell for home, passing an old gent who was walking his dog; when told that the aircraft was German he didn't believe us until he looked up at the bomber and saw the plainly visible black crosses. He then took off at a right rate of knots and left his dog standing! The aircraft was actually so low that the crew were clearly visible in the perspex nose. On reaching home I yelled to mother to take to the Anderson shelter at the bottom of our garden in the Broadway. We were half way there when a stick of bombs dropped onto the MECO works causing an explosion and a sheet of yellow flame shot up. We were nearly blown over by the blast.'*

Fred Beechey was standing in Bromyard Road opposite the Garibaldi pub when he suddenly saw the Ju 88 *'roar over at about 300' with its bomb doors wide open. Members of the Home Guard started shooting small arms fire at the raider, but two bombs tumbled out of the aircraft, hitting the ground in a horizontal attitude. There was a tremendous explosion and windows smashed all around.'*

Anne Smith had walked her younger brother and a friend along Winchester Avenue to the corner shop in Pitmaston Road. As the Ju 88 passed overheard, Anne thought *'funny looking plane, funny markings.'* She went into the shop and said *'Can I have a packet of gravy salts, please'*, when *'there was a terrific bang and the ground shook.'* As Anne ran home with her young charges, the enemy aircraft machine-gunned St John's.

Bessie Cook was standing in the kitchen of her house, the last in Bransford Road, opposite the junction with Watery Lane, and was stirring some custard. *'Suddenly I heard the plane, very low, as it came right over an apple tree outside the window. Although I saw it clearly, it was actually quite a foggy day. Within seconds it had dropped its load. The lock flew off my front door the length of the hall, and a window blew out across a bed in which someone was lying but she was unhurt.'*

Gordon Doran was at the Royal Albert Orphanage in Henwick Road, and when out in the playground saw *'the aircraft came over very low. It went away then returned. We watched it circle round, then saw the bomb doors open and a bomb fall out of the plane. The plane then came straight at the school, in fact, it may even have clipped the top of some trees in front of the building.'*

Jessie Wood: *'I was talking to my friend around the back of the house when that plane* came over the roof tops in Broadway Grove, flying towards the MECO. I remember it was 1215 pm and my husband was soon due home for lunch. I'd just gone into the house and put the oven on when there was this almighty bang. I fell to the floor thinking that my house had been hit as we were so close to the back of the factory. I don't think we had any dinner that day!'

Lesley Adams was actually working in the MECO's riveting shop:-

Lone Ju 88 over England, low and fast.
Bundesarchiv.

'Someone shouted "Jerry gone over!" but we all laughed as we thought it was a leg-pull. He said "It's true, I've seen the crosses!", so we all went out and out of the gloom came this aircraft, and true enough there were the big black crosses. Looking up I saw a bomb drop and fall towards us. I shouted "God, strewth!" and ran. The bomb went through the roof of the assembly shop, bounced through a brick wall and exploded adjacent to MECO Lane and near houses in Happy Land West. There was another which skidded and hit some houses. Then it was absolute chaos. I ran across the railway line and up the embankment. The bomber then opened fire at the factory as it flew on towards Laugherne Brook. Shaken, I then made my way back to the chaos.'

Having been dropped from such a low altitude, the bombs ricochetted due to having hit in a horizontal attitude. One SC250 had dropped into the machine shop but carved its way out through the factory's east wall. Mr Sadler was working in there at the time, and remembers that *'the bomb hit a girder, bounced and shot outside before exploding.'* The canteen was demolished and there seven men were killed, three were seriously injured, amongst them the canteen attendant, Doris Tindall, who lost an eye, and 60 others suffered minor wounds. Had the attack occurred a few minutes later when the factory en bloc were queuing to clock out, or taking lunch in the canteen, the death toll would have been enormous. The second SC250 narrowly missed the factory, bounced off a concrete base, across Happyland West and exploded in adjacent Lambert Road. Around 300 houses were damaged in total. A child, Margaret Wainwright, also tragically lost an eye, local legend being that she was standing in the window awaiting her father's arrival home for lunch at the time. Margaret Woodward, who lived in Bromyard Road, remembers that *'our window frames were never quite the same fit afterwards, although the criss-crossed sticky tape with which we all covered our windows had saved the glass.'*

One of the dead was young Terry Hulme's father, William, a foreman blacksmith and old servant of the MECO, having moved down from Sheffield during the late 1920s to help start the Worcester firm. Mrs Hulme received a War Widow's Pension of 10 shillings (50p) a week, hardly a fair exchange for the loss of the family breadwinner. Another fatal casualty was Albert Williams, 42 years old, who had lost both legs above the knees whilst fighting with the Worcestershire Regiment at the Battle of Gheluvelt in 1914. Nevertheless, he managed to be very mobile on two wooden legs, and he even rode a motor-cycle. When the Second World War broke out he was employed at the Austin works in Longbridge. As he could not get about quickly during air raids, he decided to move to Worcester, where such attacks were far less likely. It was ironic, therefore, that he should be amongst the dead that October afternoon.

Sam Beard had been mobilised with the Worcestershire Regiment's 8th Battalion at Upton, and at the time of the Worcester raid was 'R' Company's runner, which involved daily trips to Worcester:-

'On the day in question, I was making my way along Bath Road, back to barracks at Norton, on an army issue bicycle, when at the top of the bank a plane appeared flying low over the river from a direction of Worcester bridge, flying in fact towards the petrol tanks and Aston's timber yard at Diglis. I was higher than the plane. Though I could not make out the individual codes under the wing, I most definitely saw what appeared to be the French tricolour on the rudder of that plane. There was a clear view over the Diglis dock area from some railings in those days, and I tried to get a better look from there as I was confused as to the plane's identity. It next banked further down the river, and headed for Norton. We had a Bren gun put on the Keep tower, another on Whittington Tump, and one on the Cathedral tower. That at the "Tump" was manned by the Home Guard during the day, and our chaps by night. I heard small arms fire come from a direction of the barracks, and on arrival was told that the plane had machine-gunned the barracks as it passed over.'

Another who saw the raider's escape was Wally Brooks, standing in Mill Lane, between Malvern and Guarlford village and stunned to see the Ju 88 flying fast over Guarlford church in a southerly direction. *'It was at about 200' and I clearly saw the German markings. I told my dad but he wouldn't believe me!'*

Margaret Hayton was a Ward Sister at the Worcester Royal Infirmary in Castle Street, and although now 82 years old, she remembers that afternoon vividly:-

'We saw the plane going over part of the WRI just as I was dishing out the patients' mid-day meal, then soon afterwards "Bang" and "Boom!". Before long patients were being brought in from St John's. Poor Matron thought more was to come, so had the top floor patients brought down to ground level, it was bedlam! Blast was the biggest trouble, most injuries being to face and eyes, medical and opthalmic attention being given on admission.'

Bessie Cook, also now 82, remembers that *'Worcester was asleep at the time, but I can tell you it woke us up!'*

The Worcester *News & Times* was soon on the scene to report events. In the resultant article, Worcester became a *'Midlands town'* and the account was recorded in a style typical of the period, the heading being *'Women and children machine-gunned'*:-

'A few persons were killed and others injured. ARP services were quickly on the scene. The plane is reported to have flown low, estimated by one eye-witness to have been little higher than 300 feet. The Nazi airman followed his bombs with machine-gun bullets spattered near a childrens' recreation ground where youngsters and women were. A Mrs Cram and a Miss Binns spoke indignantly of German inhumanity. They said they were next to the recreation ground and had to dive into a patch of nettles. Other women also experienced the machine-gunning, some while they were standing in their back gardens. A woman returning home to lunch from the office heard the plane swoop, a man grabbed her arm and flung her beneath a hedge. She had just got down when she heard machine-gun bullets. The forewoman of the business premises hit said a bomb crashed through the roof of her department where 9 girls and more than 100 men were working. "We ran for shelter; there was not the least panic", she said. All the girls were simply marvellous and followed ARP instructions which had been in operation since the war began.'

The report also related that ambulances were quickly on the scene, and how Mr J R Hadley, of the Automobile Association patrol, had immediately begun directing traffic until the police arrived. Within minutes the Home Guard and Special Constabulary placed a cordon around the area. Mrs Alice Smith, aged 71, remarked *'If Hitler thinks he is going to break our spirit this way, he is very much mistaken.'* A woman eye-witness reported having seen the black crosses and swastika as the plane passed overhead before she dived into a ditch from where she heard bombs explode. She then saw the raider circle the stricken factory before making off. Ronald Roberts, 16, was a night-worker sleeping in a nearby house. The blast threw him out of bed, but he was unhurt. As Roberts delivered his account to the *News & Times* reporter, a rescue worker shouted *'Look out!'* as tiles fell from the roof above. Mr Falls helped to remove casualties but stated that there was no panic: *'Everyone was simply marvellous; cool and quite steady. A boy of 10 was delighted to tell his father that he had actually seen a German plane drop some bombs!'*

Ironically, it had been intended to make the weekend a rest weekend as all the men and staff at the MECO were very tired. Instead it became one of the busiest, clearing up debris and covering roofs, not only to make them waterproof but also to restore the all-important blackout. So hard did they work that full production was resumed the following Tuesday, and the night shift shortly afterwards. Employees will no doubt never forget the characteristic telegram received from the Minister of Aircraft Production, Lord Beaverbrook, shortly after the raid:-

'WIRE BACK FULL PARTICULARS DEATHS AND INJURIES
MAXIMUM EXTENT OF DAMAGE AND ESTIMATED
EARLIEST DATE OF CONTINUATION AND PRODUCTION.'

Bomb damage in Happy Land North, St John's,
Worcester, October 3rd, 1940.

Michael Grundy.

The scene in 1994.

Antony Whitehead.

Repair work being undertaken at the MECO factory.

Michael Grundy.

This raid on Worcester, although minute when compared with others elsewhere, is a perfect example of a successful nuisance hit and run raid. The enemy crew that undertook this attack did so in audacious style; to navigate across England in such awful weather, the pilot flying on instruments, then spend time correctly identifying the target before making a successful low-level attack all points towards those responsible being a somewhat combat experienced crew. As the aircraft crossed the eastern English coastline, that in itself suggests that a machine from Generalfeldmarschall Kesselring's Luftflotte 2, based in Holland, Belgium and north-west France, was responsible. Luftflotte 3's daily operations reports have survived, and are available to researchers in Germany. No mention is made of an attack against Worcester, however, also indicating that Luftflotte 2 were responsible. Unfortunately similar documentation appertaining to Luftflotte 2's air operations over England was destroyed in 1945, so we will never know exactly who was involved.

The original *News & Times* report identifies the raider as an He 111, but, as we have seen, just three days previously the Heinkel had been withdrawn from daylight operations. Virtually all eye-witness evidence points to the aircraft having been a Ju 88. Certainly the raider shot down attacking Hatfield was a Ju 88 of Stab I/KG77, a unit based at Laon and a part of Luftflotte 2. There is every possibility that the MECO raider was also from this Geschwader, which had not been fully operational during July and August but was brought to Laon, Neufchatel and Amiens during early September. During the second half of that month it suffered heavy casualties against southern England. However, III/KG1, III/KG4, Stab KG30, I & II/KG30, and Stab KG40 were also operating Ju 88s from bases in Luftflotte 2's area, so it cannot be discounted that the Worcester raider could have been from one of those units.

When compared with poor Sherborne, Worcester's brush with the Luftwaffe could clearly have been much worse. In four days time, however, the people of Yeovil would also experience the full terror of an air raid when subjected to an attack by a Gruppe of Ju 88s in an example of the enemy's alternative daylight bombing tactics.

Angriff Westland

For the populace of Yeovil, *Lord Haw Haw's* malicious warning became harsh reality on Monday, 7th October, 1940.

A ridge of relatively high pressure was moving eastwards across the British Isles. Although elsewhere suffered occasional showers, the weather was *'fair'* in the Midlands, east and south of England. At 1300 hrs the Meteorlogical Office recorded a force 4 WSW wind at Portland Bill, the sky *'partly cloudy'* with a layer of 4/10ths stratus at 4,000'.

From 0930 - 1540 hrs, Luftflotte 2 had mounted an almost endless stream of fighter sweeps and jabo attacks against the 11 Group area. All was quiet over the West Country, however, until mid-afternoon.

Between 1437 - 1446 hrs, the twin Jumo engines of 20 Ju 88s of II/KG51 *Edelweiss* roared into life. Soon afterwards the Gruppe took off from Orly, just to the south of Paris, briefed for an *Angriff auf Yeovil Westland Aircraft* (attack against the Westland aircraft factory at Yeovil). The formation carried a total of 44 SC250 HEs and 24 Flamm SC250s.

Amongst 5th Staffel's pilots setting course for England that afternoon was 25-year- old Oberleutnant Sigurd Hey, in *9K + SN* which was carrying four SC250s. Herr Hey remembers: *'as a former flight instructor I was normally selected for night raids only. On this occasion, however, I volunteered to fly on an attack against the Yeovil factory which I understood to be manufacturing ball-bearings for the aircraft industry. I took over the aircraft of a pilot who had been taken ill, and called urgently for my crew. When airborne we assumed an outer position in the Gruppe formation.'* Hey's crew were all confident and experienced, and without exception possessed the EK II. His bombardier, 28-year-old Oberfeldwebel Josef Troll, was also decorated with the Spannien Kreuz and Sudeten Medal.

Oberfeldwebel Ludwig Piller was a member of Stab II/KG51's reconnaissance flight between March 1st and December 1st, 1940. As a flying instructor he had aspired to the highest level, being a *blind flying* teacher, so generally *'only had to fly operationally at night when the weather was bad.'* There were two exceptions, however: July 3rd, when Piller had participated in a daylight attack on Bristol, and on October 7th when he was also bound for Yeovil on what was his 12th operational flight against England.

Unteroffizier Robert Ciuraj of the 4th Staffel was a similarly experienced combat flyer who steered *9K + CM* towards Westlands. Ciuraj would later fly many *Nachtangriff* against England during the forthcoming night blitz.

Robert Ciuraj's 4/KG51 Ju 88, '9K+CM'. Although pictured slightly later, and carrying long-range fuel tanks, this is the bomber that Unteroffizier Ciuraj flew on the Yeovil raid.

Chris Goss Collection.

II/KG51's fighter escort was to be provided by 39 Me 110s representing elements of all 3 Gruppen ZG26, 52 Me 109s of all 3 Gruppen JG2 and 7 of JG53. The fighters were waiting for the bombers over Cherbourg, as Oberleutnant Hey recalls: *'When we arrived the Me 109s had already been airborne for half an hour, so could only escort our Gruppe as far as the British coast, after which time, because of fuel shortage, they had to return to their bases. Thus our only fighter escort from there on consisted solely of twin engined Me 110s, hardly sufficient protection against the many Spitfires and Hurricanes that would soon be attacking from all sides.'*

The presence of the enemy formation over the sea and heading north was soon detected by British radar. At 1542 hrs, II/KG51's plot was designated *Raid 139*. Already 10 Group's squadrons were being scrambled.

Unteroffizier Robert Ciuraj at the controls of '9K+CM'.

Chris Goss Collection.

Me 110s of 5/ZG26 in line astern as seen from the air gunner's position in the Schwarm's last zerstörer.
Chris Goss Collection.

The enemy bombers were flying at 17,000' with the Me 110s behind, in line astern, and 1,000' above. From time to time the leaders of each line would turn around and so an *Abwehrkreis* was formed. When the circle broke, each line of 10 zerstörers would link up with the bombers again.

Michael Robinson had been promoted to command 609 Squadron at Middle Wallop on October 4th, and at 1530 hrs Squadron Leader Robinson led 12 Spitfires off with orders to patrol base at 20,000'. At the same time, Squadron Leader Fenton led an identical number of 238 Squadron Hurricanes off from Wallop with similar instructions. The squadron diary records that *'the weather had improved becoming bright and sunny in the afternoon with wisps of cloud.'* The Hurricanes flew on the Spitfires' left flank. Pilot Officer David Crook wrote about that afternoon:-

'I don't think that I have ever seen such a clear day in my life. From 15,000' I could see Plymouth and far beyond into Cornwall; up in the north the whole coast of South Wales was clearly visible, from the Severn at Gloucester and way beyond Swansea in the west, while on our left, to the south, the Channel glistened and sparkled in the sun, and the French coast and the Channel Islands, although seventy-five miles away, seemed to lie just under my wing-tip.

'But I can't say that I appreciated this superb view very much under the circumstances, because I was busily engaged behind the squadron anxiously scanning the sky for the Messerschmitts which we knew would soon be arriving.'

To the north-east of Warmwell, 12 Spitfires of 152 Squadron found the enemy

3,000' below. The squadron went into line astern and attacked the bombers. At the same time, 609 Squadron sighted the enemy some 15 miles south of their position. David Crook: '*The sun was so brilliant and dazzling that it was very difficult to see anything clearly in the glare, and yet this made it even more important to maintain the utmost vigilance, as the Me 109s are very good at jumping out of the sun.*' As 609 and 238 Squadrons headed for the Me 110s, suddenly the Hurricanes broke up, having been bounced by Me 109s from out of the sun. According to David Crook, '*About four people at once started to shout warnings on the R/T and there was a perfect babel of excited voices which rather added to the confusion.*' Richard Covington was amongst the Hurricanes and remembers how he was '*going to have a go at this daisy chain of Me 110s when an Me 109 got me from behind. I baled out quickly.*' His fighter crashed at 1554 hrs on the Dorset Downs at MeridenWood, Winterborne Houghton. Pilot Officer Covington was slightly injured and taken to Blandford Cottage Hospital.

Pilot Officer Jackie Urwin-Mann of 238 Squadron took evasive action when the Me 109s pounced from a thousand feet above the Hurricanes and out of the sun. Subsequently he saw the Ju 88s and Me 110s proceeding towards Bristol and in a '*straggly formation, wide vic and line astern. I dived from 2,000' above and delivered a full quarter attack on a Ju 88 of the leading section which by this time had turned back and was heading towards the coast.*' However, two Me 110s intervened and Green 1 was forced to break away.

Sergeant Shepperd of 152 Squadron attacked a Kette of Ju 88s and fired his second burst at the starboard aircraft, probably the same bomber attacked briefly by Pilot Officer Urwin-Mann, closing to just 50 yards range: '*it jettisoned its bombs, began to stream glycol and dropped back from the formation. It then turned SW losing height. At 4,000' it went into a spin, the tail fell off and it hit the ground, bursting into flames. Four crew members jumped by parachute, but one had his on fire.*'

Flying Officer Bob Doe, Yellow 1 of 238 Squadron, had also attacked the same *Edelweiss* bomber: '*my first burst stopped the starboard engine. Overtaking speed was very high so I half rolled upwards and attacked the E/A from above with a short burst from about 100 yards. I broke away and carried out a beam attack from the port side from 300 yards. E/A turned away and started diving. As it dived a burst of fire appeared in front of the tail which flew off. Three people baled out. E/A crashed in flames about 6 miles NW of Maiden Newton.*'

Doe had probably hit the Ju 88's oxygen bottles, stored together near the tail. His Hurricane was damaged too, however, and back at Middle Wallop he counted 11 bullet holes in the fighter, including one in the engine.

Although incorrectly identifying the enemy aircraft as an '*Me 110*', Pilot Officer John Bisdee of 609 Squadron also attacked the same Ju 88: '*pieces of cowling flew off the port engine and it started to smoke. The E/A turned onto its back and dived down. Just above the clouds it tried to flatten out, but could not.*'

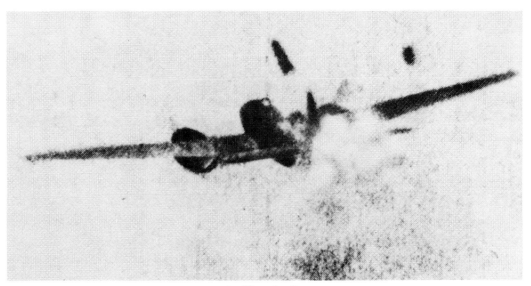

Ju 88 under fire.

Author's Collection.

The '*E/A*' concerned was actually that flown by Oberleutnant Hey: '*my starboard engine's radiator was hit. Though I dropped my bombs at once and switched the damaged motor to a feathered position, I could not hold my position in the Gruppe formation and fell behind. I then turned southwards, diving a couple of thousand feet, and tried to make the French coast on one engine. This time three fighters came up attacking from all different directions. First the controls were hit and I was only able to hold the aircraft horizontally by using the trimming system. Next the fuselage tank was hit which set the aircraft on fire. Then I gave the order to bale out, but received no reply as my crew had already left the aircraft unseen by me in the dense smoke. When the aircraft turned into a flat spin I was lucky to get out, but landed safely by parachute when I was taken prisoner by two old men armed with shot guns.*'

According to the Dorset Constabulary, Hey's Ju 88 hit the ground at 1600 hrs. Eye-witnesses recall that it impacted travelling at great speed on Tappers Hill, Upper Sydling, before coming to a grinding halt embedded in the Downs. However, although the wreck blazed fiercely, the Dorchester Fire Brigade could only stand and watch from a distance as their appliance had become stuck in the field.

John Bisdee's '*most vivid memory of the entire Battle of Britain is coming right down to see that Ju 88 burning on the Downs with a crowd of yokels waving pitchforks and dancing around it! I did a victory roll over them and went back upstairs to see what was happening.*'

Another of the Auxiliary Spitfire pilots was Flying Officer John Dundas of 'B' Flight. After attacking a defensive circle of Me 110s, he found a straggler: '*After a short turning match I got onto his tail. I fired about 12-14 seconds ammunition into this*

Oberleutnant Sigurd Hey of 5/KG51 whilst on home leave in Germany during the summer of 1940. On October 7th, 1940, he was shot down over Wessex and captured.

Chris Goss Collection.

One of the pilots responsible for Hey's demise: Sgt EE Shepperd of 152 Squadron, snapped here with the 152 Squadron mascot, 'Pilot Officer Pooch.' Two weeks later Shepperd was killed in a flying accident.

Author's Collection via Allan White.

Flg Off RFT Doe of 238 Squadron; he blew the tail off Oblt Hey's Ju 88.

Author's Collection via Wg Cdr RFT Doe.

Sqn Ldr Michael Robinson (left) and Plt Off John Bisdee of 609 Squadron. Bisdee also attacked Hey's bomber and recalls seeing locals dancing around the crash site waving pitchforks!

Chris Goss Collection.

E/A from astern at ranges starting at 400 but closing to 180 yards. His port motor soon started to stream smoke and glycol. Soon afterwards his starboard motor followed suit. His only evasive action consisted of short climbs and dives. I tried to finish him off by a series of short attacks from below and the quarter but at this time my aircraft was hit by an explosive shell from astern. My aircraft spun and I was forced to land at Warmwell. I did not see the E/A which attacked me. The Me 110 that I claim was last seen by me gliding at a fast tick-over at 14,000'. I am sure that he could not have reached France.'

Dundas, himself *temporarily u/s* with shell splinters to his legs, was right; at 1600 hrs *3U + BT* of 9/ZG26 walloped in and exploded at Hart Hill, Stoborough, near Wareham, with both crew-men still on board. The pilot, Leutnant Kurt Sidow and his Bordfunker, Gefreiter Josef Repik, were both killed instantly.

238 Squadron's Sergeant Joseph Jeka had attacked a Ju 88 from such close range that his aircraft shook from the raider's slipstream. Although the German rear gunner bravely returned Jeka's fire, the Czech later reported how he saw the *'Ju 88'* (actually believed to be an Me 110, see Appendix 4) *'crash into the sea about ten miles due south of Bridport.'*

'56 Squadron, Scramble!'

At 1530 hrs, five 56 Squadron Hurricanes roared skywards from Warmwell. About ten minutes later, *SE of Yeovil*, the *Punjab* Squadron fighters had entered the fray. One of the pilots was 19-year-old Sergeant Dennis *Nick* Nichols, who remembered those events over fifty years later:-

'We took off from Warmwell being on detachment from our base at Boscombe Down. We took off in formation with me on the left of the leader, Flight Lieutenant Brooker, and I was "Pip-squeak" man, the radio being blocked every 15 seconds. I can't remember hearing any R/T transmissions so perhaps the wireless was on the blink. I did not hear the "Tally Ho". Flying in tight formation the first I saw was tracer coming from one of our leader's guns. Quick glimpse and I saw a Ju 88 and fired my guns, still in formation, but had to break away to avoid collision with Flight Lieutenant Brooker. I then lost the squadron and pulled up, searching for the enemy. No sign of the bombers but some

Sgt Dennis 'Nick' Nichols of 56 Squadron.

Author's Collection via Flt Lt DH Nichols.

110s in a defensive spiral well above. I pulled the "tit" for maximum power and went to intercept. A Spitfire was attacking the top of the spiral so I went head-on for the bottom. I fired but, perhaps not surprisingly in view of their heavy forward-firing armament which I must have overlooked, was hit. Flames started coming from the nose of my aircraft and the windscreen was black with oil, so I broke away as I could not see out. I turned the aircraft on its back to bale out at 25,000', first time a slow roll but I remained seated. Second time I tumbled out, spinning. I told myself not to panic and gave the ripcord a steady pull. When the parachute deployed, the lanyards on one side were twisted. I tried to untangle them without success but relaxed as at about 15,000' appeared to be coming down reasonably slowly. I did not see the ground coming up and crumpled in a heap upon landing. The Home Guard then appeared on the scene and told me to stick my hands up. They thought I was German but I just laughed at them between groans as I had actually broken my back. There was a Jerry parachutist stuck up a nearby tree, from the Ju 88, but the locals would not get him down until they had seen to me.'

Schwarm 'B' of 5/ZG26 looking for trouble. This photograph was taken over France in May 1940. Note the 'ace of spades' badge usually associated with JG53.

Chris Goss Collection.

Sergeant Nichols had landed near the village of Alton Pancras, also on the Dorset Downs. At about 1600 hrs, 19-year-old Charlie Callaway was ploughing in the Vernall when he saw a parachute drifting towards Buckland Newton. He then saw the Hurricane *'coming down hard and well on fire!'* His younger brother, Sam, 17, was rabbiting nearby and he too saw the doomed British fighter *'descending at a shallow angle but all ablaze and travelling sharpish, like. It was so close that I could have reached out and touched it. There were several parachutes in the sky at the same time.'* P3154 impacted at Austral Farm, some nine miles north of Dorchester. Villagers also recall cartridge cases from the combat overhead raining down on the cobbled streets.

In the 56 Squadron charge, Sergeant Whitehead had dived on and fired at a *'Do 17'* which subsequently emitted a slight stream of glycol from its port engine. Blue 4 then overshot and broke away. Yellow Section, led by Flying Officer Wicks, had dived vertically upon the enemy. Sergeant Peter Hillwood delivered a short burst before pulling out and attacking another *'Do 17'* from behind. When he broke off, there were streams of glycol pouring from both engines. Pilot Officer Nosowicz initially fired a rapid burst at a *'Do 17'* before attacking an Me 110, the rear gunner of which returned his fire until silenced by a hail of lead from the Pole who then broke away when attacked by another 110.

56 Squadron line up after the Battle of Britain. Of interest to our story are (standing): Flg Off BJ Wicks (5th from left) , Flg Off MH Constable-Maxwell (6th from left), and (sitting) Plt Off 'Taffy' Higginson (2nd left), and Flt Lt REP Brooker (extreme right).

Author's Collection via Wg Cdr FW Higginson.

The German fighter escort appeared to have been successful in engaging the defenders as the bombers reached Sherborne, over which they turned on a *dog-leg* course for Yeovil, still only having lost Hey's machine at Sydling St Nicholas. Over Yeovil, the entire Gruppe slipped into Ketten astern in order to attack, passing over the town from east to west. The Germans were to be thwarted again, however, as a layer of cloud obscured the target, making the bombardiers' job difficult. With the cry of *'Bomben Los!'*, however, the Gruppe bombed, and as the Ju 88s turned south for home, their crews could see *'two large fires burning.'*

Unteroffizier Robert Ciuraj and crew.

Chris Goss Collection.

At 1545 hrs that afternoon when the *Alert* wailed Yeovil's 33rd air raid warning of the war, haunted by the spectre of Sherborne's recent agony, people took notice and sought shelter immediately. In what was also Yeovil's first experience of bombing, the first bombs are reported as having fallen at 1555 hrs. All fell in the town centre, causing damage and loss of life at Montague Burton's store in Middle Street, St Andrew's Road, and Summerleaze Park. Direct hits were also recorded on shelters at the Methodist Church in Vicarage Street and at 45 Grove Avenue. An engineering firm, Ricketts Ltd in Belmont Street, and nearby houses were also seriously damaged. The final civilian death toll would be 16, with nine others seriously wounded and 20 less so.

A target seen from Ciuraj's Ju 88.
Chris Goss Collection.

The Methodist Church in Vicarage Street, Yeovil, pictured in 1994. On October 7th, 1940, a direct hit was suffered by a shelter at this location killing five people outright with a sixth dying from injuries two days later.

Mark Postlethwaite.

Workers amidst the bomb damage at Ricketts factory. The spirit of the civilian population when subjected to air attack was an incredible phenomenon that Goering had not reckoned with.

Museum of South Somerset.

Bomb damage to Ricketts factory, Belmont Street, Yeovil.

Museum of South Somerset.

More damage at the Ricketts factory.
Museum of South Somerset.

Mrs Margaret Hewlett:-

'My husband and I were in Woolworth's at the time, next-door to Burton's menswear shop where there was a direct hit. Eight people were killed there. The whole front of Woolworth's was blown in, but, fortunately, we had both moved back from the front of the store. There were several people injured and a lot of panic as a gas main had burst. We all tried to get out by the back entrance and as quickly as possible. The Emergency Services did a good job, though, and the fire was soon under control.'

Yeovil, 1994. The building now occupied by 'Principles' and 'Birthdays' was Montague Burton's store on October 7th, 1940, and a billiard hall occupied the first floor. Eight people died at Burton's during the raid.

Mark Postlethwaite.

Fred Denham:-

'The bombs on Burton's and the billiard hall above it fell just 150 yards from my First Aid Post. A bomb had exploded on the steps between there and Woolworths where many were sheltering. I ran there carrying a stretcher with another chap. We got two women from the top of the steps, but the others were all dead. We did what we could for various people but swiftly moved on to the Methodist Church in nearby Vicarage Street where a shelter had been hit.'

John Chesterman:-

'I remember seeing a tremendous fighter escort flying around the bombers overhead.'

Henry Smith:-

'My elder brother, Albert, was employed at the time at the Southern Railway Station in Yeovil and was in bed following a night shift. My mother and I were in the farm cottage where we lived at Brympton D'Every. Suddenly we heard the siren followed by explosions from falling bombs. My brother got up and the three of us took shelter in a ditch at the bottom of the garden. In the adjacent field a barrage balloon was sited with two huts housing the crew, I suppose about three miles from the airfield. It would appear that one of the aircraft had overshot the target and dropped its bombs near us. An oil bomb was dropped in the ditch where we sheltered. Fortunately the ditch was dog legged which sheltered us from the blast. Another bomb, an HE, fell in front of the barrage balloon hut. Following the bombing the NCO in charge came running to look for us at the damaged cottage and said that one of his men was missing. Then the displaced earth at the edge of the crater moved and out stepped the "missing" man, shaken but otherwise unhurt!'

Once again, however, Westlands miraculously remained unscathed.

With the bombers homeward bound, the cut and thrust continued with the fighter escort. It was over the Yeovil area that 152 Squadron was able to press home its attack.

Yellow 3, Pilot Officer Cox, managed to damage a Ju 88, but Green 2, the Polish Sergeant *Zig* Klein, had ambushed three Me 110s from out of the sun. When he broke

away back into the glare, white smoke was issuing from both engines of one enemy aircraft which was losing height. His next attack was repulsed by two more Me 110s which attacked the Spitfire from astern. Green 2, Pilot Officer Dudley Williams, attacked the leading Ju 88 whilst Green 3, Sergeant Kearsey was fired at by anti-aircraft guns and forced to take evasive action. Sergeant Joseph Szlagowski, also Polish, took no part in the fight having been unable to reach the altitude involved due to a faulty oxygen system.

152 Squadron's Polish Sgt 'Zig' Klein who damaged an Me 110 on the Yeovil raid.

Author's Collection via Flt Lt EH Marsh.

152 Squadron's Blue 1, Pilot Officer Eric *Boy* Marrs, had attacked the Ju 88s without noticeable result. He later wrote:-

'I thought that I would have a crack at the fighters. These I found were going about in strings of about ten aircraft sneaking along behind the bombers. From time to time the leader of each string would come round behind the last man to form a defensive circle. After one or two attempts I found I was able to sneak up behind one of these "strings" and attach myself to the end of it for a short spell, shooting at the end machine in the line. Every time the leader came round to form a defensive circle I had to break away and wait until the circle broke again. I was, however, able to tack myself on again. In this way I was able to make the end one of one of these lines stream glycol from one of its engines. I was not able to finish it off as the leader of this particular string was forming one of the defensive circles and was coming round behind me.

'I then drew away a bit to take stock of the position. The Huns were now making for the coast again, and I saw a straggler all by himself. I swooped up on him from the starboard rear quarter. He saw me coming and opened up, but I was starting to catch him up quite easily. I opened fire and his starboard engine streamed glycol. I switched on to the fuselage and then over on to the port engine. I was by now overtaking him somewhat fast, so I drew out to his left. Suddenly the back half of his cockpit flew off and out jumped two men. Their parachutes streamed and opened and they began drifting slowly earthwards. Their aeroplane dived vertically into the sea, making a most wonderful sight and an enormous splash. I had not finished my ammunition and so looked around for something else to shoot at, but everything seemed to have cleared off, so I circled round the two Huns, still floating earthwards. They took an awful long time to come down as they baled out at 15,000'. They came down on land and I watched the army rush up and capture them.'

At 1605 hrs *3U + FM* of 4/ZG26 had crashed into Ringstead Bay, Dorset. Although the crew, Oberfeldwebel Erwin Genzzler, 26, and Unteroffizier Franz Haefner, 24, later refused to give their unit, both described how they had been attacked by a lone Spitfire before baling out when their starboard engine was hit.

After destroying an Me 110, 609 Squadron's Flt Lt Frank Howell's Spitfire was hit and he forced landed at Sutton Waldron. Here he is seen (in Mae West) whilst CO of 118 Squadron and during the making of the 'First of the Few' *(telling the story of Spitfire designer RJ Mitchell) at Ibsley in 1941. Note actor Lesley Howard leaning over the* 'crashed' *501 Squadron Spitfire's cockpit, and David Niven standing to Howell's right.*

Author's Collection via the late Wg Cdr PI Howard-Williams.

Around the same time, having claimed an Me 110 destroyed, 609 Squadron's Flight Lieutenant Frank Howell made a wheels-up forced landing at Vale Farm, Sutton Waldron, near Shaftesbury. His Spitfire's Merlin engine seized, having been damaged by return fire from the 110. Meanwhile, Sergeant Alan Feary, a Volunteer Reserve pilot, was killed. Of him the squadron archivist recorded:-

The grave of 609 Squadron's Sgt AN Feary, Holy Trinity, Warmwell.

Andrew Long.

'*He was a steady, painstaking pilot who, from becoming operational at Northolt on June 26th, 1940, had disposed of 5 and a 1/3rd enemy aircraft destroyed, 2 probables and 2 damaged. He seemed to regard his Spitfire with the kind of jealous care and affection that some others bestow upon animals, and the notion has been advanced by those who knew him well that this trait may have contributed to his loss of life, causing reluctance to bale out from a spin which he was unable to control.'*

Feary's Spitfire crashed to earth at Watercombe Farm, just south of Warmwell, and the unfortunate pilot's body landed nearby with an insufficiently deployed parachute owing to his having finally left his Spitfire too low.

Pilot Officer Michael Staples was more fortunate when his Spitfire was hit in the vicious combat above Dorset. At 21,000' he baled out with a *'big hole'* in his leg, shortly to join Pilot Officer Covington in Blandford Hospital. His Spitfire was reported by the Observer Corps to have crashed at Nutmead, Shillingstone, on the banks of the River Stour, at 1615 hrs. Mrs Doris Butt remembers later seeing the crash site *'well guarded.'*

609 Squadron's Plt Off Michael Staples who baled out wounded over Shillingstone, Dorset.

Andy Saunders Collection.

Flying Officer Forshaw claimed an Me 110 damaged in what had become a confused dog-fight with even more British fighters arriving, and Sergeant Hughes-Rees, also of 609 Squadron, claimed an Me 109 damaged.

The *Millionaires* of 601 Squadron had been scrambled from Exeter in two sections at 1545 and 1600 hrs. At 1610, Flying Officer Clyde attacked and claimed as destroyed an Me 110 over Yeovil. At the same time, Flying Officer Jankiewicz damaged another 110 above Bridport. Pilot Officer Aldwinckle claimed a *'Do 17'* as probably destroyed over Lyme Bay. At 1605 hrs, Pilot Officer Mayers, who was slightly injured, forced landed his Hurricane in a field south of Axminster with damage to the aircraft's glycol tank.

Pilots of 601 Squadron. Note the squadron's winged-sword badge, and parachute at the ready resting on the tailplane. The pilot at extreme right is Flg Off HC Mayers whose Hurricane was damaged by Me 110s over Portland on October 7th, 1940. The wounded pilot safely forced landed south of Axminster at 1605 hrs.

Author's Collection via Wg Cdr AJM Aldwinckle.

Having led 609 Squadron into the attack, and inconclusively engaged an Me 110, Squadron Leader Robinson had followed a Hurricane, possibly Flight Lieutenant Brooker of 56 Squadron, in to attack another 110 and left the enemy's port engine smoking. That aircraft is believed to have been

3U + JR of 7/ZG26. Gefreiter Bernhardt Demmig's Bordfunker, 21-year-old Obergefreiter Josef Bachmann, had been shot and killed from behind before the pilot even realised that they were under attack. At 1600 hrs, T.R. Hiett, a child evacuee from Southampton living at Church Knowle, witnessed Demmig execute a superb forced landing between a wooden fence and some trees near the Swanage Road at Corfe Castle. The schoolboy watched fascinated as the pilot got his dead gunner out of the aircraft before igniting the cockpit with a flare pistol round. Gefreiter Demmig then collapsed before being captured by the Home Guard. Young Hiett later visited the crash site and found the Me 110 still smoking but relatively intact. The forward-firing armament had not been used and each barrel remained covered in an orange coloured paper wrapper for protection.

Squadron Leader Robinson then requested from *Bandy Control* the position of any other raiders and was advised of one plot at 15,000' over Lyme Regis. 10 miles NW of Portland, Red 1 found a circle of Me 110s: *'I attacked one from dead astern and it dived vertically into the ground about 5 miles north of the coast (Little Bredy?).'*

Mrs Vestry of Kingston Russell House, Long Bredy, clearly recalled the dramatic incident:-

'My husband and I were watching the battle from the hill beside our house. There were quite a lot of planes involved but they were very high up so it was impossible to identify friend from foe. Presently, however, a German plane was hit and it nose dived into a field from about 18,000' and had literally flown into the ground.

'We were all very thankful as we thought that it was going to fall on the house. In the event it couldn't have fallen in a better place as it did no damage. There wasn't much of it left above the ground, but what there was burned furiously. It was impossible to get near it for some time due to exploding bullets.

'A military guard was put on it, and a day or two later the remains of the crew were buried in the hole made by their aeroplane. At that time the village would not consent to a burial in the churchyard here, I think because quite close by a week earlier one of our own pilots was machine-gunned whilst descending on his parachute. Also, an old ploughman had been shot at but not hit.

'We never knew whether there were one or two people in the plane, but we went on the assumption that there were two because that number of pairs of boots were found. A proper funeral was held by Canon Frotman and was attended by me in my capacity of Village Leader and Chief Air Raid Warden, the Canon's wife, the Commanding Officer of the soldiers stationed here, and a firing squad of six. Two RAF officers were also present who told us that the plane had gone down 36'.

'Our soldiers in the camp made two white wooden crosses which were put up at the edge of the field with the words "A German Soldier" painted on each.'

Robinson's victim was actually *3U + JP* of 6/ZG26 which had dived in from

20,000' with both engines pouring smoke. The crew, Oberfeldwebel K Herzog and Obergefreiter H Schilling, were indeed both killed.

After 238 Squadron had been bounced by the Me 109s and broken up, Squadron Leader Fenton had tried to intercept the enemy near Yeovil. However, he could not see the raiders there, so flew instead to Weymouth where he found four Me 110s going home at about 1620 hrs. The ZG26 machines were below and to the left, so Red Leader attacked from astern but experienced difficulty in closing with the enemy aircraft due to their high speed. Having initially fired from *'extreme range'* one of the 110s turned to port allowing the Hurricane pilot a full deflection shot from close range. The zerstörer then pitched into a steep dive towards the sea but disappeared into a bank of broken cloud at 1,000'. Being some distance out to sea, Fenton wisely broke off and returned to base.

One of Fenton's pilots, Pilot Officer Urwin-Mann, also claimed a victory over the sea. Having set the starboard engine ablaze, *'the E/A went down in a spiral dive, pulled out and went into the sea seven miles SW of Portland.'* This was *3U + DD* of III/ZG26's *Stabskette* which crashed at 1630 hrs between Arish Mell Gap and Worbarrow Bay, Lulworth. The pilot, Leutnant Botho Sommer, 26, a holder of the EK 1, later stated that he could have forced landed over England, but preferred the sea - as a result of his experience, however, he professed that dry land would actually have been preferable. His Bordfunker, Unteroffizier Paul Preuler, 22, was slightly wounded. Both stated that the bombers' target was *'Yeovil or SW Bristol'*, which suggests an alternative target at the formation leader's discretion.

Ditched Me 110.

Returning from his own lone combat over the sea off Bridport, Sergeant Jeka *'flew low, then straight for Portland, and over Weymouth Bay I saw a lifeboat going out to SE where I saw a big patch of substance in the water.'*

In the confused mayhem occurring over the West Country, Pilot Officer Roger Hall, Yellow 2 of 152 Squadron, had also become separated from his squadron. Past Yeovil he saw three aircraft, which he identified as *'He 111s'*, flying NW at 15,000'. The Spitfire pilot *'got ahead of them near the Bristol Channel at a point which I think may have been Foreland Point. I did a head-on attack on the leader of the vic, opening at 1,000 yards - one long burst - and broke away above - half rolled and saw the left hand E/A drop from the formation with glycol pouring from him. He was going down fairly steeply. I then saw what I took to be two other He 111s flying NE. I chased them but caught up a Blenheim well inland past Yatesbury. Came down to 500' to pinpoint. Found 5 gallons in one tank only so put down in a field with wheels down, the engine having cut before I had completed my last turn in to approach the field.'* In his log book, Roger Hall later recorded *'Forced landed at Barton Stacey, aircraft a write-off.'*

Informal snapshot of 152 Squadron shortly after arrival at Warmwell during the Battle of Britain. Left to right: Plt Off Warner, Sgt Wolton, Plt Off Marrs, Sgt Shepperd, Plt Off Innes, Flt Lt Withall, Plt Off Wildblood, Flg Off Deansley, Flt Lt Thomas, Flg Off Jones, Plt Off Williams, Plt Off Bayles, Sgt Akroyd and 'Pilot Officer Pooch.'

Author's Collection via Ray Johnson.

The grave of 152 Squadron's Plt Off HJ Akroyd. Shot down on October 7th, 1940, he died of burns the following day and is also buried in the churchyard of Holy Trinity, Warmwell.

Andrew Long.

Herbert Akroyd of 152 Squadron had been commissioned on September 25th, 1940, but his identity discs were still those of *Sergeant 740043*. At 1630 hrs his Spitfire was shot down, crashing at Shatcombe Farm, Wynford Eagle near Dorchester; Pilot Officer Akroyd baled out but had received fatal burns. The Dorset Constabulary noted the pilot's identity disc details and informed the RAF accordingly. Legend has it that Mrs Irene Akroyd was a WAAF at Warmwell and watched her husband's flaming Spitfire plunge from the heavens above, not knowing, of course, the identity of the young pilot trapped within the blazing inferno. Herbert Akroyd lingered on for a day in great pain before finding release in death on October 8th.

By now the disjointed and sporadic combats over the coast had all but ceased as the raiders made their exit. I/JG2, however, later claimed the destruction of two Blenheims. This was in fact an aircraft of 59 Squadron engaged on a *Moon Patrol* of Le Havre. The pilot, Pilot Officer Wenman was unhurt when his aircraft was attacked off Cherbourg at 1815 hrs by three Me 109s, but Sergeants Eric Neal and Gordon Wood were both wounded. T1874 made it back to Thorney Island but was seriously damaged. Whilst the *Richthofen* pilots claimed the destruction of two Blenheims, Wenman's crew claimed to have shot down one of their assailants *'in flames.'* However, there is no evidence to substantiate either claim.

Blenheim T1874 of 59 (Coastal Command) Squadron which had a narrow escape from the hands of
I/JG2 on October 7th, 1940. The damaged aircraft is shown here several weeks later but still unrepaired.

Chris Goss Collection.

In France the Germans assessed their losses over the West Country. The final balance sheet was one Ju 88 and seven Me 110s *vermisst* (missing). Of the aircrews lost, seven had been killed in action, and 11 had been captured, three of them wounded.

Fighter Command had lost six Spitfires and Hurricanes destroyed, with three more and the Blenheim damaged. One pilot had been killed with another fatally injured, and five, plus the two Blenheim crew members, had been wounded.

Though Yeovil was aflame, Westlands had again been spared as if by some divine intervention.

Between 1920 and 1930 hrs on Tuesday, October 8th, 1940, a small force of bombers returned to Yeovil, again bent on damaging Westlands. In the twilight some 30 HE bombs fell entirely on the residential area of Preston Grove on the far side of the airfield from the factory. 10 civilians were killed. One person was never identified. The shelter at Don Harrison's corner shop in Preston Grove received a direct hit, and amongst the dead there were two little boys, nine-year-old Laurence *Peter* Sweet and three-month-old Maxwell Fitkin.

This was the last raid of any strength against Yeovil, although eight more hit and run attacks would be made throughout the war. In total, 107 HE bombs were dropped on the town, 49 people were either killed outright or died of injuries, 32 were seriously and 90 slightly injured. 68 houses were totally destroyed and 2,754 were damaged. At no time, however, was any significant damage caused to the aircraft factory.

With autumn's golds rapidly fading to stark winter greys, perhaps somehow symbolic of wartime austerity, the threat of invasion passed. Although the Air Ministry officially deemed the Battle of Britain to have concluded on October 31st, 1940, this might not actually have been the case. The air attacks against England continued at night, and during the day frequent fighter sweeps were mounted against southern England until the winter's poor flying conditions significantly retarded this activity. Hitler had, however, already turned his true territorial ambitions eastwards and the great attack on London during a night of full moon on May 10th, 1941, saw the blitz at its zenith. Thereafter many Luftwaffe units were transferred to the Eastern Front for the war against Russia. This coincided with the RAF seeking to *lean into France* in a reversal of the Battle of Britain situation, and so began Fighter Command's *Non-Stop Offensive*.

During those 16 dramatic weeks of Summer 1940, however, the West Country had witnessed part of a battle that was to dictate the 20th century's destiny. Essential time had been bought, albeit at great cost, and the free world saw that Hitler was not invincible. Later, the West Country would provide essential bases for Allied forces which would land in Normandy on June 6th, 1944, ultimately smashing *Festung Europa* and Hitler's evils forever.

Through the Looking Glass

Flt Lt Dennis 'Nick' Nichols (2nd right) at the launch of Dilip Sarkar's third book 'Through Peril to the Stars', September 1993. Other pilots are Flt Lt WLB Walker (616 Sqn, extreme right), and Wg Cdrs 'Jimmy' Jennings and 'Grumpy' Unwin, both of 19 Sqn, extreme left and second left respectively.

Chris Carne.

'I threw it away in 1940 and I don't want it back now!' came the spirited reply from Dennis Nichols when told of the Malvern Spitfire Team's intention to investigate his Hurricane's crash site at Alton Pancras, Dorset. This came about entirely by accident after Dennis and I met when he moved to the Worcester area. With gentle persuasion, Dennis, who had later flown night fighters and after the war became a BOAC pilot before retiring with numerous flying hours, provided a personal account of the events which caused him to spend six months in hospital and my research commenced. The crash site was initially located by Dennis Williams and Andrew Long in May 1993, although several other parties had in fact recovered various items over the years. In early November 1993, Dennis Nichols and I travelled to Austral Farm on the rolling Dorset Downs where we received a warm and kindly welcome from the Ralphs. Members of the Team were already at work, probing with metal detectors and digging away, listening intently to the eye-witness accounts of the ancient Callaway brothers as they did so. Soon smashed components of the Hurricane were found, including tubular fuselage framework and a piece of armoured windscreen, the latter through which Dennis Nichols had last peered, over 53 years before, at the wrong end of an Me 110. We were joined at the site by another Battle of Britain friend, Squadron Leader Iain Hutchinson, formerly of 222 Squadron. It is heart-warming to know that the Few can

now welcome their former enemies as friends and fellow enthusiasts, and in such a manner we were also joined by Peter Wulff, formerly a Luftwaffe Leutnant who flew He 111s against the Russians before being captured when flying Fw190s in the west. The press swarmed around the site, including several television crews, and so it was that the events of October 7th, 1940, were suddenly brought vividly back to life.

Through the looking glass: Dennis Nichols (left) with former Luftwaffe pilot Peter Wulff at Austral Farm, Alton Pancras, Dorset, in October 1993. It was here that Sgt Nichols's Hurricane crashed on October 7th, 1940.

Chris Carne.

Malvern Spitfire Team line-up, Alton Pancras. Left to right: Chris Carne, Dennis Williams, Dilip Sarkar (in period hat!), eye-witness Charlie Callaway, Mark Postlethwaite, Dennis 'Nick' Nichols, eye-witness Sam Callaway, Tony Bramhall, and landowner Vic Ralph.

Chris Carne.

The Alton Pancras excavation occurred shortly after the release of my third book, *Through Peril to the Stars*, which related the stories of 11 RAF fighter pilots who failed to return, and at the time I was organising research for a proposed fourth work, *The Last of the Few*, being the stories of a similar number of friends who survived. Flight Lieutenant Dennis Nichols was to be amongst this number, and it was my intention that his chapter should also relate an account of the attack against Westlands on the day that he baled out over Dorset. However, the more I stared through the looking glass into the events of over half a century previously, two things soon became obvious: firstly that, to do the story justice, it was impossible to write about October 7th without similarly studying the raid on Sherborne of a week before, and secondly that the potential of what I had stumbled on was not a mere chapter but a book in its own right.

Some years before, when I would perhaps have been better advised to study for my imminent 'A' Level examinations, I read Alfred Price's superb account of the fighting on August 18th, 1940: *The Hardest Day*. In the book Alfred relates how his research was undertaken, and as an 18-year-old I was overawed, thinking that *'I'd give anything to do something like that!'* Shortly afterwards I became familiar with Ken Wakefield's similarly excellent *Luftwaffe Encore*, which relates the attacks against West Country targets on September 25th and 27th, 1940. Little did I know then that in the years ahead, both of these renowned authors would be numbered amongst my friends. However, the negative side when embarking upon this project was my anxiety that whatever I produced about the events of either one day or a particular raid would be judged against these two highly acclaimed works. It was not without some trepidation, therefore, that I decided to go ahead at full throttle, with perhaps nothing but bags of enthusiasm and my family and friends to help see the project through to a successful conclusion.

The first job was to glean whatever information was available at the Public Record Office. David Malpas kept me company on several pre-dawn starts to Kew where copies of RAF squadron records, combat reports and other daily information were obtained. That data provided the foundations upon which the book was built. At the same time, Ken Wakefield very kindly provided the Luftflotte 3 reports for both September 30th and October 7th, detailing not only which units were involved, but also what their bomb loads, losses and claims were. That essential information became the framework for the Luftwaffe research. These reports were translated for me by Peter Wulff who also added several extra observations based upon his own experiences as a former Luftwaffe pilot. Chris Goss, a fellow young author and contemporary, is a mine of information concerning Luftwaffe units and personnel operating over England during the Second World War, and soon various snippets of Luftwaffe related information were regularly arriving in the post from my friend. Being better placed than me geographically, Chris also helped out with minutiae at both the Public Record Office and the Ministry of Defence's Air Historical Branch. Michael Payne, an expert on all things Me 109, also freely gave of his knowledge and photographs. Allan White came up trumps with photographs of the 10 Group fighter squadrons and saved me much time. I was delighted also to trace Ray Johnson, an armourer with 152 Squadron throughout the war, who lent me his own precious album relating to his RAF service and recorded his experiences on several cassette tapes, some of which have been reproduced in this book.

Unfortunately the Royal Artillery Museum was unable to furnish any data regarding the anti-aircraft batteries in the West Country during this period, and an appeal for contact with retired fire and police officer eye-witnesses was similarly unsuccessful. However, Observer Lieutenant Neville Cullingford worked hard in extracting data from the West Country Observer Corps post logs. In fact, as the times of all other records are virtually without exception contradictory and recorded in retrospect, I have based the times of most occurrences on these Observer Corps records which were completed at the time. Civil Defence and police reports were forthcoming from the Somerset County Records Office and these too provided much essential information, particularly regarding the locations of crashed aircraft, bomb damage and casualties.

Over the Christmas 1993 holiday, Antony Whitehead, Andrew Long and I travelled to Dorset with a view to visiting Sherborne in addition to locating the crash sites of several aircraft brought down on the days under the microscope. We walked through Sherborne impressed by its medieval character, and in a bookshop I found a copy of Harry Osement's *Wartime Sherborne*; the stroll back to the car took on a completely different meaning as we matched up dramatic photographs of the bomb damage therein against the peaceful present-day scene. At nearby Burdon's Nurseries we discovered that Sergeant Walton's Hurricane had been recovered some 10 years previously, but managed to photograph two pistons in the landowner's possession. At Winterborne Houghton we found several middle-aged men who, as schoolboys, remembered Pilot Officer Covington's Hurricane crashing, and told us how, for years afterwards, they would visit the site collecting ammunition and cockpit instruments.

Pistons from Sgt Walton's Hurricane recovered from Burdon's Nurseries, Sherborne, during the mid-1980s. But where has all the wreckage gone now ?

Andrew Long.

The plaque outside the Abbey remembering those killed in Sherborne on 'Black Monday.'

Mark Postlethwaite.

Another aircraft shot down on October 7th, 1940, was Pilot Officer Staples's Spitfire at Nutmead, Shillingstone. Our search for the crash site led to some ambiguity as an eye-witness identified to me a *new* field, as opposed to the area in which both Andy Saunders, of the Tangmere Military Aviation Museum, and John Congram, a Wessex based aviation archaeologist, had previously searched and found small items of the aircraft. However, as Spitfire N2321 had been abandoned at 21,000', and crashed into soft ground so close to a river, I was certain that much more of the aircraft must remain buried at the site but deeper than the range of conventional metal detectors. Bob Williams subsequently came to our rescue by kindly sponsoring use of a Proton Magnetometer device designed and manufactured by his company, *Aquascan* of Newport, Gwent. The Magnetometer is capable of detecting metal buried many feet below the surface. We had used similar *Aquascan* equipment in 1986 to precisely locate the remains of Spitfire R6644 (see *The Invisible Thread: A Spitfire's Tale*, also by this author), but found the latest equipment more advanced with its digital control panel. On a cold and wet April Saturday, members of the Malvern Spitfire Team met John Congram at Beremarsh Farm, Shillingstone, and commenced a thorough search with the new specialist equipment. Two very encouraging readings were recorded in the originally accepted area, which also tallied with further eye-witness evidence received by John, and at the time of writing an excavation is being planned. Ultimately it is intended that parts of this Spitfire can be restored by Team expert, Dr Dennis Williams, for display at the new 609 Squadron Museum and inclusion in a travelling exhibition relating the *Angriff Westland* story in three dimensions. Also being planned is the return of 56 Squadron's Peter Fox to the crash site of his Hurricane, which will have occurred by the time this book is published.

The search for the Shillingstone Spitfire using the Proton Magnetometer supplied by 'Aquascan'. *Left to right: Antony Whitehead, Dennis Williams, Dilip Sarkar and Chris Carne.*

It is worth mentioning at this point the confusion in various published sources which state that 152 Squadron's Pilot Officer Akroyd crashed at Nutmead, and that Staples crashed at Shatcombe Farm, Wynford Eagle. The truth is the reverse of that hitherto accepted *fact*. The mystery was unravelled with the discovery of the Chief Constable of Dorset's Daily Reports to the County Air Raid Precautions Controller which correctly recorded the locations.

An appeal in the *Western Gazette* newspaper for eye-witnesses to the bombings of Sherborne and Yeovil bore much fruit, and I am particularly indebted to Sherborne School for sharing with me the boys' accounts, and also to Gerald Pitman, a local historian, for providing much information, but especially to retired PC Frank Childe for his account.

Many eye-witnesses to the Yeovil bombing told me that Preston Grove and Don Harrison's shelter had been hit on October 7th, and I was extremely moved to hear of the loss of Laurence *Peter* Sweet and Maxwell Fitkin. Roy Madelin, Chairman of South Somerset District Council and still resident in Preston Grove, related how he and young Sweet had been playing together that afternoon, but upon the siren's wail Mrs Madelin had ushered Peter off home to his mother. Whilst running by the corner shop, Mrs Harrison apparently called out to the youngster to come quickly into their shelter; minutes later all therein were dead. John Chesterman, however, was adamant that Preston Grove was bombed on October 8th, and after a check of Civil Defence records this was in fact proved to be the case.

The grave, in Yeovil cemetery, of 17-year-old Frank Rose, killed at Burton's Store in Middle Street, on October 7th, 1940. Just one of many connected sites identified to the author by local historian Jack Sweet.

Mark Postlethwaite.

My close friend, aviation artist Mark Postlethwaite, and I visited Yeovil and with Roy Madelin himself went to the Museum of South Somerset where we met local historian Jack Sweet. Having provided us with essential information concerning bomb damage and casualties in Yeovil, Jack then kindly took us on a fascinating *Sweet's Tour* of the town where various former bomb sites and existing damage were pointed out.

As research progressed, it became apparent that the *hit and run* raid mounted against Worcester's MECO factory on October 3rd, 1940, was an ideal example of a lone aircraft daylight harassing attack, especially as it had occurred during the neglected fifth phase of the Battle of Britain with which *Angriff Westland* was mainly to deal. As no significant research had ever been undertaken on this raid either, an appeal in the Worcester *Evening News* (formerly the *News & Times*) produced many eye-witnesses, each with a fascinating story to tell of the *Faithful City's* only air raid. I am particularly indebted to 22-year-old Antony Whitehead, however, who undertook much on site *leg-work* for me in respect of this part of the project, visiting the factory and its locale, matching up contemporary photographs with present day scenes, searching cemeteries for the victims' graves, and making the most stunning discovery of all throughout the entire research project: the completely intact nose section of one of the two SC250s dropped on the MECO! This is kindly being lent to us for promotional events connected with the launch of *Angriff Westland*, although it would be excellent to perhaps one day see this incredible relic on permanent display at Worcester's Tudor House Museum.

The nose cone of an SC 250 dropped on the MECO and as discovered in 1994 by Malvern Spitfire Team researcher Antony Whitehead in nearby office premises.

Antony Whitehead.

Two Luftwaffe 'Black Men' with an SC 250. The welded nose cone can clearly be seen.

Bundesarchiv.

Despite now being the author of four books and much other material besides on this subject, I had not previously studied in any detail the effect of bombing on the civilian population. Some of the eye-witness accounts were so horrifying that they were unsuitable for publication. At times it became so depressing that I wondered whether it was actually wise to dabble in the past at all. Clearly the carnage on the ground was much more real than the combat in the air, which seemed almost like a lethal sport. However, on the positive side, I hope that this book will make people understand how the ordinary man in the street felt and what he experienced at this time. I also hope that *Angriff Westland* will in itself be a memorial to all those civilians killed in Yeovil, Sherborne and Worcester, in addition to the aircrew of both sides who lost their lives fighting for causes which each believed were just.

Many Yeovil eye-witnesses also spoke of the *Hurricane* which crashed at Newton House, near Yeovil Junction railway station. Some said it happened on September 30th, others on October 7th, and others still on either September 25th or 27th when the Luftwaffe passed over during the raids dealt with by Ken Wakefield in *Luftwaffe Encore*. Mrs Sybil Robinson, however, got married on September 30th, the date on which she says the incident occurred, and a local person's diary in Jack Sweet's possession also indicates that date. However, neither Chris Goss or myself have been able to find any records relating to such a crashed aircraft on any of the dates mentioned, nor indeed on any other. Someone out there must have the relevant information, so I am hoping that with publication of this book a reader will fill in this gap for me!

Dr Alfred Price strongly advised me to obtain the weather reports for the days in question, particularly as some previously published accounts suggested that Sherborne had been bombed on September 30th because of *scattered cloud*, and others as the German bombers had been deflected from their true target by the weight of the British fighter attack. The latter I doubted anyway, as did Alfred, not least because, although perhaps overworked, KG55 was an experienced unit. Its pilots also knew that their chances of survival were considerably decreased if they broke formation and lost the mutual fire support of their comrades. Their leader also knew that unless the job was done properly, someone would have to come and do it again. As the reader will now know, the weather report confirmed that cloud was really the major cause for the mistake being made, thus to an extent exonerating the Germans.

A previously published account in a supposed accredited volume on the Battle of Britain states that Westlands was hit on October 7th and 100 workers were killed in a shelter. When I contacted Westland Helicopters, Peter Batten, of the Public Relations Department confirmed, however, that this was not the case. Peter Batten and Fred Ballam were later instrumental in providing masses of information regarding the history of Westlands and many photographs of the factory during the war years. Needless to say, their co-operation has been greatly appreciated.

The best was saved until last as I did not want to contact surviving pilots until certain of their specific parts in each combat. I am extremely mindful that the Few are not only getting older but also increasingly fewer, and therefore the task faced by authors of such books today is much harder than back in the 1970s when many such volumes were written. Then the survivors were younger, fitter and more numerous on

As ever the majority of survivors offered great support. This is Wg Cdr RFT Doe DSO DFC RAF Retd 54 years after the Battle of Britain and sitting in the cockpit of a somewhat more advanced aircraft than the Spitfires and Hurricanes he flew at that time!

Author's Collection via Wg Cdr RFT Doe.

both sides of the Channel. Furthermore, we are now at the end of a long line of people to have contacted these former pilots, and I am similarly mindful of this when forced to increase their correspondence. However, many were located via several friends, including Wing Commander NPW Hancock OBE DFC RAF Retd, in his 17th year as Honorary Secretary of the Battle of Britain Fighter Association, and most responded enthusiastically. I drove to South Wales where I met 56 Squadron's *Taffy* Higginson, now 83, and we talked of 1940 for several hours. Perhaps most riveting of all, however, was Peter Fox's lengthy written account of being shot down on September 30th. To all of these gentlemen, from all over the world, who cast their minds back to 1940 and dug out from attic boxes on my behalf long forgotten log books and faded photographs, I am eternally grateful.

Reduction gear cog recovered by John Congram from the crash site of Peter Fox's Hurricane at Wootton Fitzpaine.

John Congram.

I feel that this research has been more than justified owing to the previous errors and misconceptions about the various incidents which have been rectified by this book, in addition to producing the first ever full account of the three raids in question. Despite there already being thousands of books in print on this subject it is perhaps indicative of exactly how much work still lies ahead in our race against time. I also feel privileged to be amongst the last generation of historians who can reach out to the surviving aircrew and eye-witnesses. Certainly these very special people will be long-gone by the time that my son comes of age. His generation, and all afterwards, will only have for reference whatever legacy we leave them; it is our duty, therefore, to ensure it shall be of the highest quality.

Writing the book itself was a frustrating experience, as no two contemporary reports or records seemed to have the same time, or indeed location! As previously explained, many of the times used in the text are those recorded by the Observer Corps and which are, we feel, likely to be the most accurate. I very much doubt whether, in a half roll firing at an Me 110 with another rapidly closing from the rear, many fighter pilots would have looked at their watches to note the exact times and observed locations of specific combats! Indeed, many years ago Jeffrey Quill, Supermarine's Chief Test Pilot, remarked to me that *'Our minds were not focused upon posterity in 1940!'* Throughout the descriptions of the combat, it will be seen that numerous pilots have incorrectly identified the German aircraft involved, as if to further confuse a chaotic situation! The other difficulty was that many of the events occurred at exactly the same time and in the same area, so this was difficult to record in a story-board presentation.

After Harald Penrose test flew the first Westland-built Spitfire on July 8th, 1941, the Yeovil factory went on to produce almost 700 examples. In conjunction with

Cunliffe-Owen Aircraft, Westlands also became integrally involved in production of the Seafire - the carrier version of Mitchell's original design - and in fact produced two-thirds of the 2,400 built. In addition to Tony Bianchi's Spitfire Mk 1A, AR213, the Shuttleworth Trust's Spitfire Mk VC, AR501, is also a Westland-built survivor.

Westland survivor: the Shuttleworth Trust's Spitfire Mk VC, AR501, seen in the markings of 310 (Czech) Squadron with which the aircraft flew during 1942.

Photo Link.

Another surviving Spitfire worthy of note is Mk IA R6915, for this is the very fighter which Pilot Officer Noel Agazarian flew over Sherborne on September 30th, 1940, when he damaged an He 111, and which on October 7th was flown by Flight Lieutenant John Dundas when he destroyed the Stoborough Me 110. This Spitfire can now be seen at the Imperial War Museum, Lambeth, wearing rather weathered markings from its later days with a training unit (I am not alone in thinking that the machine should be proudly resplendent in the colours worn during its finest hour with 609 Squadron during the Battle of Britain). Sadly, however, neither Agazarian or Dundas survived the war. *Aga*, Michael Appleby's *Green Eyed Monster*, was to perish over the desert in a Hurricane, whilst John Dundas went *missing* over the Solent shortly after the Battle of Britain.

The crew of the Me 110 shot down on October 7th, 1940, and which crashed at Kingston Russell House, Long Bredy, Dorset, were both originally buried at the crash site. Later they were interred at the *Soldatenfriedhof* on Cannock Chase, Staffordshire, but as *Unbekanst* (unknown). In 1976 an aviation archaeological group excavated the zerstörer's crash site at Brickhills Field. There much of the aircraft was recovered, including a tail-wheel assembly, oxygen bottles, ammunition drums and propeller blades, in addition to more human remains found with torn flying overalls, Luftwaffe grey *fliegerblouse* and *schwimmweste*. Most importantly of all, personal papers were discovered which identified the crew as Oberfeldwebel K. Herzog and Obergefreiter H. Schilling. Initially the Central Dorset Coroner, Mr Morris Bailey, refused to accept the evidence before him as conclusive proof that the two airmen were not *Unbekanst* but were in fact Herzog and Schilling. A destruction order was placed on the human remains recovered by the archaeologists. Andy Saunders and others involved were understandably totally dissatisfied with this decision, and so petitioned the German War Graves Commission. Eventually Andy's findings were accepted, and a new headstone was installed at Cannock bearing the correct names. Nearly 20 years after it was recovered, the tail wheel is now being restored by Malvern Spitfire Team expert, Dr Dennis Williams (readers of *The Invisible Thread* & *Through Peril to the Stars* will be familiar with the exemplary standard of his work).

By 1945, many of the participants in these particular battles from both sides either lay buried on battlefields from the Soviet Union to Normandy, or worse their bones were scattered in unknown places. But all that, as they say, is another story.

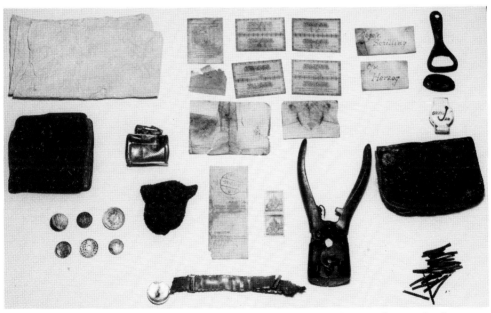

A poignant selection of personal items recovered from the crash site of the Long Bredy Me 110. The two cards at top right bore the crew's names, previously buried as 'unbekanst' and assisted in their correct identification as Oberfeldwebel K Herzog and Obergefreiter H Schilling.

Andy Saunders Collection.

A replacement headstone appeared at the Soldatenfriedhof on Cannock Chase inscribed with the names of Schilling and Herzog. Their grave is shared with Leutnant Werner Knittel of II/JG51 who died when his Me 109 was shot down over the south coast on October 28th, 1940. Similarly, his remains were recovered by archaeologists during the 1970s.

Andy Saunders Collection.

Appendix One

AFTERNOON, MONDAY, SEPTEMBER 30TH, 1940.
KNOWN RAF PARTICIPANTS, LOSSES & CLAIMS.

RAF PARTICIPANTS (AIRCRAFT SERIALS WHERE KNOWN IN BRACKETS).

87 UNITED PROVINCES (HURRICANE) SQUADRON

Flight Lieutenant IR Gleed DFC
Flying Officer JR Cock
Pilot Officer ACR McLure
Pilot Officer HT Mitchell
Pilot Officer RP Beamont
Flight Sergeant IJ Badger
Sergeant H Walton   (Possibly V7307)

The following pilots of 87 Squadron patrolled Bristol:-

Flying Officer RMS Rayner   (V7225)
Flying Officer R Watson   (P2829)
Sergeant FV Howell   (P3420)
Sergeant LA Thorogood   (P3093)

COMBAT CLAIMS.

Flight Lieutenant IR Gleed DFC: 1 Ju 88 destroyed.
Flying Officer JR Cock :   1 Ju 88 destroyed & 1 Me 109 damaged.
Pilot Officer ACR McLure: 1 Me 110 destroyed.

COMBAT LOSSES.

1. Hurricane, serial not known, of Flight Lieutenant IR Gleed DFC slightly damaged.

2. Hurricane, serial possibly V7307, of Sergeant H Walton crashed at Burdon's Nurseries, Osborne Road, Sherborne, Dorset at approximately 1640 hrs. Aircraft a write-off, pilot baled out slightly wounded and admitted to Sherborne Hospital.

238 (HURRICANE) SQUADRON

Flight Lieutenant ML Robinson	(R4099)
Pilot Officer W Rozycki	(P3618)
Pilot Officer JS Wigglesworth	(P3611)
Pilot Officer JR Urwin-Mann	(R4232)
Sergeant JW McLaughlin	(N2546)
Sergeant J Jeka	(P3219)
Flying Officer RFT Doe DFC	(V6814)
Sergeant LG Batt	(P3178)
Sergeant J Kucera	(P2920)

COMBAT CLAIMS.

Flight Lieutenant ML Robinson:	2 Me 110s destroyed, 1 Me 109 damaged.
Flying Officer RFT Doe DFC:	1 He 111 destroyed.
Sergeant J Jeka :	1 Me 110 damaged.
Sergeant J Kucera :	1 He 111 destroyed.

COMBAT LOSSES.

1. Hurricane V6814 flown by Flying Officer RFT Doe DFC suffered a damaged propeller whilst attacking an He 111.

213 *CEYLON* (HURRICANE) SQUADRON

Squadron Leader DS MacDonald	(*AK-K*)
Flight Sergeant C Grayson	(*AK-Z*)
Sergeant HJR Barrow	(*AK-W*)
Pilot Officer HW Cottam	(*AK-R*)
Pilot Officer B Wlasnowolski	(*AK-Y*)
Pilot Officer J Lockhart	(*AK-P*)
Pilot Officer WM Sizer	(*AK-X*)
Sub-Lieutenant DM Jeram	(*AK-U*)
Sergeant G Stevens	(*AK-D*)
Pilot Officer HD Atkinson	(*AK-C*)
Flying Officer RA Kellow	(*AK-B*)
Sergeant HH Adair	(*AK-E*)
Flying Officer M Duryasz	(*AK-I*)

COMBAT CLAIMS.

Squadron Leader DS MacDonald:	1 Me 110 destroyed.
Sub-Lieutenant DM Jeram :	1 Me 110 probable.
Flying Officer RA Kellow:	1 Me 110 destroyed.
Sergeant HJR Barrow:	1 Me 110 damaged.
Sergeant G Stevens :	1 Me 110 damaged.
Pilot Officer HD Atkinson:	1 Me 109 destroyed.

COMBAT LOSSES.

1. Hurricane *AK-D* flown by Sergeant G Stevens suffered slight damage when pulled out of steep dive.

152 *HYDERABAD* (SPITFIRE) SQUADRON

Squadron Leader PK Devitt
Flying Officer GJ Cox
Flying Officer IN Bayles
Flying Officer RF Innes
Pilot Officer RMD Hall
Flight Lieutenant FM Thomas
Sergeant EE Shepperd
Pilot Officer HJ Akroyd
Pilot Officer ES Marrs
Pilot Officer WD Williams
Sergeant AW Kearsey
Sergeant LAE Reddington

COMBAT CLAIMS.

Squadron Leader PK Devitt:	1 He 111 damaged.
Pilot Officer Williams :	1¹/₂ Me 110 destroyed (shared with Pilot Officer FW Higginson of 56 Squadron)
Flying Officer GJ Cox:	1 Me 110 damaged.
Sergeant EE Shepherd:	1 Me 110 damaged.
Pilot Officer ES Marrs:	1 He 111 damaged.
Sergeant AW Kearsey:	1 Me 110 destroyed.

COMBAT LOSSES.

1. Spitfire L1072 and Sergeant LAE Reddington missing. Believed shot down over the sea.

2. Spitfire, serial not known, flown by Pilot Officer ES Marrs, suffered damaged cockpit hood, petrol tank and undercarriage system. Pilot landed on one wheel at Warmwell.

504 *CITY OF NOTTINGHAM* (HURRICANE) SQUADRON

Squadron Leader J Sample DFC	(N2471)
Flight Lieutenant AH Rook	(V6702)
Pilot Officer CM Stavert	(V6695)
Flying Officer EM Frisby	(P2987, *TM-M*)
Sergeant WH Banks	(P3774, *TM-V*)
Sergeant C Haw	(P3614)
Flying Officer MEA Royce	(P3388)
Flight Lieutenant WB Royce	(V6731)
Flying Officer JR Hardacre	(P3414, *TM-K*)
Pilot Officer W Barnes	(P2908)
Sergeant BM Bush	(P3021, *TM-N*)
Sergeant HDB Jones	(V6732)
Flying Officer BEG White	(V6695)

COMBAT CLAIMS.

Sergeant HDB Jones:	2 He 111s destroyed.
Sergeant BM Bush:	1 He 111 damaged.
Flight Lieutenant WB Royce:	1 He 111 damaged.
Flying Officer MEA Royce:	1 He 111 damaged.
Flight Lieutenant AH Rook:	1 He 111 damaged.

COMBAT LOSSES.

1. Hurricane P3414, *TM-K* and Flying Officer JR Hardacre missing. Hardacre's body was washed ashore at Yarmouth on October 10th.

2. Hurricane P2987, *TM-M*, flown by Pilot Officer EM Frisby forced landed low on fuel and damaged at 1700 hrs, 1^1/$_2$ miles south of Whitcombe Church, Whitcombe, near Dorchester, Dorset. Pilot uninjured.

3. Hurricane P3021, *TM-N*, flown by Sergeant BM Bush and forced landed low on fuel at 1700 hrs near Priddy, Somerset. Pilot uninjured, aircraft damaged.

4. Hurricane P3774, *TM-V*, flown by Sergeant WH Banks also forced landed in *Yeovil area*, 1700 hrs. Pilot uninjured, aircraft damaged.

5. Hurricane V6731, flown by Flying Officer MEA Royce, damaged during attack on He 111 but returned safely to base.

56 *PUNJAB* (HURRICANE) SQUADRON

Squadron Leader MH Pinfold	(P2910)
Pilot Officer FW Higginson	(P3702)
Flight Lieutenant REP Brooker	(P3421)
Sergeant PEM Robinson	(P3862)
Pilot Officer BJ Wicks	(P3870, *US-D*)
Sergeant PH Fox	(N2434, *US-H*)
Pilot Officer MHC Maxwell	(L1674)
Pilot Officer RSJ Edwards	(P3088, *US-N*)

COMBAT CLAIMS.

Squadron Leader MH Pinfold:	1 *Do 215* destroyed.
Pilot Officer FW Higginson:	1/2 Me 110 destroyed (shared with Pilot Officer WD Williams of 152 Squadron).
Flight Lieutenant REP Brooker:	1 *Do 215* damaged.
Sergeant PEM Robinson:	1 *Do 215* damaged.

COMBAT LOSSES.

1. Hurricane N2434, *US-H*, crashed at 1630 hrs, 800 yards north of Wootton Fitzpaine to Monkton Wyld Road, at Wootton Fitzpaine near Lyme Regis, Dorset. Aircraft shot down during attack on He 111, pilot, Sergeant PH Fox, baled out wounded in right knee.

2. Hurricane P3870, *US-D*, flown by Pilot Officer BJ Wicks, damaged by return fire from He 111 and forced landed at Warmwell, pilot unhurt and aircraft repairable.

3. Hurricane L1674 flown by Pilot Officer MHC Maxwell forced landed damaged on Abbotsbury Beach, Chesil Bank, at 1700 hrs. Pilot unhurt.

4. Hurricane P3088, *US-N*, destroyed in combat over Portland, 1700 hrs. Flight Lieutenant RSJ Edwards baled out unhurt.

5. Hurricane P2910, 1705 hrs forced landed at Warmwell by Squadron Leader MH Pinfold when damaged during attack on an He 111 over Portland.

609 *WEST RIDING* (SPITFIRE) SQUADRON

Flight Lieutenant FJ Howell	(X4477)
Sergeant AN Feary	(X4179)
Pilot Officer JD Bisdee	(N3113)
Pilot Officer AK Ogilvie	(R6706)
Sergeant JA Hughes-Rees	(L1096)
Pilot Officer ME Staples	(N3231)
Pilot Officer MJ Appleby	(R6631)
Flying Officer P Ostaszewski	(P9503)
Flying Officer EL Hancock	(X4471)
Pilot Officer N le C Agazarian	(R6915)
Pilot Officer DM Crook	(X4165)
Flying Officer T Nowierski	(R6961)
Pilot Officer J Curchin	(N3223)

COMBAT CLAIMS

Flying Officer T Nowierski:	1 Me 109 destroyed.
Pilot Officer DM Crook:	1 Me 109 probable.
Pilot Officer N le C Agazarian:	1 He 111 damaged.

COMBAT LOSSES.

1. Spitfire R6915 flown by Pilot Officer N le C Agazarian hit in glycol tank during attack on He 111 inland of Warmwell at about 1700 hrs. Aircraft repairable, pilot unhurt.

NOTE: *It is believed that at about 1640 hrs a British fighter, possibly a Hurricane, crashed at Newton House, near Yeovil Junction Station. The pilot baled out safely and landed at East Coker. Neither this aircraft or its pilot have so far been identified.*

Appendix Two

AFTERNOON, MONDAY, SEPTEMBER 30TH, 1940.
KNOWN LUFTWAFFE UNITS, LOSSES & CLAIMS.

PARTICIPATING UNITS.

THE KAMPFLIEGERN.

Stab KG55 *Greifen*:	4 He 111s carrying 15 SC250 HE.
I/KG55:	16 He 111s carrying 76 SC250 HE.
II/KG55:	23 He 111s carrying 8 SC500 HE, 131 SC250 HE and 15 Flam 250.

THE JAGDFLIEGERN.

JG2 *Richthofen*:	47 Me 109s.
JG53 *Pik As*:	5 Me 109s.
ZG26 *Horst Wessel*:	40 Me 110s.

COMBAT CLAIMS.

II/JG2:	4 *Jagdflugzeuge* (fighter aircraft).		
III/JG2:	4	..	
II/JG53:	2	..	*Note: Oberfeldwebel Patho is known to have claimed 2 Hurricanes but times n/k.*
ZG26:	4	..	

Note: *Although not awarded in connection with the September 30th raid, the following members of 5/ZG26 received the EK I on that date:-*
Leutnant Fritz Mittler
Unteroffizier Heinz Schrodt
Unteroffizier Gerhardt Gröhl
Unteroffizier Mathias Nicoley
Unteroffizier Franz Beckel
Obergefreiter Günter Franke
Obergefreiter Walter Munz

COMBAT LOSSES.

KG55 *GREIFEN.*

Stab KG55
He 111P-2 (Werk Nummer: 2836). *G1 + JA.* Believed shot down into the sea. Major Dr Ernst Kühl (Geschwader Operations Officer), Unteroffizier Steglich, Gefreiter Feichtmayer and Gefreiter Becker rescued by Seenotdienst, but Unteroffizier Barabas killed.

3 Staffel/KG55
He 111P-2 (Werk Nummer: 1616). *G1 + AL.* As above, Oberleutnant Moessner, Unteroffizier Reiter, Unteroffizier Trenkmann, Gefreiter Thuemel and Flieger Geist *vermisst.*

4 Staffel/KG55
He 111P-2 (Werk Nummer: 1545). *G1 + AM.* As above, Unteroffizier Kuebler killed, Unteroffizier Eggert, Obergefreiter Geyer, Gefreiter Biedermann and Gefreiter Roesel *vermisst.*
He 111P-2 (Werk Nummer: 2643). *G1 + CM.* As above, Obergefreiter Schocke and Oberfeldwebel Guttler both killed. Gefreiters Bauer,Rudeck and Strauss all *vermisst.*

Note: *Three RAF fighter pilots claimed 4 He 111s destroyed between them in conclusive combats over the sea: Sergeant J Kucera (238 Sqn.)at 1620 hrs 20 miles south of Portland, Flying Officer RFT Doe DFC (238 Sqn.) at 1630 hrs 15 miles south of Portland, and Sergeant HDB Jones (504 Sqn.) who destroyed 2 He 111s at 1700 'south of Portland'. All of these enemy aircraft were seen to crash into the sea.*

AUFKLÄRUNGSGRUPPE 123.

1st Staffel(F)/123
Ju 88A-1 (Werk Nummer: 0385). *4U + MH* attacked by Flying Officer JR Cock of 87 Squadron over Dorset and subsequently crashed into the Solent off the Isle of Wight. Unteroffiziers Essemann and Obermeier, and Feldwebel Waack all killed, Leutnant Frenzel *vermisst.*

JG2 *RICHTHOFEN.*

5th Staffel
Me 109E-4 (Werk Nummer: 4861). Crashed 1640 hrs, 100 Acre Field, Spriggs Farm, Sydling St Nicholas, Dorset. Unteroffizier Alois Dollinger fell dead at Grimstone with unopened parachute. Shot down by Flying Officer Tadeuz Nowierski (Polish) of 609 Squadron.

Appendix Three

AFTERNOON, MONDAY, OCTOBER 7TH, 1940.
KNOWN RAF PARTICIPANTS, COMBAT LOSSES & CLAIMS.

RAF PARTICIPANTS (AIRCRAFT SERIALS WHERE KNOWN IN BRACKETS).

601 *COUNTY OF LONDON* (HURRICANE) SQUADRON

Flying Officer WP Clyde	
Pilot Officer WW Straight	(P3675)
Flying Officer J Jankiewicz	(P3831)
Pilot Officer AJM Aldwinckle	(V6666)
Pilot Officer AJ Rippon	(P3228)
Pilot Officer JH Hoare-Scott	(P3886)
Flying Officer HC Mayers	(R4218)

COMBAT CLAIMS.

Flying Officer WP Clyde:	1 Me 110 destroyed.
Flying Officer J Jankiewicz:	1 Me 110 damaged.
Pilot Officer AJM Aldwinckle:	1 *Do 17* probable.

COMBAT LOSSES.

1. Hurricane R4218 flown by Flying Officer HC Mayers suffered a damaged glycol tank in combat with Me 110s over Portland and forced landed south of Axminster at 1605 hrs. Pilot slightly injured, aircraft a write-off.

56 *PUNJAB* (HURRICANE) SQUADRON

Flight Lieutenant REP Brooker	(V7510)
Flying Officer BJ Wicks	(V7508)
Pilot Officer Z Nosowicz	(V7605)
Sergeant PEM Robinson	(P3862)
Sergeant DH Nichols	(P3514)
Sergeant C Whitehead	
Sergeant P Hillwood	

COMBAT CLAIMS.

Flight Lieutenant REP Brooker:	1 Me 110 probable, 1 *Do 17* probable.
Pilot Officer Z Nosowicz:	1 *Do 17* probable, 1 Me 110 damaged.
Sergeant C Whitehead:	1 *Do 17* damaged.
Sergeant P Hillwood:	1 *Do 17* damaged.

COMBAT LOSSES.

1. Hurricane P3514 flown by Sergeant DH Nichols shot down in solo head-on attack on defensive circle of Me 110s. Aircraft crashed 1600 hrs at Austral Farm, Alton Pancras, Dorset. Pilot baled out and landed heavily, suffering a broken back. Spent six months in hospital but returned to operational flying.

152 *HYDERABAD* (SPITFIRE) SQUADRON

Pilot Officer FH Holmes	(R6964)
Sergeant R Wolton	(P9391)
Pilot Officer IN Bayles	(R6643)
Pilot Officer RMD Hall	(R6608)
Sergeant EE Shepperd	(R6607)
Flying Officer GJ Cox	(R6763)
Pilot Officer ES Marrs	(R6968)
Pilot Officer WD Williams	(X4381)
Sergeant J Szlagowski	(L1048)
Sergeant AW Kearsey	(X4550)
Pilot Officer HJ Akroyd	(K9882)
Sergeant Z Klein	(P9386)

COMBAT CLAIMS

Pilot Officer FH Holmes:	2 Ju 88s damaged
Sergeant EE Shepperd:	1 Ju 88 destroyed
Flying Officer GJ Cox:	1 JU 88 damaged
Pilot Officer ES Marrs:	1 Me 110 destroyed, 1 Me 110 damaged
Sergeant Z Klein:	1 Me 110 damaged

COMBAT LOSSES

1. Spitfire N3039 shot down and crashed at 1630 hrs Shatcombe Farm, Wynford Eagle, near Dorchester. Pilot Officer HJ Akroyd baled out fatally burned and died in Dorset County Hospital the following day. Note that the squadron Form 541 states this aircraft to have been K9882, but Form 78 confirms N3039.

2. Spitfire R6608, forced landed at Sutton Scotney completely out of fuel, 1640 hrs, by Pilot Officer RMD Hall. Aircraft repairable, pilot unhurt.

238 (HURRICANE) SQUADRON

Squadron Leader HA Fenton	(P2920)
Pilot Officer AR Covington	(V6777)
Pilot Officer VC Simmonds	(P2681)
Flying Officer RFT Doe DFC	(V6814)
Sergeant LG Batt	(V6727)
Pilot Officer CT Davis	(V6801)
Pilot Officer BB Considine	(P3214)
Pilot Officer W Rozycki	(P3618)
Pilot Officer JS Wigglesworth	(R4699)
Pilot Officer JR Urwin-Mann	(R4232)
Sergeant J Jeka	(L1189)
Sergeant J Kucera	(P3249)

COMBAT CLAIMS

Squadron HA Fenton:	1 Me 110 destroyed
Pilot Officer RFT Doe DFC:	1 Ju 88 destroyed
Pilot Officer JR Urwin-Mann:	1 Ju 88 destroyed
Sergeant J Jeka:	1 Ju 88 destroyed

COMBAT LOSSES

1. Hurricane V6777 shot down in surprise attack by Me 109s, crashed at 1600 hrs Meriden Wood Down, Winterbourne Houghton near Blandford, Dorset. Pilot Officer AR Covington baled out slightly wounded and admitted to Blandford Cottage Hospital.

609 *WEST RIDING* (SPITFIRE) SQUADRON

Squadron Leader ML Robinson	(L1096)
Flight Lieutenant FJ Howell	(X4472)
Sergeant AN Feary	(N3238)
Pilot Officer ME Staples	(N3231)
Pilot Officer JD Bisdee	(X4630)
Sergeant JA Hughes-Rees	(X4173)
Flying Officer JC Dundas	(R6915)
Flying Officer P Ostaszewski	(R9503)
Pilot Officer DM Crook	(R3273)

Flight Lieutenant THT Forshaw   (X4471)
Pilot Officer MJ Appleby   (X4539)
Flying Officer EL Hancock   (R6651)
Pilot Officer J Curchin   (R6706)

COMBAT CLAIMS

Squadron Leader ML Robinson: 2 Me 110s destroyed
Flight Lieutenant FJ Howell: 1 Me 110 destroyed
Pilot Officer JD Bisdee: 1 Me 110 destroyed
Flying Officer JC Dundas: 1 Me 110 probable
Flight Lieutenant THT Forshaw: 1 Me 110 probable
Sergent JA Hughes-Rees: 1 Me 109 destroyed

COMBAT LOSSES

1. Spitfire N3238 shot down in combat over Warmwell, crashed at Watercombe Farm, Owermoigne, 1 mile south of Warmwell at 1600 hrs. Pilot, Sergeant AN Feary, baled out too low and killed.

2. Spitfire X4472 forced landed by Flight Lieutenant FJ Howell with damaged engine at 1600 hrs, Vale Farm, Sutton Waldron, near Shaftesbury. Pilot uninjured, aircraft repairable.

3. Spitfire N3231 shot down and crashed at *Nutmead* half-mile north of Shillingstone Railway Station, Dorset, 1600 hrs. Pilot Officer ME Staples baled out with wounded leg, admitted to Blandford Cottage Hospital.

4. Spitfire R6915 hit by return fire from Me 110, Flying Officer JC Dundas received shell splinters in both legs. Aircraft damaged but repairable.

59 (COASTAL COMMAND) SQUADRON

Blenheim T1874 was attacked by three Me 109s off Cherbourg at 1815 hrs whilst engaged on a *Moon Patrol*. The aircraft was seriously damaged but returned to Thorney Island. The pilot, Pilot Officer Wenman, was unhurt, but Sergeants Eric Neal and Gordon Wood were both wounded. This tallies with claims by Me 109 pilots providing escort for the Yeovil raid (see Appendix 4).

Appendix Four

AFTERNOON, MONDAY OCTOBER 7TH, 1940
KNOWN LUFTWAFFE UNITS, CLAIMS AND LOSSES

PARTICIPATING UNITS.

THE KAMPFLIEGERN.

II/KG51 *Edelweiss*: 20 Ju 88s with 44 SC250 HE & 24 Flamm 250.

THE JAGDFLIEGERN.

JG2 *Richthofen*:	52 Me 109s.
JG53 *Pik As*:	7 Me 109s.
ZG26 *Horst Wessel*:	39 Me 110s.

COMBAT CLAIMS.

I/JG2:	3 Spitfires & 2 Blenheims.
II/JG2:	4 Hurricanes.
III/JG2:	1 Spitfire.
I/ZG26:	1 Spitfire & 2 Hurricanes.
II/ZG26:	2 Hurricanes.

COMBAT LOSSES.

5th Staffel KG51.
Ju 88A-1 (Werk Nummer: 8064) *9K + SN*. Shot down by Sergeant EE Shepperd (152 Sqn.), Flying Officer RFT Doe DFC (238 Sqn.), en route to Yeovil. Aircraft crashed at 1620 hrs, Sydling St Nicholas, Dorset. Abandoned by crew, Oberleutnant Sigurd Hey, Leutnant Friedrich Bein,Oberfeldwebel Christian Koenig & Oberfeldwebel Josef Troll, all baled out and captured unhurt.

4th Staffel ZG26.
Me 110E-1 (Werk Nummer: 3427) *3U + FM*. Shot down by Pilot Officer ES Marrs and crashed into the sea at 1605 hrs at Ringstead Bay, Dorset. Crew baled out, Oberfeldwebel Erwin Genzzler captured unhurt, Unteroffzier Franz Haefner captured slightly wounded.

6th Staffel ZG26.

Me 110C-7 (Werk Nummer: 3418) *3U + JP*. Shot down by Squadron Leader ML Robinson (609 Sqn.) at 1600 hrs, crashed at Brickhills field, Kingston Russell House, Long Bredy, Dorset. Obergefreiter Herbert Schilling and Oberfeldwebel Karl Herzog both killed. Partial remains originally buried at crash site, but later interred at the Soldatfriedhof as *Unbekanst*. In 1976 the site was excavated by Andy Saunders whose team recovered substantial wreckage and further human remains in addition to personal papers identifying the crew. Consequently a new headstone was installed at Cannock Chase naming these two *Zerstörerfliegern*.

Stabskette III Gruppe ZG26.

Me 110E-1 (Werk Nummer: 3421) *3U + DD*. Shot down by Pilot Officer JR Urwin-Mann (238 Sqn.) at 1630 hrs over Weymouth Bay. Pilot, Leutnant Botho Sommer, ditched in the sea between Arish Mell Gap and Worbarrow Bay, Lulworth, but was captured with Unteroffizier Paul Preuler, the latter being wounded.

9th Staffel ZG26.

Me 110C-4 (Werk Nummer: 3283) *3U + BT*. Shot down at 1620 hrs by Flying Officer JC Dundas (609 Sqn.), crashed at Hart Hill, Stoborough, near Wareham, Dorset. Leutnant Kurt Sidow and Gefreiter Josef Repik both killed.

9th Staffel ZG26

Me 110C-4 (Werk Nummer: 3640) *3U + GT*. Ditched into the sea off Weymouth, 1615 hrs, Oberleutnant Grisslich captured unhurt, Unteroffizier Obermayer baled out but captured seriously wounded.

9th Staffel ZG26

Me 110C-4 (Werk Nummer: 3564) *3U + JT*. Shot down by Squadron Leader ML Robinson (609 Sqn.) and Flight Lieutenant REP Brooker (56 Sqn.) at 1600 hrs, forced landed at Corfe Castle, Dorset. Pilot, Gefreiter Bernhardt Demmig captured, *Bordfunker*, Obergefreiter Josef Bachmann killed.

II/ZG26

Me 110D-2 (Werk Nummer: 3416) *3U + HN*. Oberfeldwebel Stahl and Unteroffizier Mauer *vermisst*. Believed shot down by Sergeant J Jeka (238 Sqn.) or Squadron Leader HA Fenton (238 Sqn.) off Portland Bill.

Appendix Five

THE CIVILIAN DEATH TOLL.

SHERBORNE, MONDAY, SEPTEMBER 30TH, 1940.

Butlin, John	Jeffery, William C.	Morgan, William S.
Dawe, Leonard J.	Knobbs, Edward D.	Reason, A.H.
Gartell, Albertina, B.	Legg, Horace G.	Trask, Barry A.
Goulter, Percy H.D.	Le Gallais Albert l'E	Warren, Ronald K.
Hunt, Douglas	Lintern, Arthur J.	Warren, Robert G.
Ireland, Henry	Marden, Elizabeth A.	Warren, Paricia A.

All above remembered on plaque outside Sherborne Abbey, Sherborne, Dorset.

WORCESTER, THURSDAY, OCTOBER 3RD, 1940.

Williams, A.E.	Ricketts, W.G.	Hulme, W.
Lee, G.W.	Perry, J.W.	Santler, T.C.
	Defaye, L.C.	

All above remembered on plaque in MECO factory,
Bromyard Road, St. Johns, Worcester.

YEOVIL, MONDAY, OCTOBER 7TH, 1940.

Packard, Violet (47)	Rendell, C. (36)	Hayward, A.M. (24)
Morris, Myra (50)	Batstone, Reginald (46)	Johnson, Linda (29)
Batstone, Florence (57)	Rose, Frank (17)	Forgey, L (30)
Gay, Norman (16)	Lumber, Florence (44)	Bright, W. (37)
Palmer, Fred (65)	Smith, Elizabeth (76)	Bugler, (Mrs) (58)
	Tucker, Wendell (20)	

To date the above named are not remembered by any memorial, but at the time of writing South Somerset District Council are considering the erection of a suitable plaque in Yeovil town centre to be unveiled coinciding with the launch of 'Angriff Westland' on September 24th, 1994.

Acknowledgements

I am extremely grateful to His Royal Highness Prince Andrew, Duke of York, for contributing the foreword to *Angriff Westland*. I also owe a vote of sincere thanks to Captain Neil Blair R.N., His Royal Highness's Private Secretary, for helping to arrange this great honour.

I must thank my wife, Anita, for indulging my fascination for 1940 and joining in whenever possible.

I would like to express my sincere gratitude for the help and inspiration provided over a protracted period by Luftwaffe historian Kenneth Wakefield. As ever, Chris Goss also responded to the call and unfailingly provided otherwise unobtainable information regarding German personnel, losses and claims in addition to assisting with the tracing of RAF survivors. If not for Ken and Chris, the Luftwaffe side would have been far less detailed. Former Luftwaffe pilot Peter Wulff, and Dave Kent, kindly helped with translating German documents.

Other fellow historians and friends also helped: Dr Alfred Price, Michael Payne, Allan White, John Foreman, Andy Saunders, Michael Grundy, Jack Sweet, Gerald Pitman, Winston Ramsey, Brian Owen, Michael Grundy, Rodney Legg, Antony Whitehead, and John Congram.

Peter Batten and Fred Ballam of Westland Helicopters were both of great assistance in respect of the company's history. Mr Roy Madelin, Chairman of South Somerset District Council, and an eye-witness to the bombing of Yeovil, has given great support and encouragement. Jim Cross at Sherborne Police station pointed me in the right direction regarding the Burdon's Nursuries Hurricane. George Higgins allowed access to the MECO SC250 nose cone. Wing Commander NPW Hancock OBE DFC RAF Retd of the Battle of Britain Fighter Association and Mrs Edna Murray of the Kenley Reunion gave invaluable assistance with tracing many surviving RAF participants.

As ever a particular note of thanks must be recorded in respect of Dr Dennis Williams, whose enthusiasm, commitment and friendship I greatly value - his work as an *unofficial* editor for Ramrod Publications is much appreciated.

Once more Mark Postlethwaite G.Av.A. shared my *wavelength* and was only a telephone call away to offer encouragement and enthusiasm.Once again he has provided stunning artwork in respect of this, our third major project together.

Gilbert Davies of Victor Studios, Hay-on-Wye, has yet again done wonders in copying faded snapshots and once more I am extremely grateful to him.

Acknowledgement must also be given to the Keeper and staff of the Public Record Office, staff of the Ministry of Defence Air Historical Branch, and S10 (Air), Imperial

War Museum, Museum of South Somerset, Observer Lieutenant Neville Cullingford
& the ROC Museum, Dorset County Record Office, Somerset County Record Office,
the National Meteorological Library & Archive, and the Bundesarchiv.

The Malvern Spitfire Team would also like to publically acknowledge the kind co-
operation so freely given by the Ralph family and villagers at Alton Pancras when we
returned Dennis Nichols to his crash site. Mrs Hughes, Mrs Idda and Mr Smallwood
kindly supported our investigation into the Shillingstone Spitfire, and Bob Williams
of *Aquascan* provided the equipment which located the crash site.

Ray Johnson's memories of being an armourer on a Spitfire squadron were
fascinating and I am grateful for his involvement.

Several years ago, Mrs Dorothy Hessling, widow of Flight Lieutenant David Crook
DFC, passed on to me the original manuscript of her late first husband's book, *Spitfire
Pilot*, and I have been privileged to quote freely from this rich source of firsthand
material.

The eye-witnesses must all receive a vote of heartfelt thanks as it is perhaps not
always an enjoyable task to recollect such traumatic events. The *Western Gazette*,
Worcester *Evening News* and BBC Hereford & Worcester Radio all helped trace those
with a story to tell.

Sherborne School kindly provided over 40 accounts written by their pupils shortly
after the raid on *Black Monday*.

Aspect Print & Design have once again made production a painless experience,
and Ramrod Publications is grateful to Allan Smith and staff for their expertise.

Sherborne & Yeovil.

(Not in any order) Mr Timbrell, Mrs VM Russ, Mrs Harris, Mr DM Keys, Mr Roy
Madelin, Mr John Gaunt, Mr Martin, Mr John Gillard, Mrs Lily Powling, Mrs Morgan,
Mrs Sybil Robinson, Mr Desmond Pippard, Mrs Ellen Phillips, Mrs Stella Boce, Mr
Ronald Mitchell, Mr Dennis Howell, Messrs Henry & Albert Smith, Mrs Bulley, Mr
Cornelius, Mr John Chesterman, Mrs Molly Davies, Mrs Minterne, Mr Norman
Collard, Mr John Hall, Mr Fred Denham, Mrs M Hewlett, and the boys of Sherborne
School.

Worcester.

Mrs Bessie Thomas, Mr R Duesbury, Mr JN Chainey, Mr AR Thomas, Mrs M
Hayton, Mr BG Taylor, Mrs Taylor, Mr Martin, Mr Osborne, Mr Appleford, Mrs
Anne Smith, Mr FR Beechey, Mr Maurice Jones, Mr Sam Beard, Mr GP Doran, Mr
RW Tyler, Mrs Jessie Wood, Mr LJ Adams, Mr Terry Hulme, Mrs Margaret Woodward,
Mrs Anne Matthews.

The Defenders.

56 Squadron: Group Captain HM Pinfold, Wing Commander FW Higginson OBE DFC DFM, Flight Lieutenant DH Nichols AE, Mr PH Fox.

87 Squadron: Wing Commander RP Beamont CBE DSO DFC, Squadron Leader LA Thorogood DFC.

152 Squadron: Wing Commander FM Thomas, Flight Lieutenant RMD Hall DFC.

213 Squadron: Group Captain DSW MacDonald DSO DFC, Flight Lieutenant G Stevens.

238 Squadron: Air Commodore HA Fenton CBE DSO DFC, Wing Commander RFT Doe DSO DFC, Flight Lieutenant AR Covington, & Flight Lieutenant LG Batt.

609 Squadron: Group Captain JD Bisdee OBE DFC, Squadron Leader AK Ogilvie DFC, Flight Lieutenant MJ Appleby AE.

504 Squadron: Flight Lieutenant BM Bush DFC.

The Attackers.

Herr Sigurd Hey, Herr Robert Ciuraj, Herr Ludwig Piller (all KG51 and via Chris Goss), and Herr Robert Götz (KG55).

Bibliography

During the research for this book numerous documents were consulted at the Public Record Office. All are available to anyone with a valid reader's ticket. I have also had access to several RAF and Luftwaffe pilot's flying logbooks, and the personal papers of others. The Bundesarchiv in Germany provided certain documentation relating to Luftwaffe air operations on the dates in question.

Vital information concerning bomb damage and crashed aircraft times was found in Civil Defence and Police reports discovered at local record offices.

The following books have all proved invaluable in providing a well read understanding of 1940, and indeed are to be recommended.

German Bombers Over England, Bryan Philpott, PSL, 1978

German Fighters Over England, Bryan Philpott, PSL, 1979

Luftwaffe Fighter Units; Europe 1939-41, Jerry Scutts, Osprey Publishing Ltd, 1977

Luftwaffe Bombing Units; 1939-41, Jerry Scutts, Osprey Publishing Ltd, 1978

Messerschmitt Bf 109 Into The Battle, Michael Payne, Air Research Publications/ Kristall Productions Ltd, 1987

Arise To Conquer, Wing Commander Ian Gleed DFC RAF, Victor Gollancz Ltd, 1942

Spitfire Pilot, Flight Lieutenant DM Crook DFC RAF, Faber and Faber Ltd, 1942, but original manuscript in author's collection.

Churchill's Few, John Willis, Book Club Associates, 1985

The Story of 609 Squadron; Under The White Rose, Frank Ziegler, Macdonald & Co (Publishers) Ltd, 1971

The Luftwaffe War Diaries, Cajus Bekker, Macdonald & Co (Publishers) Ltd, 1966

Battle of Britain, Len Deighton, Jonathan Cape Ltd, 1980

RAF Fighter Squadrons In The Battle Of Britain, Anthony Robinson, Arms & Armour Press Ltd, 1987

Bob Doe, Fighter Pilot, Wing Commander Bob Doe DSO DFC RAF Retd, Spellmount Ltd, 1991

Luftwaffe Encore, Kenneth Wakefield, William Kimber & Co Ltd, 1979

Spitfire Squadron, Dilip Sarkar, Air Research Publications, 1990.

The Invisible Thread: A Spitfire's Tale, Dilip Sarkar, Ramrod Publications, 1992

Through Peril To The Stars, Dilip Sarkar, Ramrod Publications, 1993

SGT. PILOT 741474 RAF VR. A flying memoir 1938-59, LG Batt, self published, 1990

The Narrow Margin, Derek Wood and Derek Dempster, Hutchinson & Co (Publishers) Ltd, 1961

Clouds of Fear, Flight Lieutenant Roger Hall DFC RAF Retd, Bailey Brothers & Swinfen Ltd, 1975

Spitfire Survivors Around The World, Gordon Riley and Graham Trant, Aston Publications, 1986

Somerset At War 1939-45, Mac Hawkins, The Dovecote Press Ltd, 1988

Wings of the Luftwaffe, Captain Eric Brown CBE DFC AFC RN Retd, Airlife Publishing Ltd, 1987

Die Ritterkreuz Träger Der Luftwaffe 1939-45, Volume One, Jagdflieger, Ernst Obermaier and Verlag Dieter, 1966

RAF Squadrons, Wing Commander CG Jefford MBE RAF, Airlife Publishing Ltd, 1993

Messerschmitt Aces, Walter A Musciano, Tab/Aero Books, 1989

Men of The Battle of Britain, Kenneth G Wynn, Gliddon Books, 1989

Westland, David Mundey, Jane's Publishing Company Ltd, 1982

Battle Over Britain, Francis K Mason, Aston Publications Ltd, 1990

The Battle of Britain Then And Now MkV, Edited by Winston Ramsey, Battle of Britain Prints International Ltd, 1989

The Blitz Then and Now Volume 2, Battle of Britain Prints International Ltd, 1988

Wartime Sherborne, Harold Osement, privately printed, 1984

Sherborne Observed, Gerald Pitman, The Abbey Bookshop, 1983